Military Powers

Military Powers

General Editor: Stan Morse

The Military Press
New York

The Military Press
First English edition published by Temple Press
an imprint of Newnes Books 1984

This 1984 edition published by The Military Press
and distributed by Crown Publishers, Inc.
hgfedcba

Printed and bound in Italy

Created and produced by Stan Morse
Aerospace Publishing Ltd
10 Barley Mow Passage
London W4 4PH
England

All correspondence concerning the content of this volume should be addressed to Aerospace Publishing Ltd. Trade enquiries should be addressed to The Military Press, One Park Avenue, New York, NY 10016.

ISBN: 0-517-414821

Library of Congress Catalog Card Number: 83-62995

Artists: Keith Fretwell (aircraft three-views)
Tony Gibbons (ship three-views)
Peter Sarson
The Art Workshop
Ray Hutchins
Author: Lindsay Peaock (Air Force and Naval Aviation)

Typesetting: SX Composing Ltd, Rayleigh, Essex
Colour origination: Imago Publishing Ltd, Thame, Oxon

The Publishers are greatly indebted to the US Armed Forces for their help in supplying photographs for this book.

Contents

United States Navy

US naval forces have become the primary arm of American military strategy overseas. Mobile, flexible and very powerful, they can project an extremely wide range of military responses to any part of the world and are able to operate free of foreign bases. They are currently deployed to numerous trouble spots, from the Caribbean to the Gulf and from the Mediterranean to the China Sea. And they maintain the most potent element in the nuclear arsenal: the Trident submarine force.

Left: The multi-mission carrier USS *America* (CV 66) is seen passing through the Suez Canal. She has the magazine capacity to carry over 100 B-43/B-57/B-61 nuclear bombs for her air group, and can either sink a nuclear submarine or flatten a large city with them.

Below: The 'Los Angeles' class attack submarine USS *Birmingham* (SSN 695) demonstrates an emergency surfacing manoeuvre during sea trials. The 'Los Angeles' class boats are the West's fastest nuclear submarines, but are still slower than a number of Soviet submarine classes.

In late 1983, after challenging Libyan ruler Mumar Gaddafi's claim to waters in the Gulf of Sidra (where it had shot down two of his jets two years earlier), the US Navy 6th Fleet settled on station off the coast of Lebanon, supporting the US Marine Corps' role in that war-torn country. The 16-in (406-mm) guns of the battleship USS *New Jersey* (BB 62) and low-flying Grumman F-14 Tomcats from the carrier USS *John F. Kennedy* (CV 67) symbolized the awesomeness of American naval power, but there was frustration in Lebanon too: two out of 28 attack aircraft lost on an ineffective mission against Syrian targets, 239 US Marines killed by a suicidal fanatic in a truck filled with explosive.

Meanwhile, in the autumn and early winter of 1983-4, the US Navy participated in a series of complex unilateral and multi-national exercises involving 7th Fleet carrier battle groups, surface combatant task groups of cruisers and destroyers, submarines, land-based aircraft, and major amphibious units. Major operations took place in the north west Pacific, the Sea of Okhotsk, the Sea of Japan, and the East China Sea, including a fruitless search for survivors of a Korean airliner shot down by Soviet fighters.

In volatile Central America, US Navy units staged a show of strength off both coasts of Nicaragua while landing the army for an extended exercise in neighbouring Honduras. Shortly afterwards, the US Navy was the means by which Grenada was invaded.

The diversity of these activities is a reminder that a major seapower can intervene, simultaneously and worldwide, in situations which affect that power's interests. The US Navy finds itself in the limelight at a time when President Reagan is driving hard to fund a 600-ship navy, following a period of decline which saw the US Navy's numbers reduced from 800 to 450 in the

A finger on the button: this is the control room of the nuclear-powered ballistic missile submarine USS *Ohio* (SSBN 726) and she carries 24 Trident C4 missiles, each with eight multiple and independently-targeted re-entry vehicles carrying a 100-kiloton warhead. These missiles will eventually be replaced by Trident IIs with longer range, and this will enable the 'Ohio' class boats to permit targeting of the Soviet Union from remote areas of the ocean safe from anti-submarine attack.

same two decades that Soviet Admiral Sergei Gorshkov expanded his fleet to true blue-water status.

The US Navy is, in fact, a two-ocean navy charged with three-ocean responsibilities. Thinly spread, if it is to expand it must win victories not in a fight at sea, but in budgetary debates on Capitol Hill.

The US Navy is broken down into three elements. The elements' order of precedence is based on hard-won experience of World War II but should not, 40 years later, be above scrutiny.

First is the seagoing force spearheaded by a capital ship, the carrier battle group. These are in the business of sea control, establishing local superiority for a particular mission. Expensive to operate and build (the annual budget for a nuclear-powered aircraft-carrier (CVN) approaching that of the entire Royal Navy) these carriers operate effectively only with a dedicated escort and a replenishment force that extends the cost still further. As a stopgap measure, up to three of the US Navy's battle groups are temporarily headed not by carriers but by refurbished battleships of the 'Iowa' class, like the aforementioned *New Jersey*.

Second is the submarine force, which is divided into the nuclear-powered ballistic missile boats (SSBNs) that deploy the nation's seaborne nuclear deterrent and the nuclear-powered attack boats (SSNs) that prevent an adversary from using the sea for his purposes whilst preserving it for one's own. For

The fossil-fuelled carrier USS *Midway* (CV 41) is seen with five of her escorts and a replenishment ship. Such battle groups form the 'fire brigade' units of the fleets, and are deployed on presidential orders to the world's political hot spots. In recent months the *Midway* has been involved in protecting the West's vital oil highway through the Straits of Hormuz from any possible Iranian attempt to close them.

While the large and glamorous ships in service with the US Navy capture the headlines (and Congressional funding), the smaller 'bread and butter' vessels are to receive more attention. First in a projected 50-plus class, USS *Oliver Hazard Perry* (FFG 7) is typical of the frigates which are to provide the bulk of US Navy ocean-going convoy and amphibious force escort capacity.

practical purposes all-nuclear, the American submarine force remains technologically the world's most advanced. A weakness of the force is that its boats are so large that they are likely to develop into the hunted rather than the hunters. A side effect is its resolute stance against the construction of further 'conventional' or diesel-electric boats which, despite their great potential, have been squeezed out through lack of funds. They appear to be viewed as poor substitutes for nuclear boats instead of being complementary to them.

The third major element is the amphibious warfare force, that part of the fleet intended to establish and maintain a military presence for, unlike the sea which can be 'controlled', land must be occupied. Amphibious warfare ship design has become ever more complex and costly. There are becoming increasingly fewer multi-purpose ships of such high individual value as to render their hazarding off a disputed shore increasingly unlikely.

Each of these three factions has its lobby, powerful to the point that less glamorous but vital aspects of the navy such as mine warfare tend to be starved of funding.

People

Admiral James D. Watkins, Chief of Naval Operations (CNO) since mid-1982, is the first US Navy man on the Joint Chiefs of Staff to come from a nuclear background. Watkins has served aboard destroyers, submarines, a nuclear-powered guided-missile cruiser, and as commander of a nuclear attack submarine. Reflecting the view of military men receiving increased funds from a generous Congress and a conservative administration, Watkins says, 'We are a Navy alive again, actively preparing for the next decade and beyond. I am very optimistic about our current trends and course . . .'

The US Navy gets its enlisted personnel from all areas of civilian life, most of its officers from the 53 universities which offer Naval Reserve Officer Training Corps (NROTC) courses, and its elite leaders from the

At enormous cost, the Trident programme will provide the seaborne element of the US strategic deterrent for the foreseeable future. Trident I, using the 4,600-mile (7400-km) C4 missile, is to be retrofitted in 12 'Poseidon' class boats. The large D5 missile forms the basis of Trident II and will be fitted to the massive new 'Ohio' class boats.

Below: Heart of the modern US Navy is the carrier battle group, increasingly centred on a nuclear-powered carrier such as the USS *Nimitz* (CVN 68) seen here in the background with her sister ship USS *Dwight D. Eisenhower* (CVN 69) (foreground). With a close escort of the nuclear-powered cruisers USS *California* (CGN 36) and the USS *South Carolina* (CGN 37), the *Nimitz* carrier group can steam at sustained speeds in excess of 30 kts for unlimited periods to anywhere in the world at a moment's notice.

The deck of a modern aircraft carrier is no place for the untrained or incapable. Recruitment is rising after the slump induced by the Vietnam experience, and the quality of personnel is higher. These trends must continue if the Navy is to maintain its ever more complex equipment at maximum efficiency and readiness.

United States Naval Academy at Annapolis, Maryland. The US Navy has 4,527 Academy cadets, 67,062 officers and 483,680 enlisted personnel, making a total of 555,269 people on active duty. Included in this figure are about 44,000 women. In Fiscal Year 1984, $12.6 billion (£8.2 thousand million) will be allocated to naval shipbuilding and conversion alone while the US Navy's people will enjoy their share of a total defence budget still to be determined, but will be history's largest.

Even with better funding, the US Navy continues to have difficulty retaining highly skilled technical people. Retention of second-tour petty officers with skills in electronics, anti-submarine warfare and nuclear weapons is a critical personnel problem. Billy C. Sanders, master chief petty officer of the US Navy, acknowledges that the situation is improving only slightly. 'We must work harder to keep our best people,' says Sanders.

Fleet dispositions

There are four fleets in the US Navy. Of these, the 2nd Fleet is responsible for the Atlantic and is headquartered at Norfolk, Virginia. It is closely associated with the 6th Fleet which covers the Mediterranean, and both have close links with NATO fleets. The eastern Pacific is the the province of the 3rd Fleet, split between a forward element at Pearl Harbor and the remainder on the western seaboard. The 7th Fleet is also headquartered at Pearl Harbor, but its strength is scattered as far as the Philippines, Okinawa and Guam.

The Indian Ocean, once a vacuum filled by the expanding Soviet armada, may acquire the proposed 5th Fleet of the future. Diego Garcia is being developed into a 'second Pearl Harbor', with major facilities for the Rapid Deployment Joint Task Force (RDJTF).

Carriers

For 40 years, since it was proved in the Pacific, the carrier battle group has remained the linchpin of American naval strategy. The carrier has retained its pre-eminent position in American naval thinking virtually without regard to theatre or purpose. In 'brushfire' or cold war situations no vessel is more effective, but, all too often, these expensive and vital national assets are being hazarded unnecessarily where a smaller vessel could perform as well.

Today, the smallest carriers in service are the three 'Midway'-class ships of 45,000 tons, although the USS *Coral Sea* (CV 43) is slated to retire in 1989 and the USS *Midway* herself (CV 41) in 1991. To achieve the planned 15 large flight decks in the carrier force, it will, however, be necessary to keep them in service until 1991 and 1994 respectively, by which time the latter will be 50 years old. Thereafter, two new carriers will have to be ordered every five years to maintain force levels. These are World War II vessels. The modern carrier was born in 1952 when the keel for the USS *Forrestal* (CV 59) was laid down. A class of four was completed between 1955 and 1959, each able to operate about 90 aircraft, and each incorporating an angled flight deck and steam catapults.

A fifth, near-identical unit was completed in 1961. She was the USS *Enterprise* (CVN 65) and differed in

The abortive 1980 hostage rescue mission in Iran probably marked the low point in the post-Vietnam slump in efficiency which afflicted all the US armed forces. The men waiting aboard USS *Nimitz* were willing to attempt a fantastically difficult operation, but were eventually beaten back by equipment failing in tasks for which it had not been designed.

BEWARE OF JET
BLAST-PROPELLERS
AND ROTORS
AB
NAVY
300
303

The carrier USS *John F. Kennedy* (CV 67) is seen at speed with a major portion of her carrier air group arrayed on the flight deck. The four steam catapults used to launch the aircraft from the bow and waist positions are clearly visible.

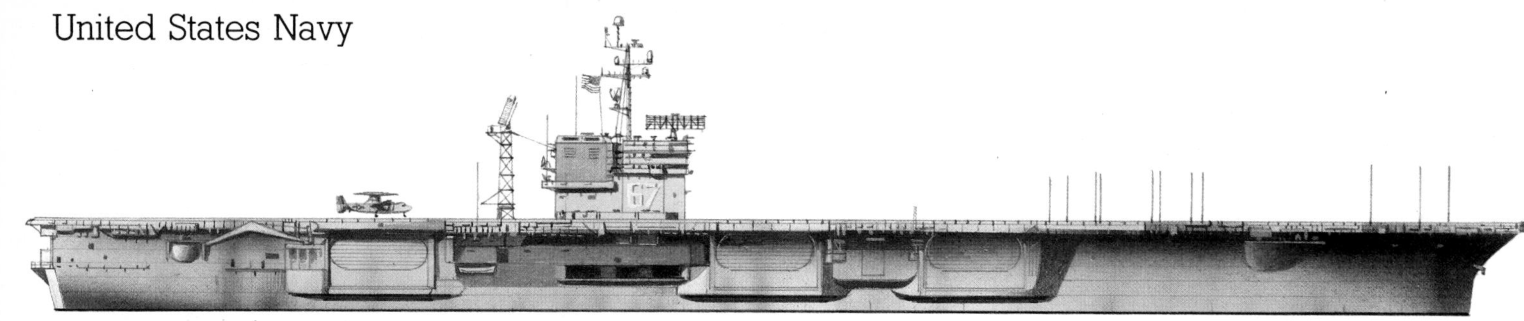

being nuclear-powered, one of a prototype squadron whose other members were the cruiser USS *Long Beach* (CGN 9) and the large frigate USS *Leahy* (CG 16) designed to explore the technical problems involved. Though officially developing the same power as the 'Forrestal' class carriers and their four improved 'Kitty Hawk' class follow-ons, *Enterprise* enjoys vastly greater endurance. If accompanied by similarly-powered escorts, she would not be hampered by regular refuellings at sea. Nevertheless, on a war footing, her crew of 5,000 needs frequent topping-up of essentials such as aviation spirit, ordnance, foodstuffs and dry stores.

The *Enterprise* proved remarkably successful, and

Considered to be a single-ship class the USS *John F. Kennedy* is a modified version of the three 'Kitty Hawk' class vessels. These four conventionally powered carriers are grouped together with the four smaller 'Forrestal' class ships in force level discussions.

Left: Commissioned in the last month of World War II, USS *Midway* is the oldest ship in front-line USN service. Likely to continue in commission until well into the 1990s, *Midway* will have been operational for half a century.

Above: A Grumman A-6E Intruder all-weather strike aircraft is about to be launched from a steam catapult aboard *Nimitz*. A single 10-aircraft squadron is carried aboard most carriers, together with four of the KA-6D tanker version. One Intruder and one Vought A-7E Corsair were lost over Syrian AA batteries in Lebanon during late 1983.

Even the broad expanse of deck and the cavernous hangar deck of a modern nuclear carrier can seem small, when you have to dispose up to 90 large jet aircraft as efficiently as possible. Here a plane director controls the movements of an F-14 on the deck of USS *Nimitz*.

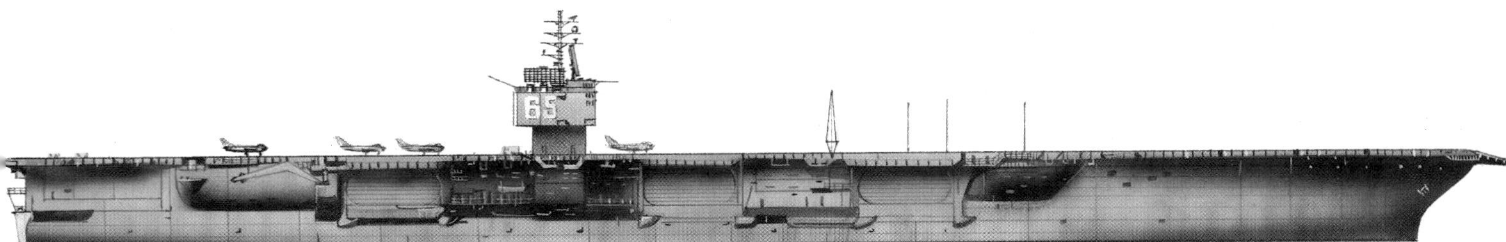

First of the nuclear-powered aircraft-carrier breed was the USS *Enterprise* (CVN 65), commissioned in November 1961. She served with an experimental nuclear-powered task force to evaluate the concept of such forces, and until the advent of the 'Nimitz' class was the largest warship yet built.

USS *Constellation* (CV 64) and her escort, the guided missile cruiser *Leahy* (CG 16), on deployment to the South China Sea. The fast combat support ship *Niagara Falls* (AFS 3) is between them providing underway replenishment.

John F. Kennedy of 1968 was to be the final steam-propelled unit, entering service only weeks after the keel-laying of the USS *Nimitz* (CVN 68) lead ship of an extended class of CVNs of which three are in service, one building, and two funded. It is a tribute to the original 'Forrestal' design that it has been remarkably little changed over the years. Inevitably the great limitation is cost, now in excess of $2 billion (£1.5 thousand million) per unit. As this, of course, inhibits the number constructed and no ship, however good, can be in more than one place at once, there is argument about the advantages of more, but smaller, decks. Smaller carriers would be less vulnerable to pre-emptive Soviet nuclear action but, so far, have not been authorized because funding them would divert financial resources from the high-capability big carriers. Senator Gary Hart of Colorado has been a lone voice among defence thinkers calling for smaller, more mobile carriers.

With the gradual disposal of older and smaller carriers, the large units have had to adopt a multi-purpose fit. Their embarked air wing now includes anti-submarine warfare (ASW) capacity as well as strike and interception, early warning, electronic warfare, reconnaissance, tanker and communications aircraft.

Despite its size, a carrier has only point-defence and close-in armament, relying on its aircraft and escorts

Now somewhat long in the tooth are the four ships of the 'Forrestal' class built back in the 1950s. To extend their service lives by another 15 years or so and to try to cut the costs entailed in new-build ships the US Navy is putting three of the class through Service Life Extension Program (SLEP) refits. Due for completion by 1987, work on the fourth ship, USS *Ranger* (CV 61), has been deferred.

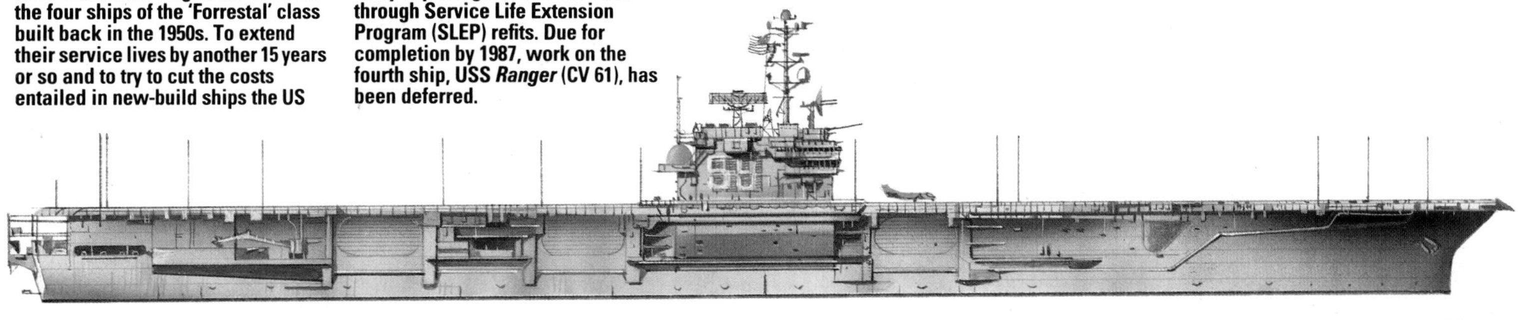

The mighty USS *Nimitz* (CVN 68) undertakes underway replenishment training off the Guantanamo operations area near Cuba with the ammunition ship USS *Mount Baker* (AE 34). Without such regular support the carriers would have to cease flight operations after only 10 days or so of sustained activity for lack of aircraft fuel and stores.

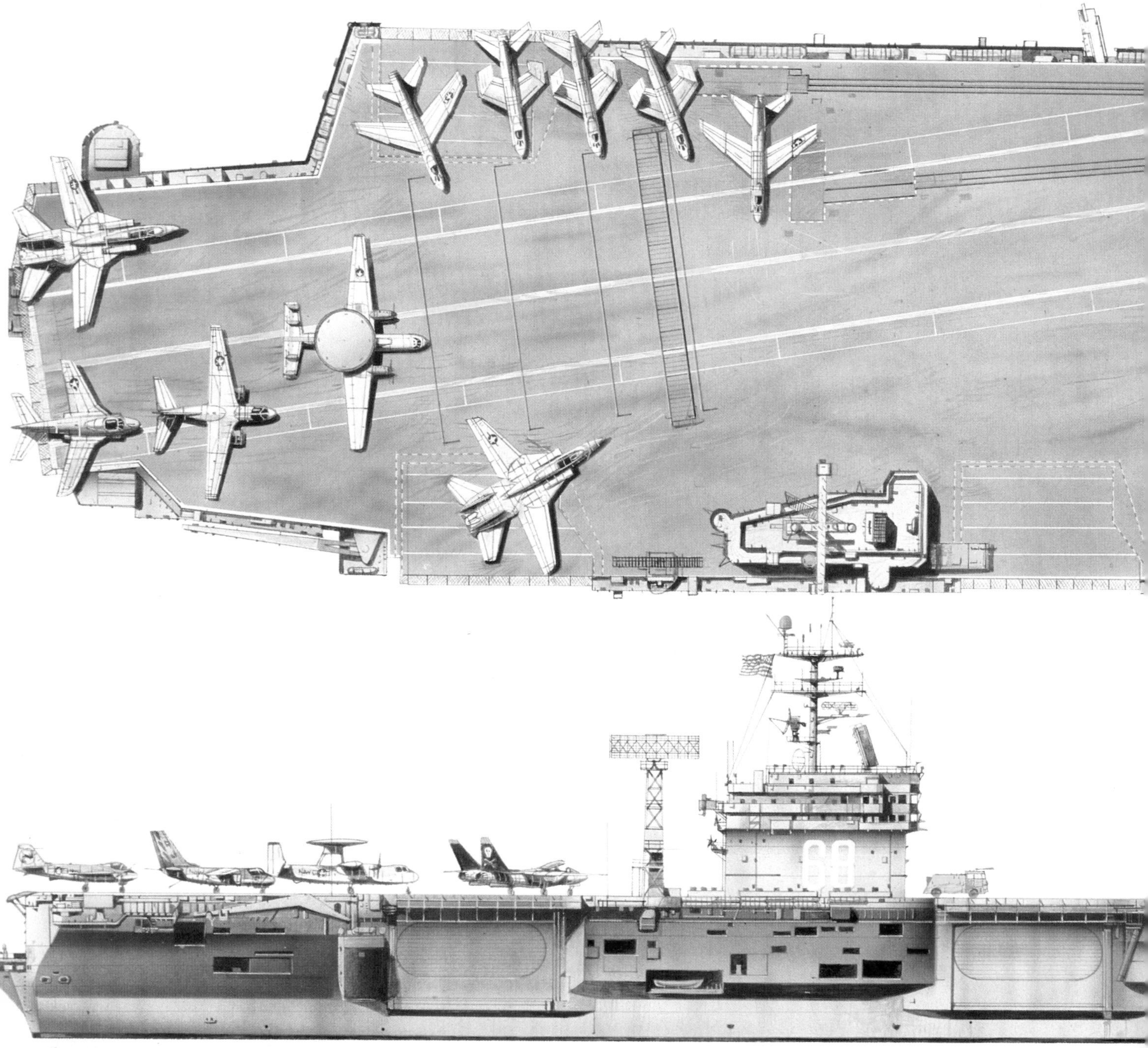

USS *Nimitz*

The 4.5-acre flight deck of the largest warship ever built can handle an air group of up to 95 large jet aircraft. Built to survive in a nuclear war environment, the USS *Nimitz*'s aircraft can attack in all weathers at all altitudes over hundreds of miles. Such a capability makes her a high-priority target in any war.

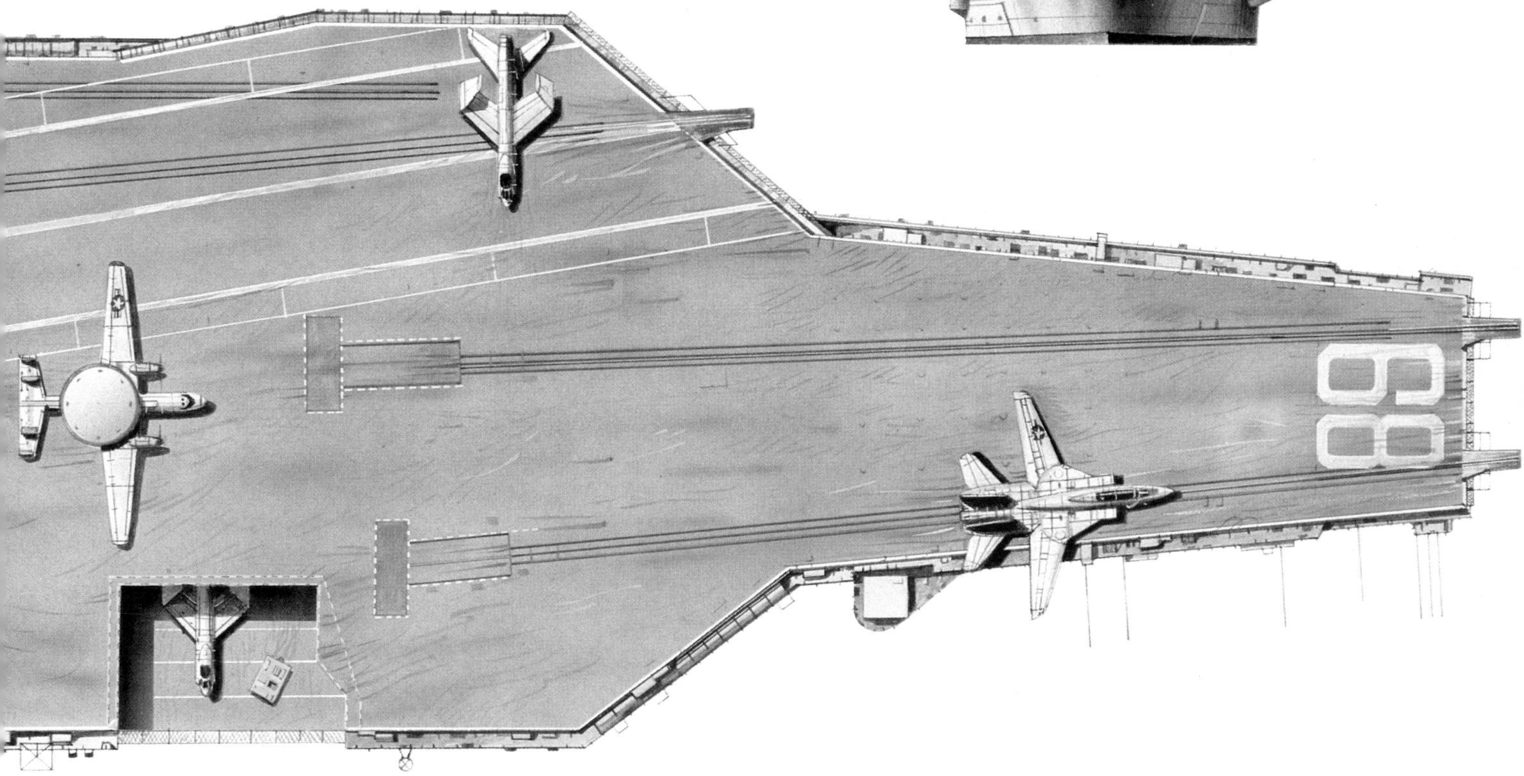

The four World War II vintage 'Iowa' class battleships are currently being modernized to enable them to operate in a modern war environment.

The USS *New Jersey* (BB 62) leads a surface action battle group. US Navy planners currently regard these vessels with their 406-mm (16-in) guns and missile armament as an asset that can survive in any form of warfare, including nuclear.

for longer-range defence. Ideally, the carrier will have an inner ring of four cruisers and an outer ring of possibly 10 destroyers, the former geared to anti-aircraft warfare (AAW) and the latter to a mix of AAW and ASW.

Cruisers

Today's first-rate cruisers are developed from the nuclear-powered USS *Bainbridge* (CGN 25) and her steam-powered sisters of the 'Leahy' class. To accommodate a second SAM system these 5,700-ton vessels dispensed with ASW armament but, stretched by only about 52 ft 6 in (16 m), the same basic layout has developed, via the 'California' class, to the USS *Virginia* (CGN 38) and identical vessels. These, at about 11,000 full load tons, have an excellent balanced armament though, even with two Standard MR launchers, they could still probably handle no more than four targets at a time. Construction was therefore halted at four in favour of a new AEGIS (CGN 42) cruiser for the late 1980s. The extra complication of the electronics will, to some extent, be offset by the adoption of a vertical

The guns of the battleship USS *New Jersey* (BB 62), seen here off Vietnam in 1968, have most recently been used in anger during the Lebanon crisis. The 406-mm (16-in) main armament fires high explosive shells weighing 1,900 lb (862 kg) apiece to a range of 41,500 yards (3790 m). The best results for a shore bombardment are achieved when the guns are directed by forward observers either on shore or in an aircraft.

Built as the world's first 'double-ended' missile ships, the 'Leahy' class units were designed to provide anti-aircraft defence for carriers. In April 1972 the vulnerability of warships to missiles was demonstrated when the USS *Worden* (CG 18) of this class was hit off Vietnam by at least two Shrike ARM missiles fired in error by friendly aircraft, the destruction caused amongst the sensors and superstructure knocking the ship out of action for a number of hours.

Developed from the large 'Spruance'-class destroyers, USS *Ticonderoga* (CG-47) is the first cruiser to be fitted for AEGIS operation. The AEGIS system promises new levels of anti-air defence of the fleet by means of the most advanced technology.

Below: a rare sight indeed is this view of the four 'Virginia' and two 'California' class nuclear-powered cruisers operating together. Their combined firepower is probably greater than any other NATO allies' surface action task forces.

Above: USS *California* (CGN 36) acts as a 'goalkeeper' escort to the carrier USS *Nimitz* (CVN 68), defending her against any aircraft that leak through the outer defences. In the late 1980s, in common with other ships equipped with Standard SM-2 missiles, she will field a W81 2/4-kiloton yield nuclear warhead version of the SM-2MR SAM missile, a capability she has not previously possessed.

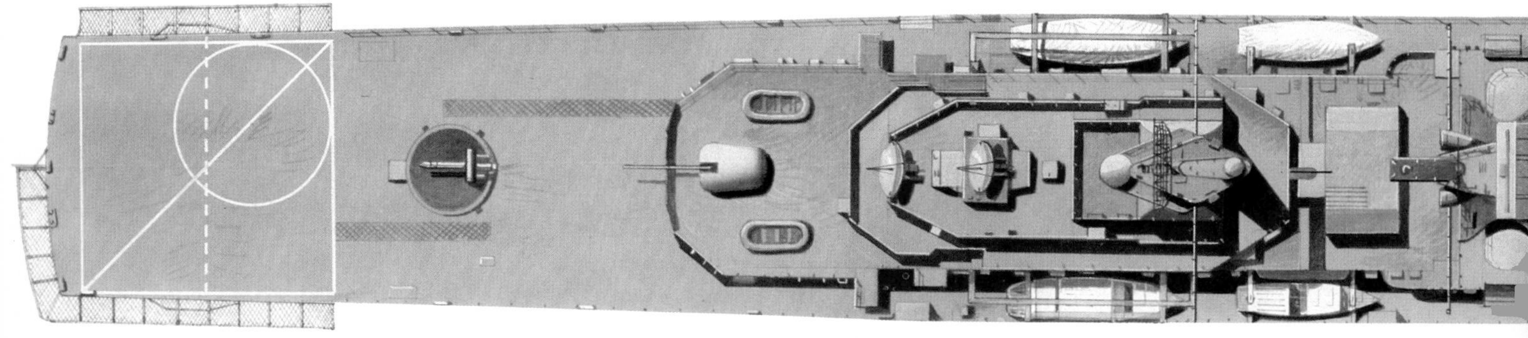

USS *California*

With an improved reactor core compared with those of earlier CGNs, the two 'California' class ships are able to operate independently for long periods at sustained high speeds as part of a carrier battle group.

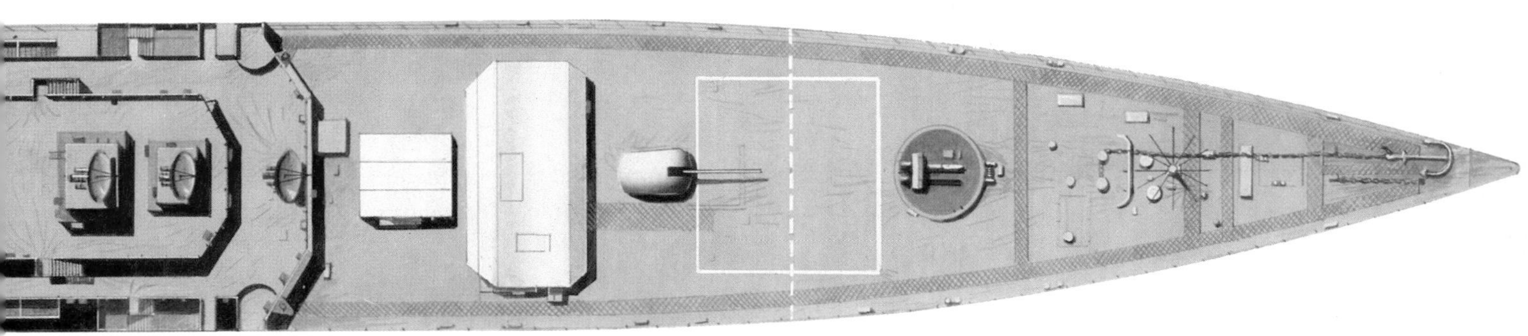

Built to replace the many obsolete 'Gearing (FRAM I)' class destroyers, the 'Spruance' class ships are the first major American combatants to employ gas turbine propulsion systems. This makes them excellent ASW platforms, and as such each such ship will eventually carry a single Sikorsky SH-3H ASW helicopter (armed with a nuclear depth charge) in place of the two Kaman SH-2F Seasprite LAMPS Mk I light helicopters carried at present.

launch system (VLS) in place of dual-function launchers. Dependent upon mission, this VLS arrangement will house SSMs, SAMs and ASMs stacked vertically below the upper deck in what resembles a milk crate in layout.

Today's cruisers are 'double enders' in having an area-defence SAM system fore and aft and, to avoid the dangers of a co-ordinated saturation attack, one of each group should be AEGIS-equipped. This system was designed to identify and track large numbers (reportedly 200) of aerial targets simultaneously. It can process its information near-instantaneously to identify friend from foe, assess each threat and, via the Naval Tactical Data System (NTDS) control and allocate the firepower of the group's defences while controlling friendly aircraft.

Destroyers

In the outer ring of the carrier battle group are ships of lesser capability, ideally destroyers but, as a result of present lack of numbers, often fast frigates. Typically, the former are older ships like the 'Coontz'- and 'Adams'-class ships for AAW and the new 'Spruance'-class ships for ASW. The last can carry two LAMPS III (Light Airborne Multi Purpose System Mk III) helicopters based on the capable new Sikorsky SH-60B Seahawk. These aircraft can deploy both ASW sensors and weapons, besides having onboard data processing to supplement the data-link with the mother ship. They can also be used to identify targets and suggest corrections to make full use of the over-the-horizon range of the ship's Harpoon SSMs.

Above: The USS *Elliott* (DD 967) is seen under way. All the 'Spruances' were built using the modular assembly technique, in which large sections of the hull were constructed in various parts of the shipyard and ultimately welded together on the slipway. This cuts costs, quickens construction and allows easier mid-life modernizations.

Right: Showing the classic ASW defence of zigzagging is the 'Spruance' class destroyer USS *Harry W. Hill* (DD 986). From 1985 onwards all 'Spruances' will be retrofitted with 61-round vertical missile launchers for SSM, SAM and ASW missile types.

Left: The USS *Farragut* (DDG 37) is lead ship of the 'Coontz' class. The ships were originally classified as missile frigates (DLG), but are now considered to be destroyers. The *Farragut* differs from her sister ships in having an ASROC ASW missile reload magazine abaft the launcher.

Below: Designed primarily for the anti-air defence mission and to screen carrier task forces, the 10 'Coontz' class ships carry the Standard SM-2 and the nuclear-armed RIM-2F Terrier missiles in their magazines.

The USS *Belknap* (CG 26) is an enlarged 'Leahy' design and was built as the first conventionally steam-powered cruiser in the US Navy with full helicopter capabilities.

Left: Lead ship of its class is the USS *Leahy* (CG 16). The two radars seen aft are the SPG-55 target-illumination systems for the SAM missiles carried. Although primarily equipped with the conventional-warhead Standard SM-2ER, the ships still carry a small number of W45 nuclear warhead-equipped RIM-2F 1.5-kiloton yield Terrier missiles for special purposes.

Below: First of the nuclear-powered frigates (later cruisers) was the USS *Bainbridge* (CGN 25). She was originally constructed to test the concept of nuclear-powered surface vessels, and served in a squadron comprising herself, the cruiser USS *Long Beach* (CGN 9) and the carrier USS *Enterprise* (CVN 65). Her maximum speed was greater than that of the carrier so that she could manoeuvre around her charge at will.

Although classified as a missile cruiser, the USS *Ticonderoga* (CG 47) is in fact an AEGIS-equipped version of the 'Spruance' class ASW destroyer design.

Above: The last 'Virginia' class nuclear-powered cruiser built was the USS *Arkansas* (CGN 41). Her flank speed is thought to be 40 kts, which is faster than most current nuclear submarines can achieve underwater. All the nuclear-powered escorts operate in pairs to protect a similarly powered carrier.

Named after World War II's audacious destroyer skipper, the USS *Arleigh Burke* (DDG 51) is now under construction as lead ship for another destroyer series. These will have VLS and a simplified AEGIS and will be a less expensive substitute for the current chosen AEGIS vehicle, the USS *Ticonderoga* (CG 47) in whose class about 20 units are planned. These expensive double enders are built onto a 'Spruance' hull and are termed cruisers based on capability rather than size.

The principle of layered defence for a task group is vital to the group's success, for the Soviets constantly practise co-ordinated saturation attacks using aircraft, surface ships and submarines. Since nuclear warheads can be fitted to all larger Soviet weapons, a near-ironclad defence is needed to avert disaster.

It works thus. Airborne early warning (AEW) from the carrier enables the combat air patrol (CAP) to intercept an enemy air strike at extreme ranges before the enemy can launch stand-off weapons. Similarly, airborne radar detects enemy surface forces before they move against the task group, laying them open to counterattack by Tomahawk cruise missiles from, possibly, 155 miles (250 km). Widely spread enemy air strikes may be beyond the capacity of the CAP and will come into the ambit of AEGIS: standard ERs will be loosed by the outer screen at 31 miles (50 km), the threat of these being nuclear-tipped keeping the

AEGIS fulfils the promise of experiments 20 years ago, when USS *Albany* (CG 10), a converted World War II heavy cruiser, made this multiple surface-to-air missile launch. AEGIS is reputedly capable of simultaneously tracking and engaging high speed targets numbered in hundreds.

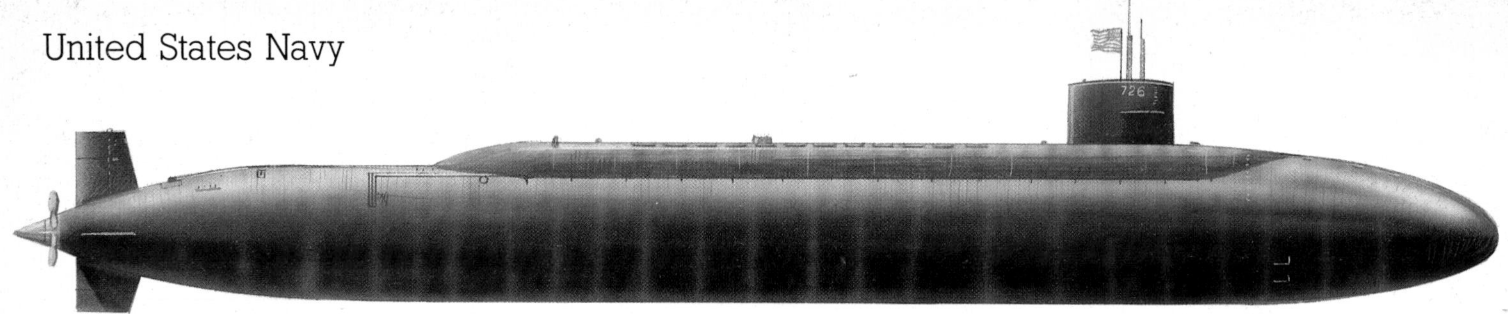

attacking aircraft well separated. Survivors which cross the task group's outer line are challenged by the outer ring's point-defence missiles just when they also come within range of the inner ring's medium-ranged weapons. Point-defence systems, which can handle crossing targets, then come into play from the inner defences and the carrier at the core of the task group. A last-ditch defence, finally, is mounted by the close-in weapons system (CIWS) which, currently, is the Vulcan Phalanx cannon able to loose about 400 rounds in two short bursts in the time that the average transonic attacker (missile or aircraft) is within its range. Critics point out that the cannon's 20-mm round lacks killing power and that, with elevation limited to 85°, a terminally diving SSM could evade it. Here at the inner core of the layered defence is a key weakness in the American inventory: the lack of an effective low-level, anti-missile missile of the calibre of the British Sea Wolf. Some US Navy vessels do carry the Sea Sparrow instead, but this, with its slow reaction time, sorely needs replacement.

Other defences, including electronic counter-measures (ECM), are also available to a carrier battle group, which usually has at least one friendly sub-marine attached to counter Soviet submarine-launched missiles. Submarines remain, in this context, the best ASW weapons.

The Submarine Force

With only a trio of ageing diesel-electric boats in service, the US Navy might as well be all-nuclear, divided into two main groups of boats, those deploying strategic missiles (SSBNs) and those designed for attack purposes (SSNs). The latter already carry the encapsulated Harpoon SSM. When they get Toma-hawk in the second half of the 1980s, they will have to be recategorized SSGN.

The 10 original SSBNs of the 'George Washington' and 'Ethan Allen' classes have been stripped of their strategic missile launching capability and the Polaris A3, still deployed by the UK, has been phased out. Backbone of the current force are the 31 'Lafayette' class submarines, some with Poseidon C3 and some converted to Trident C4 missiles. Entering service are the considerably delayed 'Ohio'-class boats, also with the C4 Trident, 24 to a hull.

As the Poseidons have a range of 'only' 2,800 miles

Only the Soviet 'Typhoon' SSBN class boats are larger than the 'Ohio' class missile submarines illustrated in the photograph and drawing above. The 'Ohios' will eventually form the bulk of the American SSBN force from the 1990s onwards, when the last of some 25 units will be completed.

The 'Sturgeon' class nuclear submarine USS *Silversides* (SSN 679) is one of nine 'Holy Stone' intelligence-gathering boats the US Navy is thought to operate off potentially hostile shores.

A Poseidon-armed nuclear missile submarine undergoes a maintenance inspection. Some of her deadly cargo has been removed, but the white foam plastic covers on a few of the tubes indicate that six missiles are still on board. A similar operation on the new 'Ohio' class submarines would reveal 24 tubes, each containing Trident missiles.

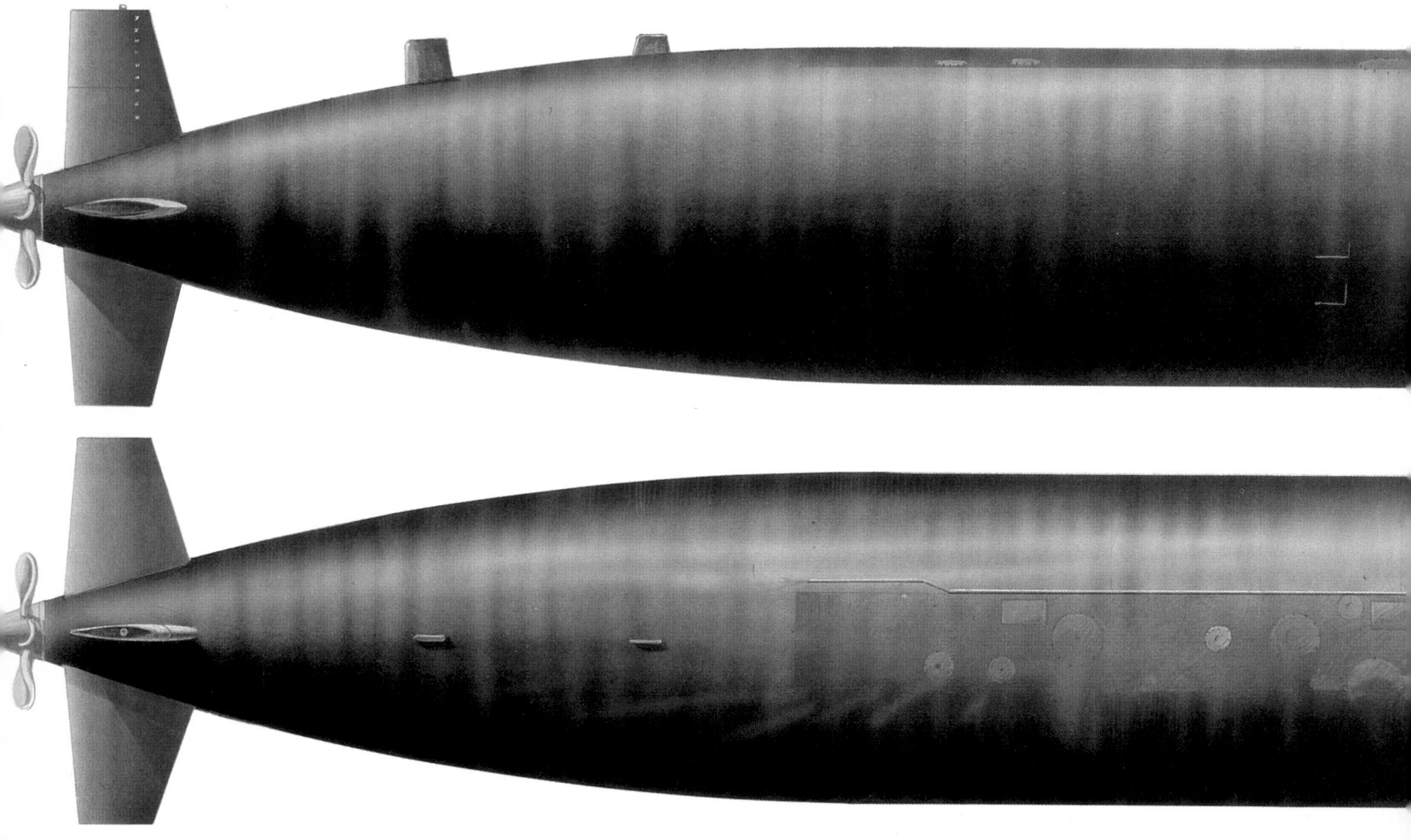

Left: The USS *Ray* (SSN 653) is a member of the 'Sturgeon' class, derived from the ill-fated USS *Thresher,* which was lost in April 1963 with all hands. The later vessels are much safer, and have vastly improved electronics.

USS *Sturgeon*

USS *Sturgeon* (SSN 637) is lead ship of an SSN class numbering 37 boats. Capable of about 18 kts on the surface, the 'Sturgeon' class is powered by the S5W reactor from the preceding 'Skipjack' and 'Permit' classes. While their increased size leads to a marginally reduced underwater speed, increased space means a more comprehensive sonar, electronic and weapon fit.

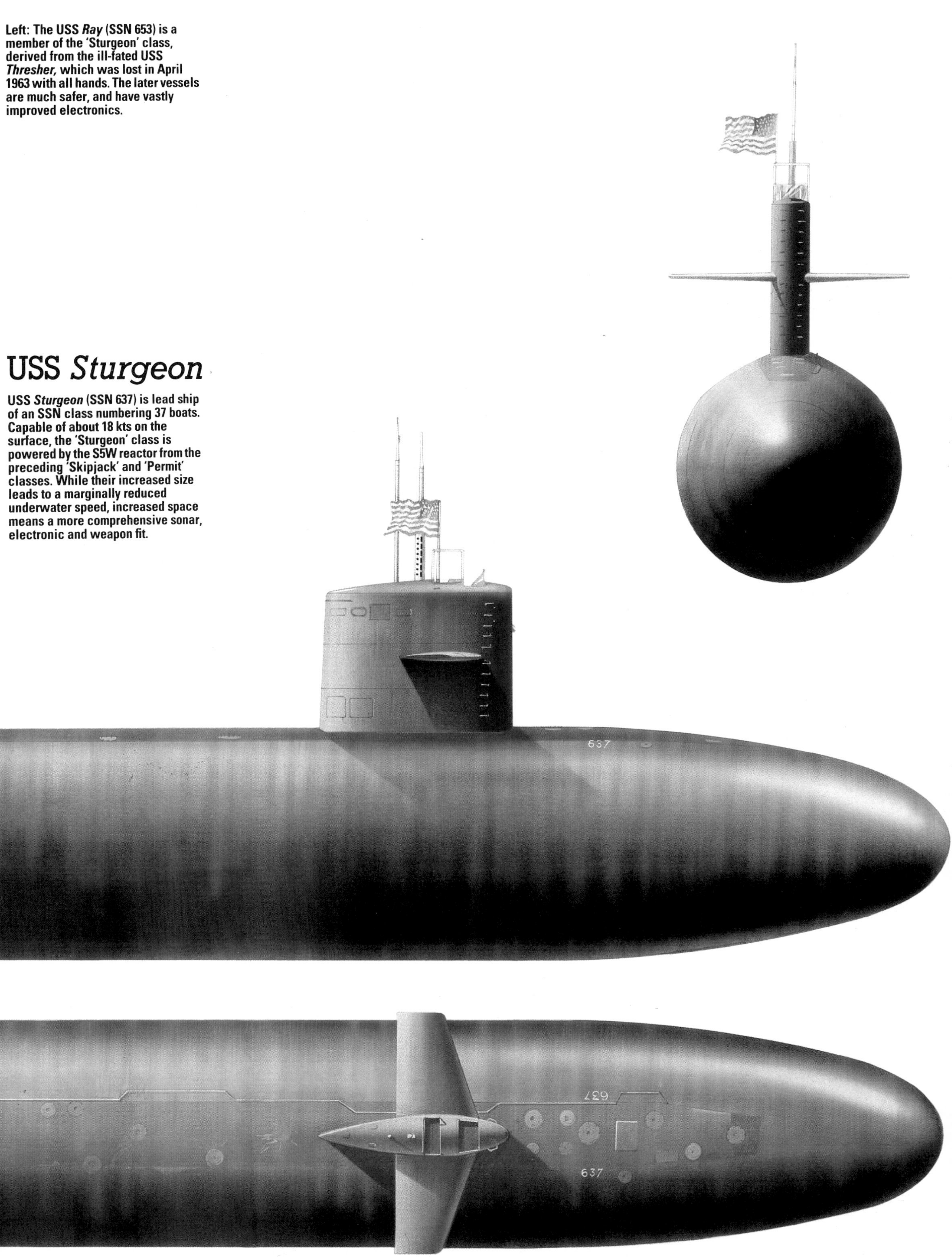

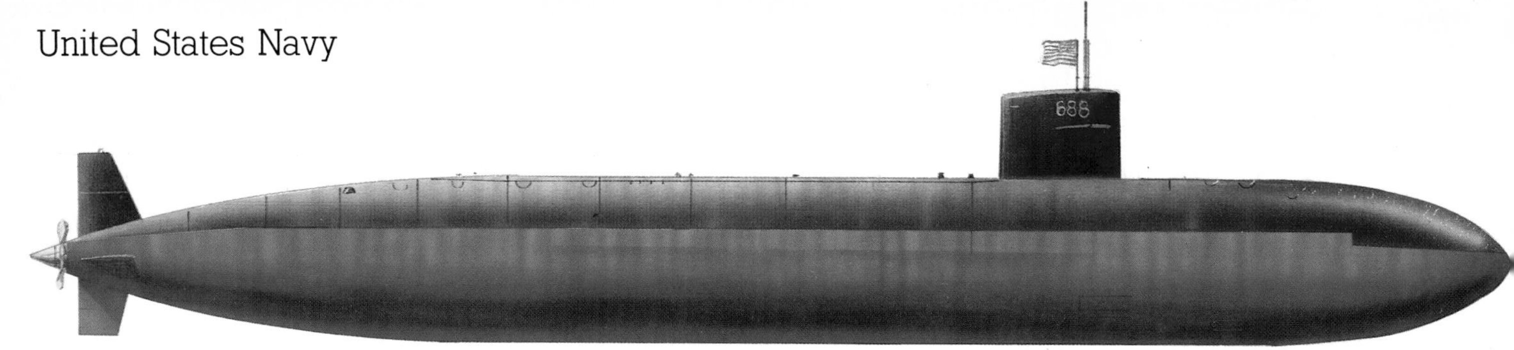

(4500 km), they are best used to target Soviet peripheral areas as, to reach the heartland, they would need to be launched from the deep oceans, leaving the submarines open to increasingly effective Soviet ASW forces. To avoid long transits and thus to increase availability, forward operational bases for SSBNs are maintained at Guam and Scotland, the base in Spain having been closed. The Trident C4 was deliberately configured to the same envelope as that of the Poseidon to allow an updating programme to be undertaken. With a 5,000-mile (8000-km) range they allow SSBNs to work from safer waters.

Later 'Ohio'-class boats will get the Trident D5, the earlier boats of the class then being retrofitted. As the Trident D5 will have an estimated 6,525-mile (10500-km) range, the SSBNs will be able to remain virtually in home waters, in areas where they can more easily be safeguarded from Soviet countermeasures.

To accommodate these large missiles, 'Ohio'-class boats are big, perhaps too big and too vulnerable, as many fear. They can hardly be dived safely in a great proportion of continental shelf waters. As long as a cruiser, no matter how quiet, they offer signatures by virtue of their length and bulk. It will be interesting to watch development of the submarine-launched Tomahawk cruise missile, for this weapon (so different from a ballistic missile in size and weight) holds forth the hope of returning to smaller, faster submarines.

Attack submarines (SSNs), like the SSBNs, are 'hot war' vessels unable to scale their response to meet a particular threat. Their defence is based on concealment. To make a deliberate appearance, to threaten overtly, is to cast aside their main advantage.

American submarine design reserves the space right forward for primary sonars. As a result, tubes are in a constricted site amidships, limited to six, or more commonly, four. Still, a wide range of weapons can be carried and launched from the same tubes: against shorter-ranged submarine targets, the Mk 37 torpedo; for longer-ranged submarines or surface ship targets, the Mk 48 torpedo, reputedly good out to about 31 miles (50 km) with a combination of wire-guidance and terminal homing, combined with a high degree of onboard electronic intelligence. SUBROC is a submarine-launched ballistic weapon with a nuclear warhead; it can 'sanitize' a considerable area to guarantee the killing of a target as important as an enemy SSBN. Now somewhat elderly, SUBROC is due to be phased out in favour of the new ASWSOW (ASW Stand-Off Weapon) currently in an advanced development stage. Surface ships can be targeted out to nearly 62 miles (100 km) by the encapsulated Harpoon and, as mentioned above, Tomahawk is under development. Finally, the same tubes can be employed for minelaying.

Mixed power

Oldest of front-line SSNs are the 'Skipjack' class boats of 1959-61, which married nuclear propulsion to the high-speed hull resulting from the 'Albacore' experiments. Their somewhat exaggerated form inhibits their sensor and armament fits, and the follow-on 'Permit' and 'Sturgeon' classes had easier lines. Running to some 50 hulls, this group forms the bulk of the US Navy's SSN strength. Despite experiments in advanced machinery, including cooling by liquid metals or natural convection, contra-rotating propellers and turbo-electric drives, all still feature the standard combination of pressurized-water-cooled (PWC) reactors upstream of conventional steam turbine plant, driving a single, centreline screw.

The 'Los Angeles'-class SSN, which first entered

At 31 kts the 'Los Angeles' class boats are the fastest attack submarines in the Western world. However, while trying to trail a Soviet titanium-hulled 'Alpha' class SSN off Iceland a 'Los Angeles' class boat was left standing when the Soviet craft increased speed to over 40 kts to elude her. In wartime it would have needed a SUBROC nuclear-tipped missile to stop the Soviet boat.

One of the 13-strong 'Benjamin Franklin' class of SSBN, the USS *Mariano G. Vallejo* (SSBN 658) was built to the same design as the earlier 'Lafayette' class but with quieter machinery and a larger crew. The SSBNs are unique in US Navy service as they are the only vessels to operate with two crews (designated Gold and Blue), one crew remaining on shore when the other is at sea on a 60-day patrol and then switching for the next patrol.

The USS *Ohio* (SSBN 726) is seen at Cape Canaveral for Trident I C4 launch trials. The Trident I is a three-stage solid-propellant missile carrying eight independently targeted Mk 4 re-entry vehicles with 100-kiloton W76 warheads. The 'Ohios' will eventually be equipped to carry the larger Trident II D5 missile carrying 10 Mk 5 re-entry vehicles each with a W87 475-kiloton warhead. Both missiles have a range of 4,600 miles (7400 km) with maximum payload.

service in 1976 and may total 60 hulls, is criticized by many as being too big and thus too vulnerable. Typified by the lead boat USS *Los Angeles* (SSN 688), the boats in this class had their installed power doubled to match recent Soviet equivalents and may be the West's fastest submarines. Their power was purchased at the expense of length, 360 ft (109.7 m) compared with 292 ft 3 in (89 m) of the 'Sturgeon' class. In comparison, the Soviet 'Victor II'- and 'Victor III'-class boats are about 328 ft 6 in (100 m) long, the British 'Swiftsure'-class boats 272 ft (82.9 m) long and the French 'Rubis'-class boats an economical 236 ft 6 in (72.1 m) long. Highly capable, the 'Los Angeles'-class vessels are also, at $600 million (£400 million) each, too expensive to be risked readily.

The purpose of this undersea armada is clear. While carrier battle groups are in the business of 'sea control', the submarine force exists for 'sea denial'. In time of war one of the SSN's main tasks would be to penetrate Soviet 'citadel' areas, where their SSBNs would be deployed as a bargaining element. They would seek to prevent older enemy SSBNs breaking out into the open oceans, needing to attack not only these SSBNs but the submarine and surface forces supporting them. The SSNs would also be needed to supplement the escort screens of carrier battle groups and to cover vital resupply convoys, which would be vigorously engaged by Soviet submarine forces. The US Navy's target is 100 SSNs and, even if realized, it will be none too large.

The Amphibious Warfare Force

Just as the island-hopping Pacific War was won by putting the US Marine and US Army ashore to occupy terrain, the permanent threat of amphibious landings to outflank defence produces uncertainty in the mind of an enemy and requires him to dissipate his strength to cover eventualities.

Over 60 assorted amphibious warfare ships are in US Navy inventory, grouped in amphibious squadrons (PHIBRONs) each capable of remaining on station with a reinforced US Marine battalion and its full equipment. At least one PHIBRON is usually attached to each fleet. Since the end of World War II a minimum of 20 kts sustained sea speed is required of each ship which, combined with a need to operate worldwide, has resulted in ever larger and more expensive ships, a tendency accelerated by the trend to combine the functions of the earlier cargo attack ships and transports with amphibious requirements. They no longer beach themselves, instead having landing craft embarked aft in floodable wells.

The 27 amphibious transport docks (LPD) and Dock Landing Ships (LSD) are closely related, each in essence being a self-propelled floating dock with the former type having the emphasis on troop accommodation and the latter on larger docking facilities. Build-

The first amphibious warfare command ships built after World War II are the USS *Blue Ridge* (LCC 19) and *Mount Whitney* (LCC 20). These provide integrated command and control for the sea, air and land force comanders involved in amphibious operations.

Right: From January 1972 to 1974 the USS *Guam* (LPH 9) served as an Interim Sea Control Ship (carrying US Marine Corps British Aerospace AV-8A Harrier V/STOL and US Navy Sikorsky SH-3D Sea King ASW helicopters) to test the Sea Control Ship concept. 'Iwo Jima' class vessels have also acted as floating bases for US Navy Sikorsky RH-53A/D Sea Stallion minesweeping helicopters used in mine-clearing operations off Vietnam and in the Suez Canal.

Left: Because of its extensive command and control facilities, the USS *Blue Ridge* (LCC 19) currently serves as the flagship of the commander-in-chief of the US 7th Fleet, and is homeported at Yokosuka in Japan. The machinery arrangement and hull are similar to those of the 'Iwo Jima' class LPHs.

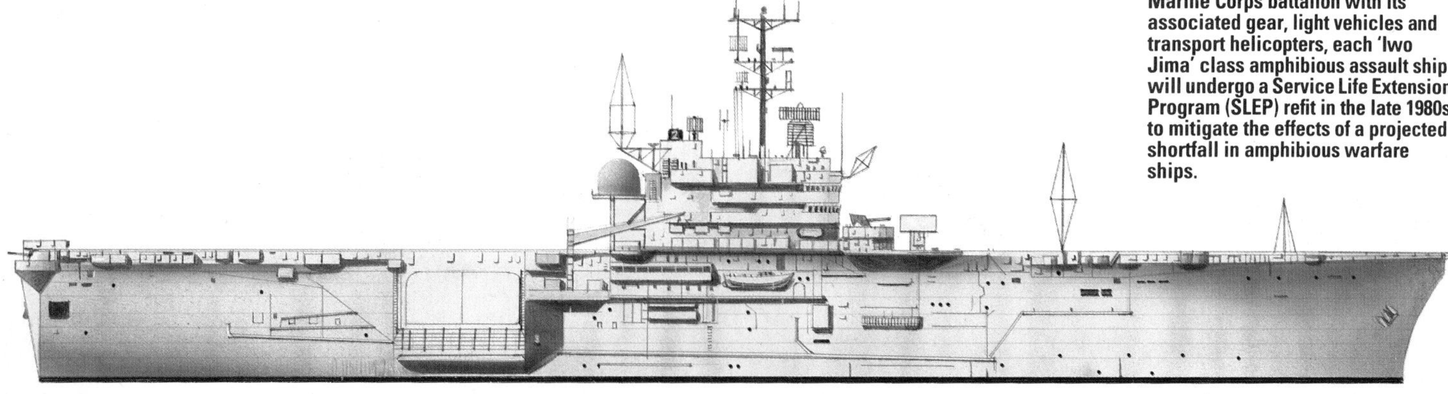

Below: Designed to carry a US Marine Corps battalion with its associated gear, light vehicles and transport helicopters, each 'Iwo Jima' class amphibious assault ship will undergo a Service Life Extension Program (SLEP) refit in the late 1980s to mitigate the effects of a projected shortfall in amphibious warfare ships.

The five vessels of the 'Tarawa' amphibious assault ship (LHA) class are multi-purpose ships designed to carry out the missions previously assigned to the LPH, LPD and LSD types of amphibious warfare craft. A slightly larger 12-ship class designated amphibious assault dock (LHD) is due to be constructed in the late 1980s both to increase amphibious-lift capacity and eventually to replace the LPH class.

ing currently are the 'Whidbey Island' (LSD 41) class, which are little changed except for the adoption of diesel machinery and a dock configured for stowage of air-cushion landing craft (flexible-skirted hovercraft).

Docked ships are essentially second-wave assets, consolidating the beach-heads seized by shock landings of spearhead troops. These arrive without warning in large helicopters such as the Boeing Vertol CH-46 Sea Knight or Sikorsky CH-53 Sea Stallion, operating from amphibious assault ships such as the 'Iwo Jima'-class LPHs or the 'Tarawa'-class LHAs.

The LPHs are like small carriers, lacking fixed-wing facilities, but carrying 1,750 combat troops, their gear, vehicles and artillery together with 20 large helicopter for their transport. Doubling the LPHs' displacement, at nearly 40,000 tons, the LHAs are highly efficient but have adopted an all-eggs-in-one-basket approach. The consequences of losing such a ship fully loaded must weigh heavily on the mind of its commanding officers.

An almost universal shortcoming among American amphibious warfare ships is an armament inadequate to meet a threat from modern weapons. The ships are utterly dependent upon their escort for protection and, with the more capable cruisers and destroyers committed largely to the carrier battle group, the US Navy's frigates will be given this task in addition to ASW and commerce protection.

Frigates

Lacking the glamour to attract funding in competition with larger projects, the frigates, as understood in West European terms, hardly existed in the US Navy before the early 1960s. The pair of 'Bronstein'-class prototypes introduced the slim, high-freeboard hull and the ASROC stand-off anti-submarine missile, matched for range by the enormous bow-mounted sonar, a combination that proved successful enough to influence all succeeding classes. ASW potency was improved in the following 'Garcia' class (10 ships) by including an organic helicopter, although half the group were completed with an area-defence SAM system.

Single-screw propulsion, which lacks redundancy and fine manoeuvring control, is a contentious feature but has been retained through the 46-strong 'Knox' class into the current 'Oliver Hazard Perry' programme of similar numbers. In the latter class, shortcomings are offset to some extent by the incorporation of a pair of retractable azimuthal thrusters. Because of the versa-

The USS *Tarawa* (LHA 1) docks down off Mindoro in the Philippines to unload assault landing craft from her stern docking well. Large vehicle parks, cargo holds and accommodation for some 1,900 US Marines make the 'Tarawas' the most capable amphibious assault ships yet built.

The 46 'Knox' class frigates are dedicated to the ASW escort role, and in fiscal year 1979 they began a retrofit programme of bow modification as they were too wet forward. This involved adding some 9 tons to the displacement and increasing the length by 3 ft 6 in (1.07m).

tility of the pair of embarked LAMPS III helicopters, the 'Oliver Hazard Perry'-class vessels have been able to discard ASROC and embark a dual-function launcher with a 40-round magazine capable of handling both the 10-mile (16-km) Standard MR SAM or the 50-mile (80-km) Harpoon SSM. This improvement in all-around capability is bought at the expense of complexity, any fault in the system robbing the ship of two major weapons. A further drawback is that these frigates' potential sees them sometimes elevated to the outer screen of a task group, a role for which they were never designed (shades of battle-cruisers). Versatility is always gained at a price, however, and the 'Oliver Hazard Perry'-class vessels are vulnerable to air attack pressed home to short ranges. They are slated to receive CIWS but lack any point-defence system, relying on the single 3-in (76-mm) gun amidships, a weapon too small for bombardment or anti-ship functions and too slow for aerial targets.

Anti-submarine warfare

While having less ASW bias than European navies, the US Navy has very considerable potential in the field. General surveillance is still based on the well-established SOSUS lines, which are strings of sensors spaced at strategic points, usually in continental-shelf waters. Each vessel crossing such a line has its acoustic signature monitored, analysed and compared with a library. The process is automatic and very rapid and, should a signal look interesting, an aircraft such as a Lockheed P-3 Orion will be brought in to pinpoint the contact. Its 17-hour endurance enables the Orion to linger, dropping active and passive sonobuoys, interrogating and processing the data on board or exchanging it with surface ships. Further aids to detection are the magnetic anomaly detection (MAD) gear, which responds to the large metallic mass of a submerged submarine, and forward looking infra-red (FLIR) gear which can detect the warm plume of air exhausted by a snorting 'conventional' boat. Carrierborne Lockheed S-3 Vikings have a similar, if more basic, fit. Both aircraft types carry a range of anti-submarine ordnance, including nuclear depth bombs.

SOSUS, though essentially passive, can be armed with advanced weapons such as CAPTOR, an encapsulated anti-submarine homing torpedo released by the correct signature. Being geared to shallow water applications, SOSUS needs supplementing in the deep oceans and this, initially, will take the form of simple 'Stalwart'-class trawler-type ocean surveillance ships (AGOS) which will operate slowly with long towed arrays known as TACTAS (Tactical Towed Array Sonar). As these are deployed at some considerable distance behind the ship and at chosen depths, their potential for detection is very high. Specialist ships are required because of the size of the winch assemblies,

The USS *Pharris* (FF 1094) of the 'Knox' class is seen during a 1982 exercise off the South American coast. Harpoon SSMs and a 20-mm Phalanx CIWS 'Gatling' mounting are to be fitted, the latter replacing the Sea Sparrow SAM on those ships currently fitted with the Mk 25 SAM launcher.

The 'Oliver Hazard Perry' class of missile frigates are anti-air warfare vessels. Fitted with a single-rail Mk 13 SAM launcher, they can also operate in the anti-ship and anti-missile roles.

Three frigates of the 'Oliver Hazard Perry' class, these ships are from left to right the USS *Jack Williams* (FFG 24), USS *Antrim* (FFG 20) and USS *Oliver Hazard Perry* (FFG 7). To counter the pop-up cruise missile and sea-skimming targets each ship carries a licence-built Italian OTO-Melara 76-mm (3-in) quick-firing gun and a Phalanx 20-mm close-in weapons system. ASW defence is limited to two LAMPS Mk III helicopters and self-defence torpedo tubes.

though smaller versions with shorter tows can be deployed by frigates. These look like replacing the earlier versions of variable-depth sonar (VDS) installations, which were introduced to counter the 'ducting' effects of the layers of water of varying temperature and salinity, which refract and distort acoustic propagation in predictable ways.

American hullborne sonars are much larger than British equivalents as they work at much lower frequencies; this confers a theoretically greater range but only at the expense of size and complexity. The bulky transducer assemblies are housed in very large bulbs at the forefoot. These are partly flooded, reducing both water noise and pitch acceleration in the ship herself but, in head seas, they can emerge and slam abominably if the ship is driven too hard. Indeed, in northern waters in winter it is unlikely that a frigate can even use a hull sonar for more than 50 per cent of the time whereas a towed array, once streamed, can operate in quite severe conditions. As in submarine practice, surface ships normally use sonar in the passive mode, necessarily at low speed to reduce self-induced noise. Passive sets will indicate bearing but not range, requiring either a bearing from another ship to give a 'fix' or, if this is not available, a quick burst of energy from an active set.

Other specialist sonars in American inventory include upward-looking sets for submarines navigating beneath ice and side/oblique scanning sets for the detection and classification of submerged objects, such as mines.

Mine countermeasures is one field where the Americans have been inactive for far too long in view of the vulnerability of the shallow approaches to the country and the known expertise of the Soviets. Only a handful of the obsolete ocean minesweepers (MSOs) remains in service; built as a result of the Korean War, these 'Aggressive' class units incorporate the means of countering mine technology of the 1950s and, even though modernized, have nothing of the capabilities of current European MCMVs, built from glass-reinforced plastic. Modern mines have considerable inbuilt intelligence, so that they can be made to react to various types and combinations of signatures, can count stimuli and ignore a set number, and even discriminate between genuine targets and sweeping gear. The only sure way to deal with them is to detect by sonar, identify and destroy by countermining with a charge dropped either by a miniature remotely-controlled submersible or by divers.

Doubtful mine countermeasures

A range of floating sleds, supporting countermeasures gear, has been developed by the Americans for towing behind RH-53D helicopters. Considerable success was claimed for them at Haiphong and in the Suez Canal, but it is difficult to see how they can deal with any remotely intelligent mine.

At long last a new class of MCM is being built with the USS *Avenger* (MCM 1) as lead ship. The programme was delayed by the need to trim a previously over-ambitious design.

As far as mine technology is concerned, the US Navy has a wide range of types available, including the CAPTOR already mentioned and an advanced weapon, named Quickstrike, under development.

After mining the major ports of North Vietnam in 1972, the USA had then to clear the mines as part of the Vietnam War's political settlement. The non-magnetic ocean minesweeper USS *Inflict* (MSO 456) is here seen entering Haiphong harbour in 1973 during Operation 'End Sweep' to clear it of influence ground mines. Since that time the US Navy has been largely inactive in Mine Countermeasures (MCM) research, although recent indications point to a change in attitude.

Apart from underway replenishment the 'Kilauea' class of ammunition ships can also undertake vertical replenishment (VERTREP) with its two Boeing Vertol UH-46 Sea Knight helicopters. The ammunition load carried is of all types, including nuclear ammunition and demolition charges for the US Marines plus the nuclear versions of the ASROC and Terrier missiles for the US Navy.

Most laying would be undertaken by submarines or aircraft but, acknowledging that the former would be in extremely short supply and the latter can lay notoriously inaccurately, the infrequent exercises in surface ship laying might well be stepped up with advantage.

Though, like most blue-water fleets, the US Navy has little peacetime use for minor combatants such as fast attack craft, the threat from them cannot be ignored as they have been transferred liberally by the Soviets to friendly states, usually those flanking shipping lanes vital to the West. Warships need to train with the real thing to establish techniques and, for this purpose, the US Navy's six 'Pegasus'-class hydrofoils (PHMs) are invaluable. These were to have launched the 'NATO hydrofoil' programme from which co-partners West Germany and Italy retired. Foilborne, these craft reach 48 kts and carry eight Harpoon SSMs, making them history's most heavily-armed craft of this size.

Imagination has gone into the development of hovercraft. Sidewall types, known as Surface Effect Ships (SES), were seen at one time as future frigate replacements, but the planned 20,000-ton SES that would have explored this concept has been shelved. Flexibly-skirted types, known as air-cushion vehicles, have been developed to the extent where the new LSD-41 assault ships will carry this style of landing craft as a standard fit.

Great interest is being shown in the Small Waterplane Area Twin Hull, or SWATH, ship. Like a semi-submersible drilling well in concept, it has a nearly square plan, its spacious deck being supported on two slim, buoyant pylons, each rising from a submerged, cylindrical hull. If successful, it promises better seakeeping in poor weather and its revolutionary layout offers an excellent and stable helicopter or V/STOL platform.

Firmly wedded to steam plant, US naval engineering came late to the gas turbine and has had to make do on just the LM 2500 powerplant for far too long. This General Electric unit develops about 20,000 hp (14915 kW) and, while reliable, needs to be complemented by a smaller model for a COGOG (COmbined Gas turbine Or Gas turbine) arrangement, allowing a ship to cruise economically without incurring the penalty of the poor specific fuel consumption exhibited by gas turbines when run at speeds other than their design point. Only recently has the LM 500 come on the market for the purpose.

Diesels are disliked, as indeed they are in the Royal Navy, mainly for their noise and maintenance levels. Continental Europe, however, is the diesel stronghold and is developing the type rapidly. If the diesel can overcome its drawbacks, its known strengths of economy and flexibility may attract American designers. Already, manufacturing licences are being taken out and diesels are going into new auxiliaries and

Located at most of the USA's foreign naval bases are floating dry docks, these constituting a vital part of the support facilities for warships overseas. Here an SSBN undergoes post-patrol repairs in the medium auxiliary floating dock USS *Richland* (AFDM 8) at the Naval Ship Repair Facility on Guam.

Below: Found wherever the SSN/SSBN submarines are based are submarine tenders. The USS *Canopus* (AS 34) illustrated here was designed specifically to service a maximum of four SSBNs simultaneously, and has the capability to repair and/or replace their missiles, to service their electronics and, if necessary, to repair their nuclear powerplants.

The fleet replenishment oiler USS *Roanoke* (AOR 7) has a cargo capacity of 175,000 barrels of fuel, 600 tons of ammunition, 425 tons of dry stores and 150 tons of refrigerated goods, and can thus keep a small escort supplied for over a week.

the LSD 41s. There is a growing interest in the 'quiet' diesel-electric frigate and the diesel will make an excellent cruising engine for medium sized CODOG (COmbined Diesel Or Gas turbine) warships. Interest is likely to grow.

On a more revolutionary note, electrical superconductivity has been attracting attention, but whether or not this will ever be satisfactorily harnessed to marine propulsion remains debatable. Though the prime mover itself would be compact, the power and bulk demanded by its associated cryogenics will be considerable with existing materials.

USS *Seattle* (AOE 3) prepares to resupply USS *America* by helicopter, an operation known as VERTREP (vertical replenishment). These large ships, known as fast combat support ships, combine the abilities of oilers and store ships.

Logistics, Operations and Maintenance

A great strength of the US Navy has always been its fleet support, the train of auxiliaries that work with a battle group for its replenishment, or act as forward bases for destroyers and submarines. The force was developed early as the US Navy never enjoyed the benefits of a worldwide chain of bases, yet needed support for out-of-area deployments.

Accompanying the fleet are the big, 20-kt replenishment oilers (AORs), ammunition ships (AEs) and fast combat support ships (AOEs). These are able to undertake underway replenishment from alongside (UNREP) or by large helicopter (VERTREP) and carry a vast range of dry stores, ordnance and fuels. They are highly valuable ships and need defending in their own right.

Though it remains American policy, where possible, to negotiate forward base rights on foreign soil, this has become politically more difficult in recent years and further destroyer tenders (ADs) and submarine tenders (ASs) have been constructed. These can service destroyers and cruisers, up to six at a time, whether gas turbine, steam or nuclear-propelled, their expertise including the repair of all types of weapons systems and electronics. Similarly, the AS ships can handle up to four SSNs and SSBNs simultaneously.

Transportation of the vast quantities of dry materials and oil needed worldwide by the fleet is the purview of the Military Sealift Command, which is also responsible for oceanographic research and missile down-range instrumentation ships. A more recent responsibility is provision of ships for the Rapid Deployment Joint Task Force (RDJTF), currently requiring vessels based in the Indian Ocean.

The ugly head of 'O & M', as Pentagon people call operations and maintenance, at times rears itself just when things seem to be going well. A General Accounting Office (GAO) report in December 1983 pointed out the danger of ignoring O & M. The GAO's figures show that US Navy appropriations to purchase new aircraft rose 83.6 per cent from 1980 to 1983, while its O & M budget for its air arm rose only 10.4 per cent to $4.6 billion (£3.0 thousand million). This disparity seems to explain the shortage of cannon rounds, bombs and ordnance with which the US Navy entered 1984. The GAO report made other charges that the US Navy is not well prepared for combat and would have difficulty getting carriers ready for more than one crisis, no matter how minor, at a time.

Whatever criticisms may be made of its equipment, doctrine, tactics and people, the United States Navy remains a world leader and an awesome fighting force. Many observers believe it is still superior to the larger Soviet navy and that it can fight and win. US Navy men share CNO Watkins' belief that the US Navy is 'alive again', and some talk of a 'rebirth' with transparent disdain toward their predecessors in Washington. Secretary of the Navy John F. Lehman Jr, complains that before he took office in 1981, 'we had serious readiness problems through 15 years of underfunding', but he insists that today's US Navy is 'ready, willing and able to do the job and do it well'.

Anyone who thinks otherwise may, in the view of many US Navy men, do so at his own peril.

A sister ship of the *Roanoke* is the USS *Kalamazoo* (AOR 6). The 'Wichita' class to which they belong is a smaller version of the fast combat support ship 'Sacramento' class.

One of the few small combatants left in service is the Harpoon SSM-armed patrol hydrofoil USS *Pegasus* (PHM 1), seen here in company with a Sikorsky Sea King helicopter and a McDonnell Douglas TA-4 Skyhawk jet trainer. All six hydrofoils of the class have been relegated to operations from Key West, Florida with the Atlantic Fleet as they are considered too complex to operate from forward bases.

Since their first deployment in the early 1960s, US Navy ballistic missile submarines have been on patrol continuously. Initially armed with Polaris missiles, followed by Poseidon and today's Trident, the missile submarines remain submerged for up to 60 days at a time until their return to port (in this case Holy Loch in Scotland).

UNITED STATES NAVY ACTIVE FLEET

SHIP BATTLE FORCES
STRATEGIC FORCES

SUBMARINES

BALLISTIC MISSILE SUBMARINES

'LAFAYETTE' CLASS
SSBN 616 *Lafayette* (Groton, Ct)
SSBN 617 *Alexander Hamilton* (Groton, Ct)
SSBN 619 *Andrew Jackson* (Groton, Ct)
SSBN 620 *John Adams* (Charleston, SC)
SSBN 622 *James Monroe* (Charleston, SC)
SSBN 623 *Nathan Hale* (Charleston, SC)
SSBN 624 *Woodrow Wilson* (Charleston, SC)
SSBN 625 *Henry Clay* (Charleston, SC)
SSBN 626 *Daniel Webster* (Groton, Ct)

'JAMES MADISON' CLASS
SSBN 627 *James Madison* (Charleston, SC)
SSBN 628 *Tecumseh* (Charleston, SC)
SSBN 629 *Daniel Boone* (Charleston, SC)
SSBN 630 *John C. Calhoun* (Charleston, Sc)
SSBN 631 *Ulysses S. Grant* (Groton, Ct)
SSBN 632 *Von Steuben* (Charleston, SC)
SSBN 633 *Casimir Pulaski* (Charleston, SC)
SSBN 634 *Stonewall Jackson* (Charleston, SC)
SSBN 635 *Sam Rayburn* (Groton, Ct)
SSBN 636 *Nathanael Greene* (Groton, Ct)

'BENJAMIN FRANKLIN' CLASS
SSBN 640 *Benjamin Franklin* (Charleston, SC)
SSBN 641 *Simon Bolivar* (Charleston, SC)
SSBN 642 *Kamehameha* (Groton, Ct)
SSBN 643 *George Bancroft* (Charleston, SC)
SSBN 644 *Lewis and Clark* (Charleston, SC)
SSBN 645 *James K. Polk* (Charleston, SC)
SSBN 654 *George C. Marshall* (Groton, Ct)
SSBN 655 *Henry L. Stimson* (Newport News, Va)
SSBN 656 *George Washington Carver* (Newport News, Va)
SSBN 657 *Francis Scott Key* (Newport News, Va)
SSBN 658 *Mariano G. Vallejo* (Charleston, SC)
SSBN 659 *Will Rogers* (Newport News, Va)

'OHIO' CLASS
SSBN 726 *Ohio* (Bangor, Wa)
SSBN 727 *Michigan* (Bangor, Wa)
SSBN 728 *Florida* (Bangor, Wa)

MOBILE LOGISTIC SHIPS

MATERIAL SUPPORT SHIPS

'HUNLEY' CLASS
AS 31 *Hunley* (Holy Loch, Scotland)
AS 32 *Holland* (Charleston, SC)

'SIMON LAKE' CLASS
AS 33 *Simon Lake* (Kings Bay, Ga)
AS 34 *Canopus* (Charleston, SC)

SUPPORT SHIPS

OTHER AUXILIARIES

'NORWALK' CLASS
TAK 282 *Marshfield* (no home port assigned)

'VEGA' CLASS
TAK 286 *Vega* (no home port assigned)

BATTLE FORCES

AIRCRAFT CARRIERS

'MIDWAY' CLASS
CV 41 *Midway* (Yokosuka, Japan)
CV 43 *Coral Sea* (Norfolk, Va)

'FORRESTAL' CLASS
CV 60 *Saratoga* (Mayport, Fl)
CV 61 *Ranger* (San Diego, Ca)
CV 62 *Independence* (Norfolk, Va)

'KITTY HAWK' CLASS
CV 63 *Kitty Hawk* (San Diego, Ca)
CV 64 *Constellation* (Bremerton, Wa)
CV 66 *America* (Norfolk, Va)

'JOHN F. KENNEDY' CLASS
CV 67 *John F. Kennedy* (Norfolk, Va)

'ENTERPRISE' CLASS
CVN 65 *Enterprise* (Alameda, Ca)

'NIMITZ' CLASS
CVN 68 *Nimitz* (Norfolk, Va)
CVN 69 *Dwight D. Eisenhower* (Norfolk, Va)
CVN 70 *Carl Vinson* (Alameda, Ca)

SURFACE COMBATANTS

BATTLESHIPS

'IOWA' CLASS
BB 62 *New Jersey* (Long Beach, Ca)

CRUISERS

'LEAHY' CLASS
CG 16 *Leahy* (San Diego, Ca)
CG 17 *Harry E. Yarnell* (Norfolk, Va)
CG 18 *Worden* (Pearl Harbor, Hi)
CG 19 *Dale* (Mayport, Fl)
CG 20 *Richmond K. Turner* (Charleston, SC)
CG 21 *Gridley* (San Diego, Ca)
CG 22 *England* (San Diego, Ca)
CG 23 *Halsey* (San Diego, Ca)
CG 24 *Reeves* (Yokosuka, Japan)

'BELKNAP' CLASS
CG 26 *Belknap* (Norfolk, Va)
CG 27 *Josephus Daniels* (Norfolk, Va)
CG 28 *Wainwright* (Charleston, SC)
CG 29 *Jouett* (San Diego, Ca)
CG 30 *Horne* (San Diego, Ca)
CG 31 *Sterett* (Subic Bay, Rp)
CG 32 *William H. Standley* (San Diego, Ca)
CG 33 *Fox* (Long Beach, Ca)
CG 34 *Biddle* (Norfolk, Va)

'TICONDEROGA' CLASS
CG 47 *Ticonderoga* (Norfolk, Va)

'LONG BEACH' CLASS
CGN 9 *Long Beach* (San Diego, Ca)

'BAINBRIDGE' CLASS
CGN 25 *Bainbridge* (Bremerton, Wa)

'TRUXTUN' CLASS
CGN 35 *Truxtun* (Bremerton, Wa)

'CALIFORNIA' CLASS
CGN 36 *California* (Alameda, Ca)
CGN 37 *South Carolina* (Norfolk, Va)

'VIRGINIA' CLASS
CGN 38 *Virginia* (Norfolk, Va)
CGN 39 *Texas* (San Diego, Ca)
CGN 40 *Mississippi* (Norfolk, Va)
CGN 41 *Arkansas* (Alameda, Ca)

DESTROYERS

'SPRUANCE' CLASS
DD 963 *Spruance* (Norfolk, Va)
DD 964 *Paul F. Foster* (Long Beach, Ca)
DD 965 *Kinkaid* (San Diego, Ca)
DD 966 *Hewitt* (San Diego, Ca)
DD 967 *Elliot* (San Diego, Ca)
DD 968 *Arthur W. Radford* (Norfolk, Va)
DD 969 *Peterson* (Norfolk, Va)
DD 970 *Caron* (Norfolk, Va)
DD 971 *David R. Ray* (San Diego, Ca)
DD 972 *Oldendorf* (San Diego, Ca)
DD 973 *John Young* (San Diego, Ca)
DD 974 *Comte De Grasse* (Pascagoula, Ms)
DD 975 *O'Brien* (San Diego, Ca)
DD 976 *Merrill* (San Diego, Ca)
DD 977 *Briscoe* (Norfolk, Va)
DD 978 *Stump* (Brooklyn, NY)
DD 979 *Conolly* (Norfolk, Va)
DD 980 *Moosbrugger* (Charleston, SC)
DD 981 *John Hancock* (Charleston, SC)
DD 982 *Nicholson* (Charleston, SC)
DD 983 *John Rodgers* (Charleston, SC)
DD 984 *Leftwich* (San Diego, Ca)
DD 985 *Cushing* (San Diego, Ca)
DD 986 *Harry W. Hill* (San Diego, Ca)
DD 987 *O'Bannon* (Charleston, SC)
DD 988 *Thorn* (Charleston, SC)
DD 989 *Deyo* (Charleston, SC)
DD 990 *Ingersoll* (San Diego, Ca)
DD 991 *Fife* (San Diego, Ca)
DD 992 *Fletcher* (San Diego, Ca)
DD 997 *Hayler* (Norfolk, Va)

'CHARLES F. ADAMS' CLASS
DDG 2 *Charles F. Adams* (Philadelphia, Pa)
DDG 3 *John King* (Norfolk, Va)
DDG 4 *Lawrence* (Norfolk, Va)
DDG 5 *Claude V. Ricketts* (Norfolk, Va)
DDG 6 *Barney* (Norfolk, Va)
DDG 7 *Henry B. Wilson* (San Diego, Ca)
DDG 8 *Lynde McCormick* (San Diego, Ca)
DDG 9 *Towers* (Yokosuka, Japan)
DDG 10 *Sampson* (Mayport, Fl)
DDG 11 *Sellers* (Charleston, SC)
DDG 12 *Robison* (San Diego, Ca)
DDG 13 *Hoel* (Long Beach, Ca)
DDG 14 *Buchanan* (San Diego, Ca)
DDG 15 *Berkeley* (San Diego, Ca)
DDG 16 *Joseph Strauss* (Pearl Harbor, HI)
DDG 17 *Conyngham* (Norfolk, Va)
DDG 18 *Semmes* (Charleston, SC)
DDG 19 *Tattnall* (Mayport, Fl)
DDG 20 *Goldsborough* (Pearl Harbor, HI)
DDG 21 *Cochrane* (Yokosuka, Japan)
DDG 22 *Benjamin Stoddert* (Pearl Harbor, HI)
DDG 23 *Richard E. Byrd* (Norfolk, Va)
DDG 24 *Waddell* (San Diego, Ca)

'FARRAGUT' CLASS
DDG 37 *Farragut* (Philadelphia, Pa)
DDG 38 *Luce* (Mayport, Fl)
DDG 39 *Macdonough* (Charleston, SC)
DDG 40 *Coontz* (Norfolk, Va)
DDG 41 *King* (Norfolk, Va)
DDG 42 *Mahan* (Charleston, SC)
DDG 43 *Dahlgren* (Philadelphia, Pa)
DDG 44 *William V. Pratt* (Charleston, SC)
DDG 45 *Dewey* (Charleston, SC)
DDG 46 *Preble* (Norfolk, Va)

'KIDD' CLASS
DDG 993 *Kidd* (Norfolk, Va)
DDG 994 *Callaghan* (San Diego, Ca)
DDG 995 *Scott* (Norfolk, Va)
DDG 996 *Chandler* (San Diego, Ca)

FRIGATES

'BRONSTEIN' CLASS
FF 1037 *Bronstein* (San Diego, Ca)
FF 1038 *McCloy* (Norfolk, Va)

'GARCIA' CLASS
FF 1040 *Garcia* (Charleston, SC)
FF 1041 *Bradley* (Long Beach, Ca)
FF 1043 *Edward McDonnell* (Mayport, Fl)
FF 1044 *Brumby* (Charleston, SC)
FF 1045 *Davidson* (Pearl Harbor, HI)
FF 1047 *Voge* (Mayport, Fl)
FF 1048 *Sample* (Pearl Harbor, HI)
FF 1049 *Koelsch* (Mayport, Fl)
FF 1050 *Albert David* (San Diego, Ca)
FF 1051 *O'Callahan* (San Diego, Ca)

'KNOX' CLASS
FF 1052 *Knox* (Yokosuka, Japan)
FF 1053 *Roark* (San Diego, Ca)
FF 1055 *Hepburn* (San Diego, Ca)
FF 1056 *Connole* (Newport, RI)
FF 1057 *Rathburne* (Pearl Harbor, HI)
FF 1058 *Meyerkord* (San Diego, Ca)
FF 1059 *W. S. Sims* (Mayport, Fl)
FF 1062 *Whipple* (Pearl Harbor, HI)
FF 1063 *Reasoner* (San Diego, Ca)
FF 1064 *Lockwood* (Yokosuka, Japan)
FF 1065 *Stein* (San Diego, Ca)
FF 1066 *Marvin Shields* (San Diego, Ca)
FF 1067 *Francis Hammond* (Yokosuka, Japan)
FF 1068 *Vreeland* (Mayport, Fl)
FF 1069 *Bagley* (San Diego, Ca)
FF 1070 *Downes* (San Diego, Ca)
FF 1071 *Badger* (Pearl Harbor, HI)
FF 1073 *Robert E. Peary* (Pearl Harbor, HI)
FF 1074 *Harold E. Holt* (Pearl Harbor, HI)
FF 1075 *Trippe* (Charleston, SC)
FF 1076 *Fanning* (San Diego, Ca)
FF 1077 *Ouellet* (Pearl Harbor, HI)
FF 1078 *Joseph Hewes* (Charleston, SC)
FF 1079 *Bowen* (Charleston, SC)
FF 1080 *Paul* (Mayport, Fl)
FF 1081 *Aylwin* (Charleston, SC)
FF 1082 *Elmer Montgomery* (Mayport, Fl)
FF 1083 *Cook* (San Diego, Ca)
FF 1084 *McCandless* (Norfolk, Va)
FF 1085 *Donald B. Beary* (Norfolk, Va)
FF 1086 *Brewton* (Pearl Harbor, HI)
FF 1087 *Kirk* (Yokosuka, Japan)
FF 1088 *Barbey* (Long Beach, Ca)
FF 1089 *Jesse L. Brown* (Charleston, SC)
FF 1090 *Ainsworth* (Charleston, SC)
FF 1092 *Thomas C. Hart* (Norfolk, Va)
FF 1093 *Capodanno* (Newport, RI)
FF 1094 *Pharris* (Norfolk, Va)
FF 1095 *Truett* (Norfolk, Va)
FF 1097 *Moinester* (Norfolk, Va)

'GLOVER' CLASS
FF 1098 *Glover* (Norfolk, Va)

'BROOOKE' CLASS
FFG 1 *Brooke* (San Diego, Ca)
FFG 2 *Ramsey* (Long Beach, Ca)
FFG 3 *Schofield* (San Diego, Ca)
FFG 4 *Talbot* (Mayport, Fl)
FFG 5 *Richard L. Page* (Norfolk, Va)
FFG 6 *Julius A. Furer* (Charleston, SC)

'OLIVER HAZARD PERRY' CLASS
FFG 7 *Oliver Hazard Perry* (Mayport, Fl)
FFG 8 *McInerney* (Mayport, Fl)
FFG 9 *Wadsworth* (Long Beach, Ca)
FFG 11 *Clark* (Mayport, Fl)
FFG 12 *George Philip* (San Diego, Ca)
FFG 13 *Samuel Eliot Morison* (Mayport, Fl)
FFG 14 *Sides* (San Diego, Ca)
FFG 15 *Estocin* (Mayport, Fl)
FFG 16 *Clifton Sprague* (Mayport, Fl)
FFG 19 *John A. Moore* (San Diego, Ca)
FFG 20 *Antrim* (Mayport, Fl)
FFG 21 *Flatley* (Mayport, Fl)
FFG 22 *Fahrion* (Mayport, Fl)
FFG 23 *Lewis B. Puller* (San Diego, Ca)
FFG 24 *Jack Williams* (Mayport, Fl)
FFG 25 *Copeland* (Long Beach, Ca)
FFG 26 *Gallery* (Mayport, Fl)
FFG 27 *Mahlon S. Tisdale* (San Diego, Ca)
FFG 28 *Boone* (Mayport, Fl)
FFG 29 *Stephen W. Groves* (Mayport, Fl)
FFG 30 *Reid* (Long Beach, Ca)
FFG 31 *Stark* (Mayport, Fl)
FFG 32 *John L. Hall* (Mayport, Fl)
FFG 33 *Jarrett* (Long Beach, Ca)
FFG 34 *Aubrey Fitch* (Mayport, Fl)
FFG 36 *Underwood* (Mayport, Fl)
FFG 37 *Crommelin* (Long Beach, Ca)
FFG 38 *Curts* (Long Beach, Ca)
FFG 39 *Doyle* (Mayport, Fl)
FFG 40 *Halyburton* (Charleston, SC)
FFG 41 *Mc Clusky* (Long Beach, Ca)
FFG 42 *Klakring* (Charleston, SC)
FFG 45 *Dewert* (Charleston, SC)

SUBMARINES

ATTACK SUBMARINES

'DARTER' CLASS
SS 576 *Darter* (Sasebo, Japan)

'BARBEL' CLASS
SS 580 *Barbel* (Pearl Harbor, HI)
SS 581 *Blueback* (San Diego, Ca)
SS 582 *Bonefish* (Charleston, SC)

'SEAWOLF' CLASS
SSN 575 *Seawolf* (Vallejo, Ca)

'SKATE' CLASS
SSN 578 *Skate* (Pearl Harbor, HI)
SSN 579 *Swordfish* (Pearl Harbor, HI)
SSN 583 *Sargo* (Pearl Harbor, HI)
SSN 584 *Seadragon* (Pearl Harbor, HI)

'SKIPJACK' CLASS
SSN 585 *Skipjack* (Groton, Ct)
SSN 588 *Scamp* (Groton, Ct)
SSN 590 *Sculpin* (Groton, Ct)
SSN 591 *Shark* (Groton, Ct)
SSN 592 *Snook* (Groton, Ct)

'PERMIT' CLASS
SSN 594 *Permit* (Vallejo, Ca)
SSN 595 *Plunger* (San Diego, Ca)
SSN 596 *Barb* (San Diego, Ca)
SSN 603 *Pollack* (San Diego, Ca)
SSN 604 *Haddo* (San Diego, Ca)
SSN 605 *Jack* (Portsmouth, NH)
SSN 606 *Tinosa* (Portsmouth, NH)
SSN 607 *Dace* (New London, Ct)
SSN 612 *Guardfish* (Vallejo, Ca)
SSN 613 *Flasher* (Vallejo, Ca)
SSN 614 *Greenling* (New London, Ct)
SSN 615 *Gato* (New London, Ct)
SSN 621 *Haddock* (San Diego, Ca)

'TULLIBEE' CLASS
SSN 597 *Tullibee* (Groton, Ct)

'GEORGE WASHINGTON' CLASS
SSN 598 *George Washington* (New London, Ct)
SSN 599 *Patrick Henry* (Bangor, Wa)

'ETHAN ALLEN' CLASS
SSN 609 *Sam Houston* (Bangor, Wa)
SSN 611 *John Marshall* (Bremerton, Wa)
SSN 618 *Thomas Jefferson* (Charleston, SC)

'STURGEON' CLASS
SSN 637 *Sturgeon* (Charleston, SC)
SSN 638 *Whale* (Groton, Ct)
SSN 639 *Tautog* (Pearl Harbor, HI)
SSN 646 *Grayling* (Charleston, SC)
SSN 647 *Pogy* (Vallejo, Ca)
SSN 648 *Aspro* (Pearl Harbour, HI)
SSN 649 *Sunfish* (Charleston, SC)
SSN 650 *Pargo* (New London, Ct)
SSN 651 *Queenfish* (Pearl Harbor, HI)
SSN 652 *Puffer* (Pearl Harbor, HI)
SSN 653 *Ray* (Charleston, SC)
SSN 660 *Sand Lance* (Charleston, SC)
SSN 661 *Lapon* (Norfolk, Va)
SSN 662 *Gurnard* (San Diego, Ca)
SSN 663 *Hammerhead* (Norfolk, Va)
SSN 664 *Sea Devil* (Charleston, SC)
SSN 665 *Guitarro* (San Diego, Ca)
SSN 666 *Hawkbill* (Pearl Harbor, HI)
SSN 667 *Bergall* (Norfolk, Va)
SSN 668 *Spadefish* (Norfolk, Va)
SSN 669 *Seahorse* (Charleston, SC)
SSN 670 *Finback* (Norfolk, Va)
SSN 672 *Pintado* (San Diego, Ca)
SSN 673 *Flying Fish* (Norfolk, Va)
SSN 674 *Trepang* (New London, Ct)
SSN 675 *Bluefish* (Norfolk, Va)
SSN 676 *Billfish* (New London, Ct)
SSN 677 *Drum* (San Diego, Ca)
SSN 678 *Archerfish* (Portsmouth, NH)
SSN 679 *Silversides* (Norfolk, Va)
SSN 680 *William H. Bates* (San Diego, Ca)
SSN 681 *Batfish* (Charleston, SC)
SSN 682 *Tunny* (Pearl Harbor, HI)
SSN 683 *Parche* (Vallejo, Ca)
SSN 684 *Cavalla* (Pearl Harbor, HI)
SSH 686 *L. Mendel Rivers* (Charleston, SC)
SSN 687 *Richard B. Russell* (Vallejo, Ca)

'NARWHAL' CLASS
SSN 671 *Narwhal* (Charleston, SC)

'GLENARD P. LIPSCOMB' CLASS
SSN 685 *Glenard P. Lipscomb* (Norfolk, Va)

'LOS ANGELES' CLASS
SSN 688 *Los Angeles* (Pearl Harbor, HI)
SSN 689 *Baton Rouge* (Norfolk, Va)
SSN 690 *Philadelphia* (Groton, Ct)
SSN 691 *Memphis* (Norfolk, Va)
SSN 692 *Omaha* (Pearl Harbor, HI)
SSN 693 *Cincinnati* (Norfolk, Va)

SSN 694 *Groton* (Groton, Ct)
SSN 695 *Birmingham* (Norfolk, Va)
SSN 696 *New York City* (Pearl Harbor, HI)
SSN 697 *Indianapolis* (Pearl Harbor, HI)
SSN 698 *Bremerton* (Pearl Harbor, HI)
SSN 699 *Jacksonville* (Norfolk, Va)
SSN 700 *Dallas* (Groton, Ct)
SSN 701 *La Jolla* (San Diego, Ca)
SSN 702 *Phoenix* (Norfolk, Va)
SSN 703 *Boston* (Groton, Ct)
SSN 704 *Baltimore* (Norfolk, Va)
SSN 705 *City of Corpus Christi* (Groton, Ct)
SSN 706 *Albuquerque* (Groton, Ct)
SSN 707 *Portsmouth* (Groton, Ct)
SSN 711 *San Francisco* (Pearl Harbor, HI)
SSN 712 *Atlanta* (Norfolk, Va)
SSN 713 *Houston* (San Diego, Ca)
SSN 714 *Norfolk* (Norfolk, Va)
SSN 715 *Buffalo* (Norfolk, Va)

PATROL COMBATANTS

PATROL SHIPS

'PEGASUS' CLASS
PHM 1 *Pegasus* (Key West, Fl)
PHM 2 *Hercules* (Key West, Fl)
PHM 3 *Taurus* (Key West, Fl)
PHM 4 *Aquila* (Key West, Fl)
PHM 5 *Aries* (Key West, Fl)
PHM 6 *Gemini* (Key West, Fl)

AMPHIBIOUS WARFARE SHIPS

AMPHIBIOUS HELO/LANDING CRAFT CARRIERS

'TARAWA' CLASS
LHA 1 *Tarawa* (San Diego, Ca)
LHA 2 *Saipan* (Norfolk, Va)
LHA 3 *Belleau Wood* (San Diego, Ca)
LHA 4 *Nassau* (Norfolk, Va)
LHA 5 *Peleliu* (Long Beach, Ca)

'RALEIGH' CLASS
LPD 1 *Raleigh* (Norfolk, Va)
LPD 2 *Vancouver* (San Diego, Ca)

'AUSTIN' CLASS
LPD 4 *Austin* (Norfolk, Va)
LPD 5 *Ogdon* (Long Beach, Ca)
LPD 6 *Duluth* (San Diego, Ca)
LPD 7 *Cleveland* (San Diego, Ca)
LPD 8 *Dubuque* (San Diego, Ca)
LPD 9 *Denver* (San Diego, Ca)
LPD 10 *Juneau* (San Diego, Ca)
LPD 12 *Shreveport* (Norfolk, Va)
LPD 13 *Nashville* (Norfolk, Va)
LPD 14 *Trenton* (Norfolk, Va)
LPD 15 *Ponce* (Norfolk, Va)

'IWO JIMA' CLASS
LPH 2 *Iwo Jima* (Norfolk, Va)
LPH 3 *Okinawa* (San Diego, Ca)
LPH 7 *Guadalcanal* (Norfolk, Va)
LPH 9 *Guam* (Norfolk, Va)
LPH 10 *Tripoli* (San Diego, Ca)
LPH 11 *New Orleans* (San Diego, Ca)

LANDING CRAFT CARRIERS

'CHARLESTON' CLASS
LKA 113 *Charleston* (Norfolk, Va)
LKA 114 *Durham* (San Diego, Ca)
LKA 115 *Mobile* (Long Beach, Ca)
LKA 116 *Saint Louis* (Sasebo, Japan)
LKA 117 *El Paso* (Norfolk, Va)

'THOMASTON' CLASS
LSD 28 *Thomaston* (San Diego, Ca)
LSD 30 *Fort Snelling* (Little Creek, Norfolk, Va)
LSD 32 *Spiegel Grove* (Little Creek, Norfolk, Va)
LSD 33 *Alamo* (San Diego, Ca)
LSD 34 *Hermitage* (Little Creek, Norfolk, Va)
LSD 35 *Monticello* (San Diego, Ca)

'ANCHORAGE' CLASS
LSD 36 *Anchorage* (San Diego, Ca)
LSD 37 *Portland* (Little Creek, Norfolk, Va)
LSD 38 *Pensacola* (Little Creek, Norfolk, Va)
LSD 39 *Mount Vernon* (San Diego, Ca)
LSD 40 *Fort Fisher* (San Diego, Ca)

'NEWPORT' CLASS
LST 1179 *Newport* (Little Creek, Norfolk, Va)
LST 1180 *Manitowoc* (Little Creek, Norfolk, Va)
LST 1181 *Sumter* (Little Creek, Norfolk, Va)
LST 1182 *Fresno* (San Diego, Ca)
LST 1183 *Peoria* (San Diego, Ca)
LST 1184 *Frederick* (San Diego, Ca)
LST 1185 *Schenectady* (San Diego, Ca)
LST 1186 *Cayuga* (Sand Diego, Ca)
LST 1187 *Tuscaloosa* (San Diego, Ca)
LST 1188 *Saginaw* (Portsmouth, Va)
LST 1189 *San Bernardino* (San Diego, Ca)
LST 1192 *Spartanburg County* (Little Creek, Norfolk, Va)
LST 1193 *Fairfax County* (Little Creek, Norfolk, Va)
LST 1194 *La Moure County* (Little Creek, Norfolk, Va)
LST 1195 *Barbour County* (San Diego, Ca)
LST 1196 *Harlan County* (Little Creek, Norfolk, Va)
LST 1197 *Barnstable County* (Little Creek, Norfolk, Va)
LST 1198 *Bristol County* (San Diego, Ca)

MISCELLANEOUS AMPHIBIOUS WARFARE SHIPS

'BLUE RIDGE' CLASS
LCC 19 *Blue Ridge* (Yokosuka, Japan)
LCC 20 *Mount Whitney* (Norfolk, Va)

MINE WARFARE SHIPS

MINESWEEPERS

'AGGRESSIVE' CLASS
MSO 443 *Fidelity* (Panama City, Fl)
MSO 448 *Illusive* (Charleston, SC)
MSO 490 *Leader* (Charleston, SC)

MOBILE LOGISTIC SHIPS

UNDERWAY REPLENISHMENT SHIPS

'SURIBACHI' CLASS
AE 21 *Suribachi* (Weapon Station Earle, NJ)
AE 22 *Mauna Kea* (Vallejo, Ca)

'NITRO' CLASS
AE 23 *Nitro* (Weapons Station Earle, NJ)
AE 24 *Pyro* (Vallejo, Ca)
AE 24 *Haleakala* (Concord, Ca)

'KILAUEA' CLASS
AE 27 *Butte* (Weapons Station Earle. NJ)
AE 28 *Santa Barbara* (Weapons Station Charleston, SC)
AE 29 *Mount Hood* (Concord, Ca)
AE 32 *Flint* (Concord, Ca)
AE 33 *Shasta* (San Diego, Ca)
AE 34 *Mount Baker* (Weapons Station Charleston, SC)
AE 35 *Kiska* (Concord, Ca)

'MARS' CLASS
AFS 1 *Mars* (Oakland, Ca)
AFS 2 *Sylvania* (Norfolk, Va)
AFS 3 *Niagara Falls* (Guam, HI)
AFS 4 *White Plains* (Yokosuka, Japan)
AFS 5 *Concord* (Norfolk, Va)
AFS 6 *San Diego* (Norfolk, Va)
AFS 7 *San Jose* (Guam, HI)

'JUMBO'/'ASHTABULA' CLASS
AO 98 *Caloosahatchef* (Norfolk, Va)
AO 99 *Camisteo* (Norfolk, Va)

'CIMARRON' CLASS
AO 177 *Cimarron* (Pearl Harbor, HI)
AO 178 *Monogahela* (Norfolk, Va)
AO 179 *Merrimack* (Norfolk, Va)
AO 180 *Willamette* (Pearl Harbor, HI)
AO 186 *Platte* (Norfolk, Va)

'SACRAMENTO' CLASS
AOE 1 *Sacramento* (Bremerton, Wa)
AOE 2 *Camden* (Bremerton, Wa)
AOE 3 *Seattle* (Norfolk, Va)
AOE 4 *Detroit* (Norfolk, Va)

'WICHITA' CLASS
AOR 1 *Wichita* (Alameda, Ca)
AOR 2 *Milwaukee* (Norfolk, Va)
AOR 3 *Kansas City* (Alameda, Ca)
AOR 4 *Savannah* (Norfolk, Va)
AOR 5 *Wabash* (Alameda, Ca)
AOR 6 *Kalamazoo* (Norfolk, Va)
AOR 7 *Roanoke* (Alameda, Ca)

'KILAUEA' CLASS
TAE 26 *Kilauea* (no home port assigned)

'RIGEL' CLASS
TAF 58 *Rigel* (no home port assigned)

'SIRIUS' CLASS
TAFS 8 *Sirius* (no home port assigned)
TAFS 9 *Spica* (Oakland, Ca)
TAFS 10 *Saturn* (no home port assigned)

'JUMBO'/'MISPILLION' CLASS
TAO 105 *Mispillion* (no home port assigned)
TAO 106 *Navasota* (no home port assigned)
TAO 107 *Passumpsic* (no home port assigned)
TAO 108 *Pawcatuck* (no home port assigned)
TAO 109 *Waccamaw* (no home port assigned)

'NEOSHO' CLASS
TAO 143 *Neosho* (no home port assigned)
TAO 144 *Mississinewa* (no home port assigned)
TAO 145 *Hassayampa* (no home port assigned)
TAO 146 *Kawishiwi* (no home port assigned)
TAO 147 *Truckee* (no home port assigned)
TAO 148 *Ponchatoula* (no home port assigned)

SUPPORT FORCES

MOBILE LOGISTIC SHIPS

MATERIAL SUPPORT SHIPS

'DIXIE' CLASS
AD 15 *Prairie* (Long Beach, Ca)
AD 18 *Sierra* (Charleston, SC)
AD 19 *Yosemite* (Mayport, Fl)

'SAMUEL GOMPERS' CLASS
AD 37 *Samuel Gompers* (San Diego, Ca)
AD 38 *Puget Sound* (Gaeta, Italy)

'YELLOWSTONE' CLASS
AD 41 *Yellowstone* (Norfolk, Va)
AD 42 *Acadia* (San Diego, Ca)
AD 43 *Cape Cod* (San Diego, Ca)
AD 44 *Shenandoah* (Norfolk, Va)

'VULCAN' CLASS
AR 5 *Vulcan* (Norfolk, Va)
AR 6 *Ajax* (San Diego, Ca)
AR 7 *Hector* (NSC Oakland, Ca)
AR 8 *Jason* (Pearl Harbor, HI)

'FULTON' CLASS
As 11 *Fulton* (Quincy, Ma)
AS 18 *Orion* (La Maddalena, Italy)

'PROTEUS' CLASS
AS 19 *Proteus* (Guam, HI)

'L. Y. SPEAR' CLASS
AS 36 *L. Y. Spear* (Norfolk, Va)
AS 37 *Dixon* (San Diego, Ca)

'EMORY S. LAND' CLASS
AS 39 *Emory S. Land* (Norfolk, Va)
AS 40 *Frank Cable* (Charleston, SC)
AS 41 *McKee* (San Diego, Ca)

SUPPORT SHIPS

FLEET SUPPORT SHIPS

'BOLSTER' CLASS
ARS 39 *Conserver* (Pearl Harbor, HI)
ARS 40 *Hoist* (Little Creek, Norfolk, Va)
ARS 41 *Opportune* (Little Creek, Norfolk, Va)
ARS 42 *Reclaimer* (Pearl Harbor, HI)
ARS 43 *Recovery* (Little Creek, Norfolk, Va)

'CHANTICLEER' CLASS
ASR 9 *Florikan* (San Diego, Ca)
ASR 13 *Kittiwake* (Norfolk, Va)
ASR 14 *Petrel* (Charleston, SC)
ASR 15 *Sunbird* (Groton, Ct)

'PIGEON' CLASS
ASR 21 *Pigeon* (San Diego, Ca)
ASR 22 *Ortolan* (Charleston, SC)

'EDENTON' CLASS
ATS 1 *Edenton* (Little Creek, Norfolk, Va)
ATS 2 *Beaufort* (Pearl Harbor, HI)
ATS 3 *Brunswick* (Pearl Harbor, HI)

'POWHATAN' CLASS
TATF 166 *Powhatan* (no home port assigned)
TATF 167 *Narragansett* (no home port assigned)
TATF 168 *Catawba* (no home port assigned)
TATF 169 *Navajo* (no home port assigned)
TATF 170 *Mohawk* (no home port alssigned)
TATF 171 *Sioux* (no home port assigned)
TATF 172 *Apache* (no home port assigned)

OTHER AUXILIARIES

'FURMAN' CLASS
TAK 280 *Furman* (no home port assigned)

MOBILIZATION FORCES CATEGORY A

SURFACE COMBATANTS

DESTROYERS

'HULL' CLASS
DD 946 *Edson* (Newport, RI)

FRIGATES

'KNOX' CLASS
FF 1054 *Gray* (Long Beach, Ca)
FF 1060 *Lang* (Long Beach, Ca)
FF 1061 *Patterson* (Philadelphia, Pa)
FF 1072 *Blakely* (Charleston, SC)
FF 1091 *Miller* (Newport, RI)
FF 1096 *Valdez* (Newport, RI)

'OLIVER HAZARD PERRY' CLASS
FFG 10 *Duncan* (Long Beach, Ca)

AMPHIBIOUS WARFARE SHIPS

LANDING CRAFT CARRIERS

'NEWPORT' CLASS
LST 1190 *Boulder* (New York, Ny)
LST 1191 *Racine* (Long Beach, Ca)

LOCAL DEFENCE AND MISCELLANEOUS SUPPORT FORCES

AUXILIARIES AND SEALIFT FORCES

SUPPORT SHIPS

OTHER AUXILIARIES

'POINT LOMA' CLASS
AGOS 2 *Point Loma* (San Diego, Ca)

'LA SALLE' CLASS
AGF 3 *La Salle* (Philadelphia, Pa)

'CORONADO' CLASS
AGF 11 *Coronado* (Philadelphia, Pa)

'DOLPHIN' CLASS
AGSS 555 *Dolphin* (San Diego, Ca)

'NORTON SOUND' CLASS
AVM 1 *Norton Sound* (Port Hueneme, Ca)

'LEXINGTON' CLASS
AVT 16 *Lexington* (Pensacola, Fl)

'NEPTUNE' CLASS
TARC 3 *Neptune* (no home port assigned)

'AEOLUS' CLASS
TARC 2 *Aeolus* (no home port assigned)

'ALBERT J. MEYER' CLASS
TARC 6 *Albert J. Myer* (no home port assigned)

'AK-C337D' CLASS
TAK 2035 *Gulf Shipper*

'AK-C346D B-SHIP' CLASS
TAK 2032 *Hay*

'AC-C4-S66A' CLASS
TAK 2043 *Letittia Lykes*

'COLORADO' CLASS
TAK 1003 *American Spitfire* (no home port assigned)
TAK 1008 *American Titan*
TAK 1010 *American Trojan*
TAK 1004 *Austral Lighting* (no home port assigned)
TAK 1005 *Austral Rainbow* (no home port assigned)

'LASH' CLASS
TAK 1015 *George Wythe*

'HEAVY LIFT' CLASS
TAK 2005 *Transcolorado*

'MERCURY' CLASS
TAKR 10 *Mercury* (no home port assigned)
TAKR 11 *Jupiter* (no home port assigned)

'LYRA' CLASS
TAKR 112 *Lyra* (no home port assigned)

'OVERSEAS' CLASS
TAOT 1204 *Overseas Valdez*
TAOT 1207 *Mormac Star*

'SEALIFT PACIFIC' CLASS
TAOT 174 *Sealift Caribbean* (no home port assigned)

'COLUMBIA' CLASS
TAOT 182 *Columbia* (no home port assigned)
TAOT 185 *Susquehanna* (no home port assigned)

MOBILIZATION FORCES CATEGORY B

MINE WARFARE SHIPS

MINESWEEPERS

'AGGRESSIVE' CLASS
MSO 427 *Constant* (San Diego, Ca)
MSO 433 *Engage* (Mayport, Fl)
MSO 437 *Enhance* (Tacoma, Wa)
MSO 438 *Esteem* (Seattle, Wa)
MSO 439 *Excel* (San Francisco, Ca)
MSO 440 *Exploit* (Newport, RI)
MSO 441 *Exultant* (Mayport, Fl)
MSO 442 *Fearless* Charleston, SC
MSO 446 *Fortify* (Little Creek, Norfolk, Va)
MSO 449 *Impervious* (Mayport, Fl)
MSO 455 *Implicit* (Tacoma, Wa)
MSO 456 *Inflict* (Little Creek, Norfolk, Va)
MSO 464 *Pluck* (San Diego, Ca)
MSO 488 *Conquest* (Seattle, Wa)
MSO 489 *Gallant* (San Francisco, Ca)
MSO 492 *Pledge* (Seattle, Wa)

'ACME' CLASS
MSO 509 *Adroit* (Little Creek, Norfolk, Va)
MSO 511 *Affray* (Newport, RI)

SUPPORT SHIPS

FLEET SUPPORT SHIPS

'ESCAPE' CLASS
ARS 8 *Preserver* (Little Creek, Norfolk, Va)

'BOLSTER' CLASS
ARS 38 *Bolster* (Long Beach, Ca)

'ABNAKI' CLASS
ATF 105 *Moctobi* (Long Beach, Ca)
ATF 110 *Guapaw* (Port Hueneme, Ca)

'ACHOMAWI' CLASS
ATF 159 *Paiute* (Mayport, Fl)
ATF 160 *Papago* (Little Creek, Norfolk, Va)

The 'Oliver Hazard Perry' class of frigate is a major new programme to modernize US escort potential. Like any completely new vessel, USS *Oliver Hazard Perry* (FFG 7) had to be thoroughly tested, such testing including the detonation of large explosive charges close to the hull to check the designed ability to withstand shock.

NE

United States Naval Aviation

US Naval Aviation is the sharp end of the maritime force. It is charged with the tasks of protection and projection: protection of the fleet from air and sea attack, and projection of its firepower far beyond the scope of its ships. As the British found in their Falklands campaign, air superiority is paramount and the US Navy has the finest shipboard air power in the world, able to challenge all comers.

Left: A Vought A-7A Corsair II of light attack squadron VA-147 returns to the USS *Ranger* following a strike mission against a target in North Vietnam in 1968. Operating from the so-called 'Yankee Station' in the Gulf of Tonkin, two or three carriers were usually present at any given time.

Below: No less than six examples of the long-range Hughes AIM-54A Phoenix air-to-air missile are carried by this Grumman F-14A Tomcat of VF-32. A most capable fleet-defence fighter, the Tomcat can also operate medium- range AIM-7F Sparrow and short-range AIM-9L Sidewinder missiles.

Like its sister services in the US Armed Forces, the United States Navy has since the end of the conflict in South East Asia been engaged in major modernization efforts, these manifesting themselves in different ways. Purchase of new equipment (such as the Grumman F-14 Tomcat, McDonnell Douglas F/A-18 Hornet and updated variants of the Lockheed P-3 Orion patrol aircraft) has played a significant part in bringing about enhanced capability, but the US Navy has also subscribed heavily to a concept known as CILOP (Conversion In Lieu Of Procurement), by which substantial numbers of older aircraft are fitted with new internal systems to permit their continued deployment as front-line elements of the combat forces. Notable examples of CILOP updating include modification of Grumman A-6A Intruders to A-6E configuration and updating of McDonnell Douglas F-4B and F-4J Phantoms to F-4N and F-4S standard respectively.

Occupying a position of clear-cut supremacy as the world's major operator of large aircraft-carriers, the US Navy fleet of these vessels currently numbers 14, including four nuclear-powered, examples; three further nuclear carriers are on order for delivery by 1991, and it is anticipated that availability of these will eventually permit the two surviving 'Midway' class vessels to be retired after more than 40 years of service. Ultimately, US Navy planning calls for the carrierborne striking force to peak and be maintained at a level of 15 Carrier Air Wings (CVWs), there being 13 such organizations in existence at the present time, with a thirteenth in the process of forming. There appears to be no great degree of urgency attached to forming the additional two CVWs, largely one assumes because of the limited availability of older 'Forrestal' class vessels which are gradually being submitted for major lengthy SLEP (Service Life Extension Program) overhauls.

By virtue of the fact that it literally constitutes a mobile floating air base, the aircraft-carrier remains the single most powerful element within the US Navy, and it is usual for such vessels to deploy with an organization known as a Carrier Air Wing. For the most part, composition of these CVWs follows standard patterns and, with the exception of those assigned to the two surviving 'Midway' class vessels, usually incorporates fighter, attack, airborne early warning, electronic countermeasures and anti-submarine warfare aircraft so as to permit the conduct of operations across virtually the entire spectrum of military aviation. A typical CVW includes nine squadrons operating no less than 86 aircraft. Fighter elements comprise two squadrons each with 12 aircraft, either F-4 Phantoms or F-14 Tomcats, paired sister squadrons invariably using the same type. The light attack component also consists of two squadrons: at present these are universally equipped with the Vought A-7E Corsair, but the first US

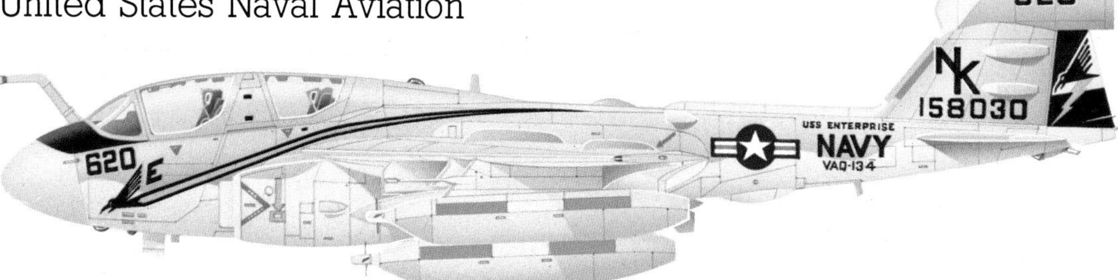

US Navy and US Marine Corps electronic countermeasures capability was significantly enhanced during the 1970s following the introduction of the Grumman EA-6B Prowler. A development of the two-seat A-6 Intruder, the Prowler has demonstrated remarkable 'growth' potential since it attained operational status in 1972.

Navy squadron to convert to the F/A-18 (VFA-113 of the Pacific Fleet) is now well advanced with training in anticipation of operational deployment in 1985, and the remainder of the 1980s should witness widespread introduction of this type. Returning to the CVW, one medium attack squadron uses the Intruder, the number of aircraft embarked usually being 14, made up of nine or 10 A-6E attack models plus four or five KA-6D tanker variants for inflight-refuelling support of all CVW assets requiring this service. ASW elements comprise one S-3A Viking squadron with 10 aircraft and one Sikorsky SH-3 Sea King squadron with six helicopters. ECM assets consist of a single squadron with a quarter of Grumman EA-6B Prowlers. Finally, airborne early warning support is provided by one squadron of four Grumman E-2 Hawkeyes.

Recon disadvantage

Until quite recently, it was also normal for a CVW to include a handful of dedicated reconnaissance aircraft but, following the retirement of the Vought RF-8G Crusader and the Rockwell RA-5C Vigilante, there is now no specialist machine to fulfil this mission, a situation which is unlikely to change in the immediate future. As a temporary solution, most of the Tomcat-capable carriers now deploy with three TARPS (Tactical Air Reconnaissance Pod System) configured aircraft amongst the 24 fighters embarked. Reconnaissance capability has been developed for the F/A-18A Hornet but is not yet on order.

In recent years there has been some imbalance in the quantity and quality of the carriers assigned to each of the two major fleets, the Atlantic Fleet having as many as eight of the so-called 'super carriers' whilst the Pacific Fleet had only four, these latter being supported by the two remaining 'Midway' class vessels, one of them operating on permanent forward-deployed status with its homeport at Yokosuka, Japan. During the summer of 1983, however, the first attempt at redressing this imbalance witnessed the transfer of the 'Midway' class vessel USS *Coral Sea* to the Atlantic Fleet whilst the nuclear-powered USS *Carl Vinson* was reassigned in the opposite direction, both carriers adopting their new assignments upon completion of world cruises.

Although each of the two major fleets is a separate and distinct organization, the past few years have also witnessed greater flexibility in operations and, whilst carrier assignments remained constant until 1983, there have been several instances of Pacific Fleet CVWs operating aboard Atlantic Fleet carriers both off the United States and in the Mediterranean. Increasing emphasis on naval activity in the Indian Ocean, formerly the sole preserve of the Pacific Fleet, has also seen carriers of both fleets deploying to this area on a regular basis, albeit at the cost of reductions in the number of Carrier Battle Groups in the Mediterranean (6th Fleet) and Western Pacific (7th Fleet) from two to one. By and large, however, carriers tend to go where the action is, and the recent troubles in Chad and the Lebanon will almost certainly have resulted in the number of carriers available to the 6th Fleet again increasing to at least two.

From the organization point of view the US Navy is a fearsomely complex agency and one that would require almost a book to itself to describe adequately.

Some idea of the power possessed by the modern aircraft-carrier is conveyed in this view of the forward flight deck of the USS *John F. Kennedy*. No less than 38 aircraft are visible, these including examples of the Grumman A-6 Intruder, Vought A-7 Corsair, Grumman F-14A Tomcat, Grumman EA-6B Prowler and Sikorsky SH-3 Sea King.

Undoubtedly the finest air defence fighter ever developed, the F-14 is the only aircraft in the world capable of simultaneously engaging at long range a series of targets, from high-altitude supersonic intruders to low-level cruise missiles.

Sikorsky Aircraft is scheduled to start deliveries of at least 40 MH-53 airborne mine countermeasures (AMCM) helicopters in 1986. A version of the successful CH-53E Super Stallion, the MH-53E's most obvious external modification is the enlargement of the fuselage sponsons for extra fuel.

Responsibility for logistical support of aircraft carriers at sea is largely entrusted to the Grumman C-2A Greyhound, a type which has recently been reinstated in production to meet future needs in this area. The example depicted here is from VR-24 which is based at Sigonella, Sicily in support of the 6th Fleet.

Essentially aviation elements of the two fleets report either to the Commander Naval Air Force Atlantic Fleet (ComNavAirLant) at Norfolk, Virginia, or to ComNavAirPac at North Island, California, both of these being subordinate to their respective Fleet Commander-in-Chief. To provide a clearer understanding of the way in which aviation assets are further organized, it is worth examining NavAirLant in greater detail, for this is essentially representative of both Atlantic and Pacific organization apart from a few fairly minor details.

To assist ComNavAirLant in control of the various assets which comprise this command, numerous smaller sub-commands exist, most being responsible for fairly specific areas of activity. It is these subordinate commands which shoulder the burden of ensuring smooth running on a day-to-day basis. Heading the list are four Carrier Groups (CarGrus), namely CarGru2 at Naples, Italy; CarGru4 at Norfolk, Virginia; CarGru6 at Mayport, Florida, and CarGru8, also at Norfolk. It is to these that the active aircraft-carriers are attached although it should be noted that CarGru2 has no permanent carriers of its own, normally controlling those detached from the three US-based groups for tours of duty with the 6th Fleet in the Mediterranean. The Carrier Groups also exercise control over the CVWs, each of the latter being headed by a commander who, in turn, reports to the captain of the carrier to which his wing is assigned. Currently, the Atlantic Fleet possesses six active CVWs, a seventh being in the initial stages of forming as part of the US Navy's long-term expansion programme. Pacific Fleet organization follows similar lines, there also being four CarGrus and six active CVWs, a figure which may eventually increase to eight later in the present decade.

Tactical assets (fighter, attack and airborne early warning aircraft) normally report direct to the commander of the CVW to which they are attached for operational control, but since most of these spend far more time ashore than at sea there are also a number of 'functional' commands which look after the more routine non-operational aspects. Since the early 1960s it has been a feature of US Navy policy to form 'communities' at certain shore bases and thus all deployable Atlantic Fleet fighter and medium attack squadrons are nominally located at Oceana, Virginia, when not at sea, whilst light attack squadrons have been gathered together at Cecil Field, Florida. Overall responsibility for the various functional commands is vested in Tactical Wings Atlantic Fleet (TacWingsLant) at Oceana, this overseeing four separate and distinct 'communities' comprising Carrier Airborne Early Warning Wing Twelve (CAEWW-12) at Norfolk (E-2C Hawkeye squadrons); Fighter Wing One (FitWingOne) at Oceana (F-14 Tomcat squadrons); Light Attack Wing One (LatWingOne) at Cecil Field (A-7 Corsair squadrons) and Medium Attack Wing One (MatWingOne) at Oceana (A-6 Intruder squadrons).

Pacific organization

As far as the Pacific Fleet is concerned, the 'community' concept is also normal, although there is no intermediate link in the chain of command, the various functional wings reporting directly to ComNavAirPac. For the record, and to illustrate the subtle differences in organization, these are as follows: Fighter and Air-

A Grumman F-14A Tomcat of VF-32 comes aboard the USS *John F. Kennedy* in December 1975 when this type was making its maiden operational deployment with the 6th Fleet in the Mediterranean. Most US Navy fighter and attack squadrons have now lost their brightly coloured markings in favour of low-visibility insignia.

From experience of target saturation in the Vietnam War evolved the ALFA or co-ordinated strike concept, whereby as many as 40 aircraft, each with a specific mission such as flak suppression or target strike, would attack as a single force. Today, this concept is still practised with F-14s, A-7s, A-6s and EA-6Bs. Shown here in low-visibility markings are aircraft from Carrier Air Wing One.

110
110
ENS RICH MURPHY
LT BILL WELCH
110
RESCUE
PC ANSAN JOHNSON
JET
DANGER
INTAKE

Grumman F-14 Tomcat

One of the latest production examples of the Grumman F-14A Tomcat is depicted in the accompanying illustration. Shown in the insignia of VF-143 aboard the USS *Dwight D. Eisenhower*, it carries the standard maximum weapons load of four AIM-54A Phoenix, two AIM-7F Sparrow and two AIM-9L Sidewinder air-to-air missiles, a mix which permits it to counter threats across virtually the entire air-defence spectrum. In addition to the missile armament, the F-14A is also equipped with an integral Vulcan M61 20-mm cannon for close-in air combat.

Originally conceived as a general-purpose utility helicopter, the Kaman Seasprite has demonstrated great versatility over the years although it is now mainly employed on anti-submarine warfare tasks from surface combatant vessels such as destroyers, frigates and cruisers. The definitive SH-2F variant is depicted here.

borne Early Warning Wing Pacific (FitAEWWingPac) at Miramar with F-4, F-14 and E-2 squadrons; Light Attack Wing Pacific (LatWingPac) at Lemoore with A-7 and F/A-18 squadrons; and Medium Attack/Electronic Warfare Pacific (Mat/VAQWingPac) at Whidbey Island with A-6 and EA-6B squadrons. Although nominally grouped together under the aegis of the Pacific Fleet it should be noted that EA-6B Prowler units deploy operationally with both major fleets while one other notable point concerning the Pacific Fleet centres around the forward-basing of the USS *Midway* for this has necessitated the provision of a similarly forward-based CVW, namely CVW-5 which has fighter, attack, electronic warfare and airborne early warning squadrons shore-based at Atsugi, Japan, when not embarked. Nevertheless, all seven squadrons of CVW-5 are still nominally grouped within the functional wing commands despite the fact that most have not been shore-based within the USA for some 10 years.

Whilst dealing with functional commands it is also worth pointing out that these do also administer the needs of the various non-deployable fleet replacement squadrons that are engaged solely in training duties. Using equipment identical with that of their sea-going counterparts, these are non-operational units tasked with bringing newly-qualified naval aviators ('nuggets') and Naval Flight Officers (NFOs) up to operational standard before assignment to a front-line squadron; with overseeing the transition of squadrons to new equipment; with provision of refresher courses for aviators returning to flying after a tour of non-aviation duty; and with training of maintenance personnel. Each of the respective communities normally has at least one such squadron to ensure a constant flow of qualified personnel to fleet units.

Sub watch

One of the most important missions of today's US Navy is that of keeping track of the ever expanding fleet of Soviet submarines, sea- and land-based elements having this as their prime function. In the case of the former, an organization known as Sea-based Air Anti-Submarine Warfare Wings Atlantic Fleet (Sea-basedAirASWWingsLant) exists, this controlling three subordinate functional wings plus an additional direct-reporting squadron from its headquarters at Jacksonville, Florida.

Following the introduction of the multi-purpose 'CV' concept in the early 1970s, all of the large carriers now routinely deploy with ASW-configured aircraft and helicopters, and these also adhere to the 'community'

A brace of Lockheed S-3A Vikings maintain tight formation as they prepare to return to their parent carrier, the USS *Dwight D. Eisenhower*. Introduced to operational service during 1975, the Viking has greatly enhanced sea-borne anti-submarine warfare capability and is now a valued element of the typical carrier air wing.

Now more than 20 years old, Sikorsky's Sea King ASW helicopter is a candidate for early replacement although progressive updating has permitted it to take advantage of many recent developments in the field of submarine detection and tracking. The example shown here was originally built as an SH-3A but has been modified to SH-3H configuration.

practice, Air Anti-Submarine Warfare Wing One (AirASWWingOne) at Cecil Field having six S-3A Viking squadrons while Helicopter Anti-Submarine Warfare Wing One (HelASWWingOne) at Jacksonville controls six deployable SH-3 Sea King squadrons as well as a similarly equipped and permanently shore-based training unit. In addition, there is another organization (Helicopter Sea Control Wing One, or HelSeaConWingOne, at Norfolk) with several squadrons engaged in two very different aspects of helicopter operations. Four of these squadrons are equipped with the Kaman SH-2F Seasprite, detachments from these embarking aboard the large number of surface combatants (cruisers, destroyers and frigates) which have helicopter operating facilities for the dual purposes of ASW and anti-ship missile defence. Reinstated in production recently, the SH-2F's capability in the latter task is rather limited but the forthcoming introduction of the Sikorsky SH-60B Seahawk should greatly improve potential in this area and will almost certainly result in the formation of additional squadrons within HelSeaConWingOne. The second major area of activity concerns mine countermeasures, there being three Sikorsky RH-53D squadrons engaged on this mission, notable operations of recent years being the clearance of Haiphong harbour following the 1973 Vietnam ceasefire and the sweeping of the Suez Canal in the spring of 1974. Deployment methods vary according to circumstances, Military Airlift Command C-5A Galaxies being used on occasion to ferry the Sea Stallions to their operating location whilst they are equally at home aboard amphibious vessels and aircraft-carriers. Capability in this area should also improve greatly when the three-engine MH-53E variant of Sikorsky's massive helicopter begins to enter service in the near future.

Finally, Air Test and Evaluation Squadron One (VX-1) serves as the US Navy's principal ASW operational test agency from Patuxent River, Maryland, being equipped with a few examples of the P-3 Orion, S-3 Viking, SH-2 Seasprite, SH-3 Sea King and SH-60B Seahawk.

In the case of the Pacific Fleet, organization of sea-based ASW assets is rather different, these being grouped together in a single command known as the Anti-Submarine Warfare Wing Pacific (ASWWingPac) at North Island. This controls SH-3 Sea King, SH-2 Seasprite and S-3 Viking units, the majority of which are to be found at North Island whilst shore-based between periods of sea duty.

Airborne early warning tasks have been conducted by the Grumman Hawkeye since the mid-1960s, and this type is still in production, the latest E-2C model being far superior to those which were originally deployed. This picture shows an E-2C about to be launched for a patrol over the Mediterranean Sea.

303
RESCUE
VFA11
NO STEP
DANGER

McDonnell Douglas F/A-18 Hornet

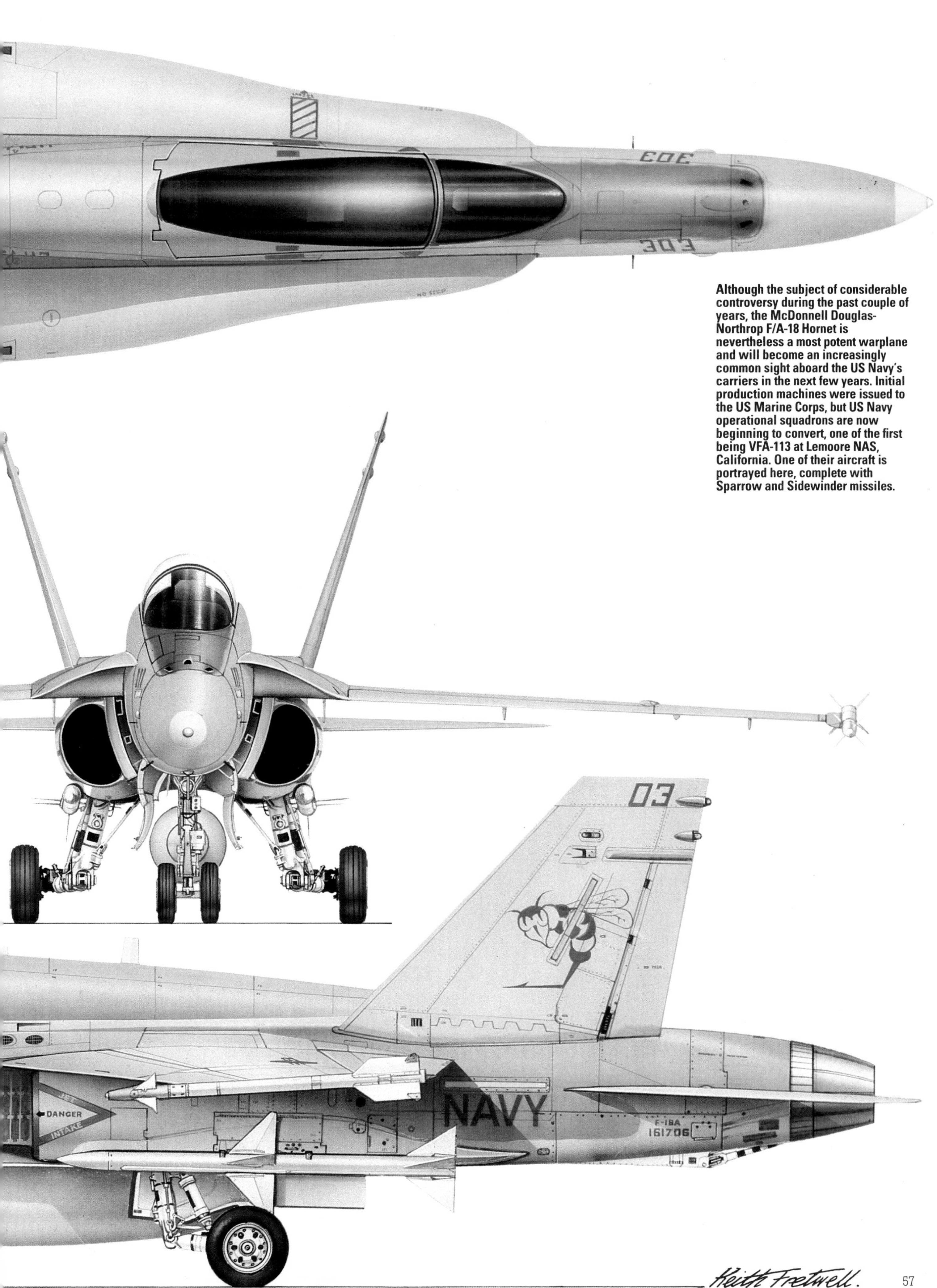

Although the subject of considerable controversy during the past couple of years, the McDonnell Douglas-Northrop F/A-18 Hornet is nevertheless a most potent warplane and will become an increasingly common sight aboard the US Navy's carriers in the next few years. Initial production machines were issued to the US Marine Corps, but US Navy operational squadrons are now beginning to convert, one of the first being VFA-113 at Lemoore NAS, California. One of their aircraft is portrayed here, complete with Sparrow and Sidewinder missiles.

Keith Fretwell.

Almost merging into the sea background, this early production Sikorsky SH-60B Seahawk, was photographed during the final stages of testing before service introduction. Training of aircrews to operate this type from surface combatant vessels is now beginning at North Island, California.

As far as land-based ASW elements are concerned, the US Navy has no less than 24 operational patrol squadrons equipped with variants of the Lockheed P-3 Orion, as well as two further squadrons tasked with training. Equally distributed between the two major fleets, these are home-ported at just four US bases, deploying periodically in much the same way as carrierborne forces for extended periods of overseas duty. East coast units are administered by an organization known as Patrol Wings Atlantic Fleet (PatWingsLant) with headquarters at Brunswick, Maine, its 12 front-line squadrons being assigned to two equal-sized Patrol Wings at Brunswick (PatWing5) and at Jacksonville (PatWing11) whilst the training squadron reports directly to PatWingsLant headquarters. Patrol Wings Pacific Fleet (PatWingsPac) is similarly organized with five squadrons at Barbers Point, Hawaii, under PatWing2 and seven squadrons plus the training unit at Moffett Field, California, under PatWing10. A third subordinate element (PatWing1) at Kamiseya, Japan) oversees the activities of forward-deployed units operating from bases at Misawa in Japan, Agana in Guam, Kadena in Okinawa and Cubi Point in the Philippines, whilst Atlantic Fleet deployment bases include Keflavik in Iceland, Sigonella in Sicily, Rota in Spain, Kindley Field in Bermuda and Lajes in the Azores.

Most of the remaining Atlantic Fleet aviation units are grouped together within Fleet Tactical Support Wing One (FleTacSupWingOne) at Norfolk and, as its title implies, this body is principally concerned with fulfilling a multitude of support functions ranging from carrier offshore delivery through target towing to helicopter combat support and communications between fleet commanders and sea-based forces. Pacific Fleet support elements do not constitute a separate command, most of the half-dozen or so squadrons reporting to the functional wing commands which most closely approximate to their mission or which place greatest demands upon their services.

Overseas

The few remaining front-line units are all stationed at bases outside the continental USA and, accordingly, come under local control. In the Mediterranean area there are three such units, namely Fleet Air Reconnaissance Squadron Two at Rota, plus Fleet Logistic Support Squadron 24 and Helicopter Combat Support Squadron Four at Sigonella. Operational control of all these units rests with the Commander Fleet Air Mediterranean (ComFAirMed) at Naples whilst administrative control is exercised by ComNavAirLant. Pacific Fleet forward-based units engaged on similar duties

Carrying practice Sidewinder missiles on the wing-tip weapons rails, this McDonnell Douglas F/A-18A Hornet was one of the first of the type to be delivered and carries the insignia of VFA-125, the Lemoore-based training unit.

Featuring the markings of the base rescue flight at NAS Agana, Guam, this Bell UH-1N is typical of the many Hueys which still serve with the US Navy. Most are assigned to rescue flights, although it is common for a single example to be attached to amphibious vessels for liaison and communications duties.

are grouped together to form the Fleet Air Western Pacific (FAirWestPac) organization.

Responsibility for the training of aircrew before assignment to a fleet replacement squadron rests with the Naval Air Training Command, which maintains its headquarters at Corpus Christi, Texas, exercising control over six Training Wings with a total of 20 squadrons at six different bases in the southern states of Mississippi, Florida and Texas.

Like the front-line forces, the training syllabus and equipment have been updated significantly in recent years, with further improvements in prospect when British Aerospace's T-45B Hawk begins to enter service later in the present decade. Considerable emphasis is now placed on 'self-help', at least in the early stages of pilot training, which is presently accomplished on the Beech T-34C Turbo-Mentor and North American T-28 Trojan although the latter type is to be phased out by early 1984. Pilots destined to fly combat jet aircraft then proceed to the Rockwell T-2C Buckeye and McDonnell Douglas TA-4J Skyhawk whilst those earmarked for the more sedate patrol community progress via the Beech T-44A King Air. Helicopter crews receive basic training in much the same way, moving on to the Bell TH-57A SeaRanger for initial helicopter conversion, this being followed by advanced tuition on variants of the ubiquitous Bell Iroquois.

All Naval Flight Officer (NFO) training is principally centred on Pensacola, Florida, where, after basic non-pilot instruction, candidates are assigned to one of four courses for specialist studies, these being radar intercept, basic jet navigation, airborne electronic warfare and airborne intercept control. These provide a thorough grounding in technique, students putting classroom theory into practice aboard the T-2C Buckeye, TA-4J Skyhawk and Rockwell T-39D Sabreliner before moving on to a fleet replacement squadron where they receive training on the aircraft type that they will eventually crew when they join an operational unit. All T-39Ds will be phased out by May 1985 and, beginning in August 1984, replaced by the Cessna T-47A Citation II.

Patrol and tests

As it has done for many years now, maritime patrol remains a major feature of activity, there being two Reserve Patrol Wings (one for the Atlantic and one for the Pacific) controlling 13 squadrons with a mixture of P-3A and P-3B Orions, whilst the remaining element (the Reserve Tactical Support Wing) is essentially a transport force predominantly equipped with the McDonnell Douglas C-9B although a few Douglas C-118Bs and Convair C-131Hs are still in use.

The only other aircraft-operating agency within the US Navy is the Naval Air Systems Command (NASC), which has responsibility for development, procurement and service support of those items necessary to permit the respective Naval Air Forces to fulfil their missions. To assist in this task, NASC has nine major field centres, these principally being engaged in various aspects of RDT&E (Research, Development, Test and Evaluation) and they do vary in size quite remarkably, ranging from the massive Naval Air Test

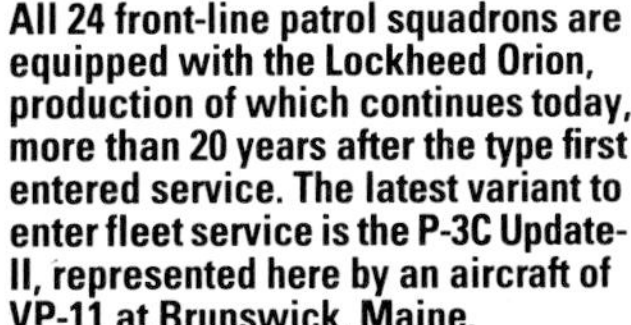

All 24 front-line patrol squadrons are equipped with the Lockheed Orion, production of which continues today, more than 20 years after the type first entered service. The latest variant to enter fleet service is the P-3C Update-II, represented here by an aircraft of VP-11 at Brunswick, Maine.

Grumman A-6 Invader

One of 122 A-6As purchased by the US Navy in FY 67, this aircraft is part of attack squadron VA-35 'Panthers', based at NAS Oceana in Virginia, and (as illustrated here) attached to carrier air wing CVW-9. The aircraft is shown with a typical attack load of 18 Mk 82 free-fall bombs and two drop tanks. Note the squadron insignia on the fin, the blackened fuselage airbrakes (later replaced by wingtip-mounted brakes), and the complex nose landing gear, which is designed for catapult launching. A twin nosewheel arrangement is required for compatibility with the catapult shuttle. Note also the nosewheel tow bar and diagonal tie-rod.

10
NG
152940
USS ENTERPRISE
NAVY
VA-35

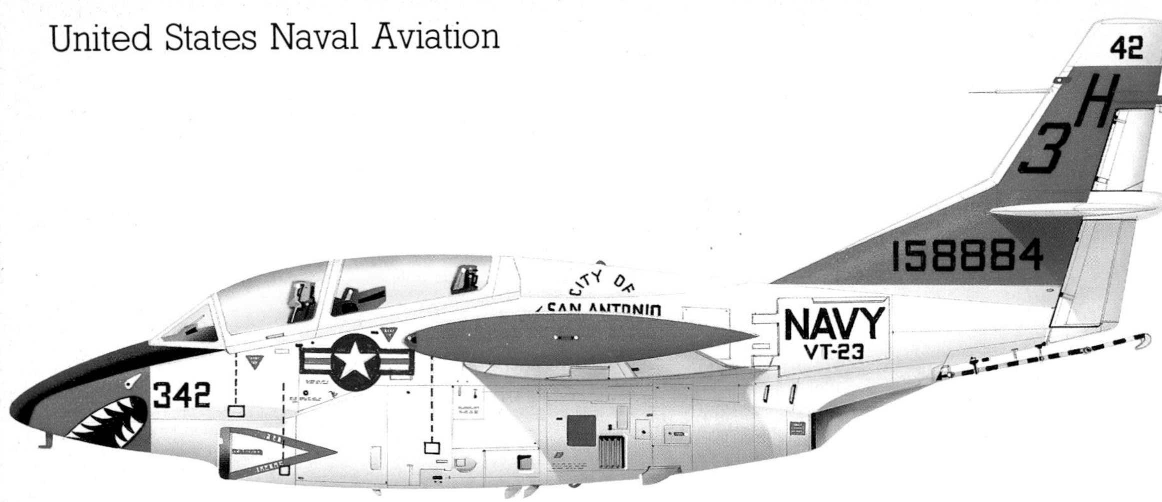

Upon completion of initial flight tuition, pilots destined to join fighter or attack squadrons progress to the Rockwell T-2C Buckeye, which presently equips six training units in Florida, Mississippi and Texas.

Left: Initial training of future pilots for both the US Navy and US Marine Corps is accomplished on the Beechcraft T-34C Turbo-Mentor, successful candidates then progressing to either the Rockwell T-2C Buckeye or the Beech T-44A King Air depending on whether they are destined to fly combat jet or patrol aircraft.

Right: The final phase of training before a pilot joins a Fleet Replacement Squadron, or 'RAG' as they are usually known, is accomplished on the McDonnell Douglas TA-4J Skyhawk, a type which is due to be replaced by the British Aerospace T-45 Hawk during the latter half of the 1980s.

Center complex at Patuxent River, Maryland, to the small Naval Weapons Evaluation Facility at Kirtland AFB, New Mexico. Examples of virtually every type to be found in the current US Navy inventory (and quite a few that are not) are on hand, the total test fleet almost certainly numbering in excess of 250 aircraft whilst NASC is also responsible for management of the six Naval Air Rework Facilities (NARFs). Mainly concerned with the overhaul of US Navy aircraft, the NARFs generally tend to specialize on certain types, this being beneficial in that it enables the predominantly civilian workforce to acquire a high degree of expertise and proficiency. In addition to airframes, other activities include the overhaul and repair of engines, components, spare parts and the guidance and control systems of air-to-air missiles.

In addition to front-line and training elements, the US Navy also possesses a quite powerful Reserve Force, the organization of which follows lines similar to those of the regular US Navy. With headquarters at New Orleans, this body is spearheaded by two Reserve Carrier Air Wings (CVWRs), each of which consists of two F-4 Phantom squadrons, three A-7B Corsair squadrons, one RF-8G Crusader squadron, one McDonnell Douglas KA-3B Skywarrior squadron, one EA-6A Intruder squadron and one E-2B Hawkeye squadron. Modernization of these elements is very much in prospect, with F/A-18 Hornets due to enter service within the next couple of years, whilst it is also proposed to re-equip one of the three A-7B squadrons assigned to each wing with the A-6E Intruder.

Second-line helicopter squadrons, for which there are seven in all, are grouped together within the Helicopter Wing Reserve (HelWingRes) and consist of two light attack units with the HH-1K Iroquois, four ASW units with the SH-3 Sea King and one unit with the HH-3A Sea King, the last being unique in that it is now the only active repository of combat search and rescue expertise in the entire US Navy.

Pilots destined to join patrol or transport squadrons move from the T-34C to the Beechcraft T-44A King Air, about 60 examples of which equip two training units at Corpus Christi, Texas.

NAVY
VT-25
500
NAVY
VT-25
501
02
NAVY
VT-25
502
03
NAVY
VT-25
503

US ARMY

United States Army

No matter what the battle, no matter what part the Air Force and Navy might play, the ground has to be secured by the Army, and that is a massive task indeed. The task is twofold; any advance by the Soviets in Europe will have to be stopped in its tracks and that requires a substantial army with heavy and large equipment. But at the same time the service must be able to respond rapidly to brushfire situations around the world and that means light, mobile airborne forces. Two armies for the price of one, or one for the price of two?

Left: A Patriot surface-to-air missile leaves its launcher during trials in the United States. Patriot will replace both the HAWK and Nike Hercules missile systems and has greatly increased range and kill probability. Development has however taken a long time and costs have risen, but units of Patriot are expected to be operational in Europe in 1984.

Below: American infantryman stands guard with his 5.56-mm (0.22-in) M16 series automatic rifle. When first issued in Vietnam this weapon was not liked, but the early problems have now been overcome.

In the Pentagon, a lieutenant colonel in office worker's suit and tie angrily breaks a pencil in half, shifts his bifocals to the tip of his nose, and groans at cost-analysis figures for a Congressional budget sub-committee. At Grenada's Point Salines Airport, a buck sergeant in Ranger garb snaps erect, grimaces, and empties the clip of his M16 in a staccato burst of rifle fire at a pair of fleeing Cuban advisers. In the Joint Security Area at Panmunjom, a military policeman in starched fatigues and spit-shined boots keeps a hand alertly over his holstered .45 and returns the menacing glare of a North Korean guard outside the building called the 'ice cream parlor' where meaningless armistice negotiations enter their 31st year. Astride the fog-shrouded Fulda Gap in Germany, a battle-garbed three-star general on inspection grabs up binoculars and peers warily in the direction of the massed armoured forces of the Warsaw Pact.

The budget man, the buck sergeant, the MP and the general are breathing symbols of the diverse human problems and multitudinous military tasks confronting the modern US Army, the most widely dispersed and most powerful ground force in the non-Soviet world.

From its home base in the continental USA, this army garrisons large forces in West Germany, South Korea, Italy, Japan and the Panama Canal Zone. It stands behind seven major defence treaties, the most crucial being the North Atlantic Treaty Organization (NATO)

A convoy of M113 series armoured personnel carriers of the 1st Cavalry Division move through West Germany during Exercise 'REFORGER '83'. The division is normally based in Fort Hood, Texas as part of III Corps but in time of war would be deployed to West Germany. The timely arrival of American forces in Europe could be a deciding influence on the outcome of any future conflict in Europe. While the troops would come by aircraft of the Military Airlift Command (such as the Lockheed C-141 StarLifter and Lockheed C-5 Galaxy), much of their equipment and supplies would have to come by sea across the Atlantic in convoys that would be open to attack not only by numerous Soviet submarines but also aircraft carrying long range anti-ship missiles.

and the US-Republic of Korea Mutual Defense Treaty. Additionally, the US Army operates Foreign Military Sales (FMS), International Military Education and Training (IMET) and Military Assistance Groups (MAG) in 53 nations. Army attaches, who are on detail to the Defense Intelligence Agency for their diplomatic postings abroad, serve at embassies in 76 capitals.

Vast force

The US Army has 781,648 soldiers on active duty, of whom 74,360 are women. A further 901,153 soldiers can be called to active duty from the ranks of the Army Reserve and the Army National Guard.

This vast force naturally influences many areas of American society (veteran Dwight D. Eisenhower warned Americans of the impact of a 'military-industrial complex'), but throughout its history the US Army has remained faithful to the civilian leadership it serves. A military coup would be unimaginable. The US constitution and American tradition place command of the military in the hands of elected civilians or their civilian appointees. In wartime, the National Command Authority passes from President to Vice President to Secretary of Defense.

Pre-dating the formation of the United States itself, the US Army had its nucleus in the rebel force which ousted the British in the Revolutionary War (1776-1783). The US Army was formally established in 1783 and defeated British forces again in the War of 1812. Thereafter, at times neglected and down to a few companies while state militias predominated, the US Army throughout the 1800s fought its series of Indian wars far from the centres of population and power. Torn asunder by the Civil War (1861-5), where West Point officers commanded on opposing sides and casualties were staggering, the US Army then became an insular body, separate from the rest of the nation: a professional fighting force which took men, trained them, and sent them off to war on the western plains, in the Caribbean and as far as the Philippines. With the entry of the United States into World War I, a newly-expanded US Army backed by the nation's industrial might helped determine the outcome. Then the US Army settled down to garrison duties until 1941, when it again went to war and helped assure Allied victory over Germany and Japan.

The years since VJ-Day have seen the conflict in Korea (1950-3), and the longest war ever fought by Americans, in Vietnam. The built-up US Army in Vietnam suffered from eroded discipline, drug abuse and racial strife, but on the battlefield the American soldier acquitted himself well. Low morale resulting from failure in Vietnam followed by lean budgets during the Carter years is now beginning to pick up. Under a conservative administration generous in seeking funds from the Congress, the US Army has managed to bring itself back to its traditional sense of purpose.

Failure, of course, must be blamed on the decision-maker and the diplomat while success, all too often, must be wrought by brave young men in battle. The American soldier is, in the end, no more than the final resort on the cutting edge of American policy. Whether a private or a general, his equipment, training, doctrine and valour must come from what he is given and what he is told to do. In Fiscal Year 1984, he will be given an unprecedented $274.1 billion (about £183 billion) in the US defence budget. He will be given AH-64 helicopters, M1 tanks, and an unpopular new-style helmet. And he will be told to take on challenges equally without precedent in a nuclear world which is a nightmare for the Pentagon's planners. Three examples indicate the problem.

In Europe, while people demonstrate in the streets against it, the NATO force bulwarked by the US Army confronts a numerically overwhelming Soviet threat, a five-to-one disadvantage in armoured strength, and a potential lightning war which could leave the defenders no choice but to initiate use of nuclear weapons to blunt a Warsaw Pact onslaught.

A member of an American airborne unit takes aim with his 7.62-mm (0.3-in) M60 general-purpose machine gun during 'Reforger '82'. The role of American and allied airborne forces in any future European conflict is open to considerable discussion as their use in their primary role would depend on the Allied air forces securing air superiority over the battlefield, and it is by no means certain that this could be accomplished in any future operation.

Right: An American soldier prepares to engage an aerial target with his General Dynamics (Pomona Division) Stinger man-portable surface-to-air missile system. This is now rapidly replacing the older Redeye missile system and is much more effective as it has an improved warhead and can engage attacking aircraft from almost any angle. The older missile could only be used after the aircraft had passed, and probably dropped its bombs, as it homed onto the target's exhaust emissions.

In Korea, where one million men under arms face each other across 2.5 miles (4 km) of no man's land, a monstrously built-up North Korean war machine can, even without Soviet or Chinese help, by official Pentagon estimate overrun the peninsula on any day and create a catastrophe in some of the world's worst fighting terrain.

Policy and pragmatism in the 1980s require a rapid deployment force able to fight and win in the heat and sands of Middle East oilfield country, in the raging cold of the Arctic, or wherever Washington decides. Some of the troopers who saw their equipment snarled by sand on manoeuvres in Egypt, and who lost mates in the daring but fruitless April 1980 rescue raid in Iran, found themselves under fire recently on the little-known Caribbean island of Grenada.

The US Army: People

Some idea of the US Army's leadership can be gleaned from its top brass. Chairman of the Joint Chiefs of Staff (JCS) General John W. Vessey Jr, is a calm-mannered but steel-tough combat fighter who rose from the ranks to win a battlefield commission at Anzio. He has a special interest in early warning of an enemy's intentions and a firm grasp of Soviet doctrine, which calls for disproportionately massed firepower at selected assault corridors. Army Chief of Staff General John A. Wickham Jr, is a battle-hardened West Pointer and a technocrat-soldier. Both men have commanded the field army in Korea which, because its United Nations mandate includes Republic of Korea (ROK) as well as US forces, bringing troop strength to 710,000, is the largest unified force an American general can command today. Although JCS officer Vessey and Wickham do not formally command the vast US Army whose senior slots they occupy, their decision-making role and access to the President make reality very much as if they do.

Current manpower of the US Army is 781,648 of whom 218,913 serve in Europe, 31,000 in the Far East (mostly in Korea) and 7,900 in the Canal Zone.

The US Army's enlisted men and women volunteer from all walks of life for an initial three-year tour of duty. The draft was eliminated with the creation of the 'all-volunteer Army' in 1974 (although registration for the

A Bell UH-1 'Huey' series helicopter hovers above the ground while troops armed with 5.56-mm (0.22-in) M16 rifles jump out. Although now an old design, the 'Huey' is still used in large numbers by the US Army and many other countries for the troop transport role. Many have been fitted with a door-mounted 7.62-mm (0.3-in) machine-gun, which can be used to give suppressive fire during landing operations.

draft for 18-year-olds was reinstated in 1981) and a return to general conscription is probably a political impossibility today. Critics charge that this means that the USA no longer has a 'citizen army', and for the first time since 1940 a generation of young Americans includes many who have never donned a uniform. For a time, the 'all-volunteer' concept attracted disproportionate numbers of racial minorities and new immigrants, creating a low educational level and a mentality where 'comic books' were needed to teach a man how to drive an armoured personnel carrier. It remains true that blacks, 13 per cent of the US population, make up 29.3 per cent of the US Army. But the economic recession and better pay benefits have recently attracted better-qualified recruits of all backgrounds. A private can reach non-commissioned officer (NCO) status in three years and retire with a pension after 20 years, a strong inducement for men and women who can receive a pension beginning as early as age 37. Retention of skilled NCOs, especially those with technical credentials needed by industry, remains the US Army's critical personnel problem.

The US Army long ago eliminated its segregated Women's Army Corps (WAC) and opened up most career ladders to the fair sex, with encouraging results. Since 1978 the number of women in the US Army has rocketed from about 12,000 to the current 74,360. Although women are precluded by law from assuming combat duties, nearly all military occupation specialities (MOS) are open to them, and the US Army recently re-opened 13 out of 26 specialities which had earlier been defined as 'combat' duties.

The bulk of the officer corps now comes to the US Army from the 303 colleges and universities which offer Reserve Officer Training Corps (ROTC) programmes. ROTC training is only incidental to a four-year university education, and is voluntary. It leads to a reserve commission as a second lieutenant who then, on entering active duty, proceeds to his branch Service school. A few US Army officers in the Medical Corps, the Army Nurse Corps, and the Chaplains' ranks come directly from civilian life, and recruiting of these highly-qualified people, especially doctors, remains difficult.

Airborne and Ranger courses

The elite US Army officer comes from the 'long gray line' (for the uniform colour) of the United States Military Academy at West Point, the ivy-covered institute in upstate New York which has bred the nation's lieutenants, generals and heroes since the 1800s. Competition to enter West Point is fierce, and its four-year mix of military and university education is gruelling. Cadets may take Airborne and Ranger training during their course and, on graduation, must serve five years. Entering cadets are college students; upon entering, they become members of the armed forces in the special category of cadet, not fully 'officer' or 'enlisted'. During their senior year, each selects the branch of service (Infantry, Artillery, Corps of Engineers, etc.) in which he or she will receive a regular commission as a second lieutenant. The sense of tradition in the halls and on the parade grounds at West Point is chilling: West Pointers have fought in all the nation's wars except the first, and 21 per cent of the Class of 1964 died in Vietnam. In his final public appearance in 1962, an ageing General of the Army Douglas MacArthur (Class of 1904) talked to the Point's cadets about his own days there and concluded with an impromptu speech which has become one of the most famous in American history, centring on the three words essential to a West Point officer's life: duty, honour and country.

Right: The General Dynamics Land Systems Division M1 Abrams main battle tank, which is now entering service in large numbers. The current model is armed with the well known 105-mm (4.13-in) M68 tank gun, which is essentially the British Royal Ordnance Factory Nottingham L7 manufactured in the United States. The M1 features a gas turbine engine and advanced armour that provides a high degree of protection against many of the weapons found on the battlefield of today.

Below: American troops leap from their Sikorsky UH-60 Black Hawk transport helicopter. The US Army has a total requirement for 1,107 of these helicopters. So far over 500 have been built, first deliveries being made to the 101st Airborne Division in June 1979. It is the replacement for the old UH-1 helicopter which has been the backbone of army aviation units for some 20 years. The prototype of an electronic warfare version has been evaluated under the designation EH-60.

General Dynamics Land Systems Division M1 Abrams Main Battle Tank

The M1 is currently being built at the Detroit Tank Plant and the Lima Army Tank Plant in Lima, with just over 60 tanks a month being produced from both plants. The US Army has a total requirement for 7,058 M1/M1A1 MBTs, with final deliveries due at the end of this decade. So far the tank has not been adopted by any other country, although it has been tested by Switzerland and Saudi Arabia.

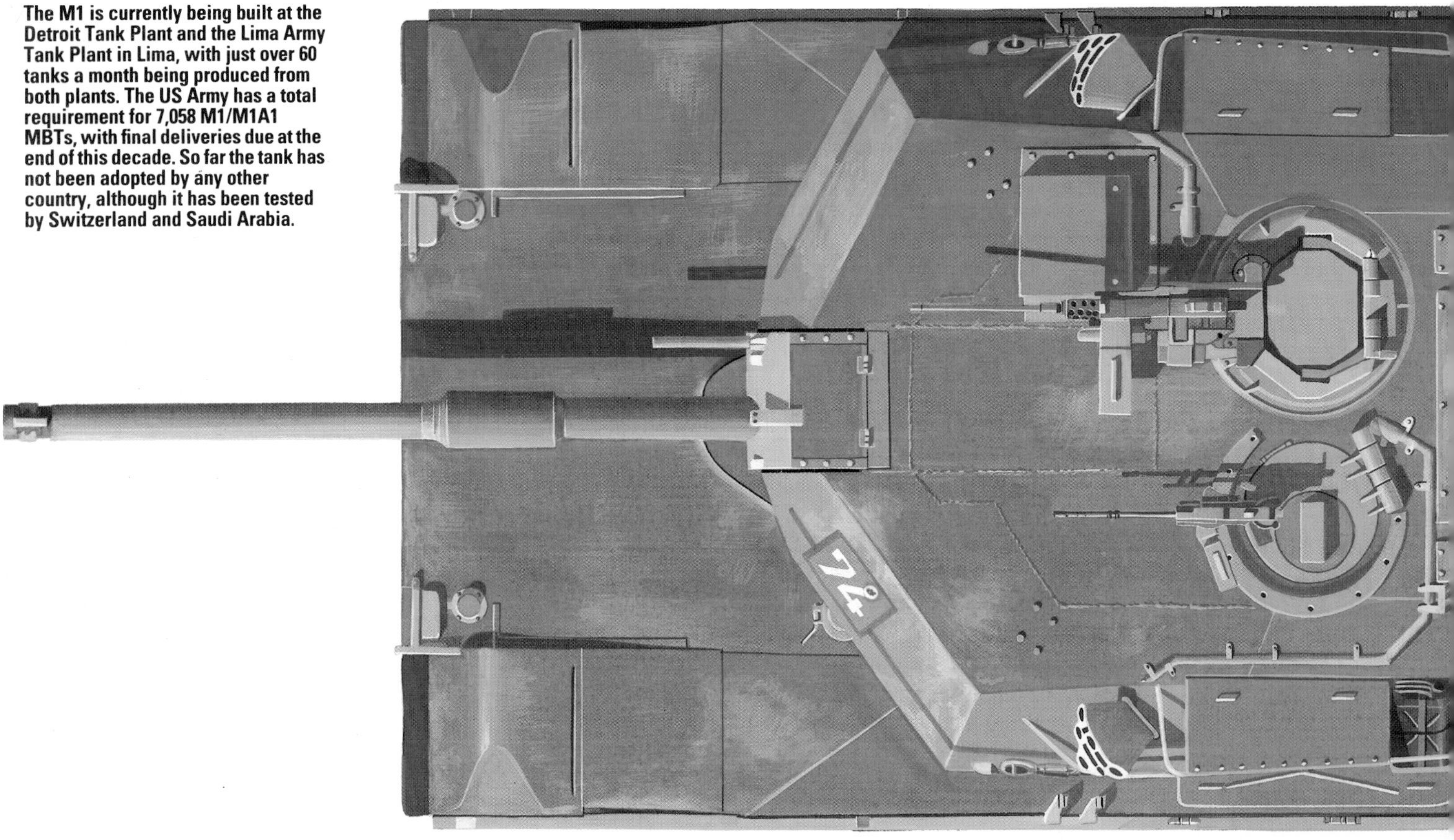

74
S. Nohara

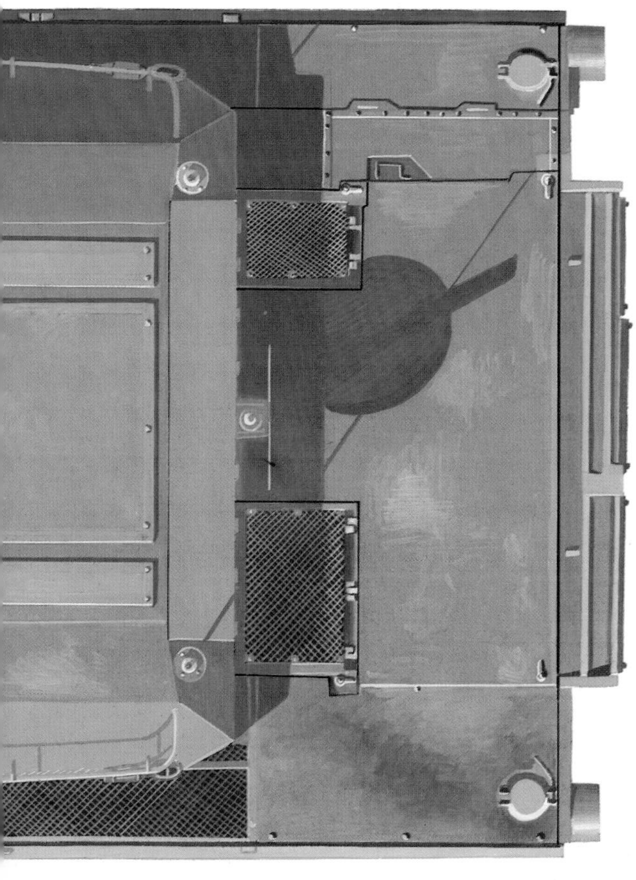

Currently entering US Army service in increasing numbers, the M2 Bradley AIFV is equipped with Hughes TOW anti-tank missiles. With procurement of the M2 planned to reach levels of 6,500 or more, the Army can expect a considerable enhancement in its anti-armour capability.

The Hughes AH-64 Apache is currently entering service with the US Army, and will greatly improve the firepower previously offered by the Bell AH-1 Cobra.

AM General High-Mobility Multipurpose Wheeled Vehicle is fitted with a roof mounted 40-mm grenade-launcher. The HMMWV is now in production and will replace a number of vehicles at present in use, including the M151 Jeep and the M561 Gama Goat. The HMMWV has excellent cross-country mobility, will also carry TOW ATGWs and Stinger surface-to-air missiles.

A Raytheon HAWK surface-to-air missile blasts away from its trailer launcher. The HAWK has been in service with the US Army since 1960. The current model is the Improved HAWK.

Once accepted for active duty, whether recruited as a private or commissioned at the Point, the US Army soldier is trained in one of over 400 military occupation specialities at one of several dozen training establishments. Enlisted recruits begin with an eight-week 'boot camp' indoctrination at one of three locations and then proceed, as do new officers, to their Army Service Schools.

For officers, further leadership and military technical training comes at each stage in a career. For those at field grade (major or above), the most important is the Command and General Staff College at Fort Leavenworth, Kansas. The course at this institute runs for one year, and without it no officer is likely to ever wear a general's star on his shoulder. Other key institutes are the Armed Forces Staff College, an inter-service establishment at Norfolk, Virginia; the Industrial College of the Armed Forces (ICAF) and the National War College, both located at Fort McNair, Washington, DC. Army officers are also eligible for courses given for senior managers by other branches of the government, such as the Department of State and the Central Intelligence Agency. A successful course, like a combat decoration, is seen as a 'ticket' to promotion and to an important command slot.

The US Army: Organization

The US Army is divided into 14 major commands. On a functional basis, it is perhaps more illuminating to think of the army as divided into two basic branches, the Arms and the Services, although these have some overlapping responsibilities.

The Arms, listed in order of precedence, are the Infantry, the Corps of Engineers, Air Defense Artillery, Field Artillery, Armor, the Signal Corps, the Military Police, and Army Intelligence.

The Services are the Adjutant General's Corps, the Finance Corps, the Quartermaster Corps, the Army Medical Department, the Chaplains, the Judge Advocate General's Corps, the Ordnance Corps, the Chemical Corps, and the Transportation Corps.

Overlap occurs with the Corps of Engineers, the Military Police, and the Signals Corps, for these are considered both Arms and Services because they have a dual combat and service function. Some entities fall into neither category, such as the Army Intelligence and Security Command (INSCOM) and Army Aviation, numerically the largest 'air force' in the world, but not permitted to operate fixed-wing combat aircraft, which have become the concern of the US Air Force.

Operationally, the US Army is formed of divisions, grouped into corps along three basic lines. These divisions are the four armoured divisions, six mechan-

ized infantry divisions, and four infantry divisions. There is also a single paratroop division, the 82nd Airborne, considered the army's crack fighting force.

Each armoured division has five or six tank battalions and four mechanized infantry battalions. Each mechanized infantry division possesses four tank battalions and five mechanized infantry battalions; in addition there are three or four artillery battalions, a helicopter battalion, an air-defence missile battalion, an air cavalry squadron, and supporting units. Each infantry division has one tank battalion, six mechanized infantry battalions and, usually, six or more infantry battalions. The 82nd Airborne is formed of three brigades, each with three parachute battalions and an artillery battalion.

The above are basic outlines. Some divisions have more units assigned, others are merely at cadre strength. The infantry and mechanized infantry divisions have National Guard components and some divisions rely on the Reserves to fill out their totals.

National Guard units, and there are 3,285 of them, represent the individual states' role in contributing to national defence. Under control of state governors until activated as part of the regular army, National Guard units are theoretically required only in times of national emergency, but have been mobilized for internal policing and disaster relief functions. Full mobilization of the National Guard would produce two armoured divisions, a mechanized infantry division, five infantry divisions and 22 independent brigades (four armoured, eight mechanized infantry and 10 infantry) of which four would join regular divisions. They would in addition form four armoured cavalry regiments, eight air-defence battalions, and supporting units. Included are five independent tank battalions, two mechanized infantry battalions, 50 artillery battalions, four anti-tank battalions armed with TOW missiles, an infantry reconnaissance group for use in the Arctic, two Special Forces groups, and Army Aviation units that fly 2,568 aircraft.

Every year 49,000 US Army Reserves serve temporarily with regulars, adding 3,410 units and 556 aircraft. The Reserves include 12 training divisions, a mechanized infantry division, two independent combat brigades, and 67 support battalions. Not all Reserve units are up to full strength, some being cadres only.

To back up conventional forces, the US Army maintains at full strength nine artillery groups, each with from 12 to 16 artillery battalions, and four anti-aircraft artillery (AAA) groups. There is a single independent armoured brigade and four independent infantry brigades. The spirit of the old horse cavalry is kept up by one independent air cavalry brigade and three armoured cavalry regiments.

Special Forces

The US Army's heavy punch comes from four Pershing missile battalions, one of which is a training battalion capable of use in the field if required. To back these longer-range units are eight Lance battalions. Pershing and Lance can be fitted with nuclear warheads, and will soon be joined in inventory by Patriot air-defence missiles in nine battalions.

Also distinct from conventional field units are the US Army's three Special Forces groups and two Ranger battalions. Men from these elite units were included in the tri-service 'Blue Light' outfit which made the Iranian rescue attempt. Special Forces and Rangers are the US Army's 'SAS' and train for everything from foiling airline hijackings to dropping behind the lines into Czechoslovakia.

Army Aviation supports the ground fighters, and its units are assigned to various headquarters for reconnaissance, scouting, tactical support, casualty evacua-

Above: A well camouflaged 20-mm M163 Vulcan self-propelled anti-aircraft gun system keeps a watchful eye on the sky. The power-operated turret is armed with a six-barrelled 20-mm Vulcan cannon developed from the air weapon originally installed in the Lockheed F-104 Starfighter aircraft; the gun has two rates of fire in this application, 1,000 or 3,000 rounds a minute, the former normally being selected for the ground-support role and the latter for the anti-aircraft role. A total of 1,000 rounds of ready use ammunition are carried, with a further 1,100 rounds in reserve.

Right: The Hughes Helicopters AH-64 Advanced Attack Helicopter (AAH) is armed with a nose-mounted 30-mm Chain Gun and pods of air-to-ground rockets. The US Army has a total requirement for 572 of these expensive helicopters. The first production helicopter was handed over late in 1983 and the type is expected to become operational in 1984. In addition to its cannon, a typical weapon load would be eight Hellfire missiles and two pods of folding-fin rockets.

Left: General Dynamics Stinger (Pomona Division) man-portable surface-to-air missile at the point of launch. Notice that both crew members are wearing flak jackets to protect them from debris kicked up to the rear of the missile during launch. In addition to issue at battalion level, the Stinger will also be assigned to the air-defence battalion of each 'Division 86', which will have a total of 75 Stinger teams. Of these the Stinger battery will have two platoons each with 15 Stinger teams, while each of the three Sgt York batteries will have 15 Stinger teams.

Right: The Beechcraft RU-21J Super King Air aircraft is part of the US Army's fleet of special-mission aircraft, originally developed from 1974 under the 'Cefly Lancer' programme. The similar RC-12D is also a special-mission aircraft and is also called Guardrail; it is fitted with antennae above and below the wings as well as wingtip pods. The RC-12D is deployed in Europe and South Korea as well as the United States, and is fitted with signals intelligence (SIGINT) equipment as well as direction finders. It is designed to fly behind friendly lines to monitor enemy communications systems.

Left: Virtually every item in the Army's inventory can be loaded aboard the capacious Lockheed C-5A Galaxy and transported between 2,300 and 5,000 miles, depending on the load.

tion, and other work. The army operates Beech RU-21D 'Guardrail' electronics aircraft on snooping missions. A new generation of helicopters is typified by the Sikorsky UH-60A and Hughes AH-64.

Dry organizational charts, jokingly called 'wiring diagrams' by the US Army's senior NCO, crusty, Kojak-bald Sergeant Major Glen E. Morrell, do not convey human images: in rain, under the high pines at Fort Bragg, North Carolina, women soldiers with helmets, field packs and M16s drive stakes into the soggy earth, then banter with the men over field chow in the mess tent. Amid a blizzard at Bad Kreuznach, chilled and weary soldiers risk frostbite repairing the tread of an M60A1 tank out-of-doors, talking about how their West German counterparts do this work inside heated buildings. In parched heat on the Somalia coast, temporary duty soldiers (aware of an airlift handicap, the fact that no one ever designed vehicles to fit inside planes and that the largest US Air Force transport, the Lockheed C-5A, can carry only one tank) prepare vehicles and supplies for a contingency, in what the US Army calls 'pre-positioning'. From Korea to the Middle East, as Morrell puts it, 'The US Army means people.'

People spread all over the globe, that is. The US Army's order of battle is a vast array of units in the continental United States (CONUS) and outside. There is also the multi-service Rapid Deployment Joint Task Force (RDJTF) with its headquarters at MacDill Air Force Base near Florida's breathtaking Tampa Bay. This force can at any time be despatched anywhere, witness Grenada. The US Army's contribution to the RDJTF is its XVIII Airborne Corps, bulwarked by the vaunted 82nd Airborne Division.

Various CONUS units are designated for the rapid reinforcement of divisions in Germany. These are known as REFORGER (Reinforcement in Germany) and frequently deploy to Germany to test readiness.

Apart from the field forces in its order of battle, the US Army has units in Greece, Italy, The Netherlands and Turkey, plus small units in the United Kingdom. To back up its major commitment in Korea, base and support personnel are stationed in Japan.

Of special interest, especially to those pondering the army of the 21st century, is the 9th Infantry Division at Fort Lewis, Washington. Part of the RDJTF, trimmed of fat, beefed up on weaponry, the 9th Infantry Division is an experimental and trials division known as the High Technology Test Bed (HTTB). It is the model for the projected Division '86, a new type of US Army division scheduled to take to the field in 1986.

The US Army: Equipment and Weapons

Just about every item in US Army inventory is superb, though some raise the eyebrows of Congressional watchdogs like Michigan Senator William Proxmire, a defence expert troubled over rising costs. The American soldier has always gone to war with the best that his nation can provide, and no effort is spared to guarantee that he will not find his equipment wanting. It does not always work: some items prove faulty under the stress of in-service or combat experience. But as a rule, strict research and development standards and rigorous testing eradicate flaws an item may conceal. While gratifying for the soldier, this has its price. Some weapon systems are too complex, where a simpler design would do. Some are 'gold-plated' to a degree to cause even the exchequer of the richest nation on Earth to blanch.

An example, say critics, is the Hughes AH-64 Apache. This armed helicopter resulted from long development and research to counter the threat of Warsaw Pact armed helicopters (such as the latest Mil 'Hind' variants) and of massed armour attack. From studies, the AH-64 design was chosen and from it a superb combat helicopter has emerged. The two-seat AH-64 can operate in all weather and has important 'survivability' features, including complex navigation

The Ford Aerospace and Communications Corporation M48 Chaparral low-level self-propelled surface-to-air missile system is seen in travelling configuration. Before the missiles can be fired the cab roof has to be removed and the windscreen folded down.

M247 Sgt York Twin 40-mm Division Air Defence Gun (DIVAD)

It has been recognized since its earliest days that the M163 Vulcan self-propelled AA gun was not entirely suitable in the face of modern attack jets. The M247 Sgt York is now being introduced as a replacement. The Sgt York, a twin 40-mm gun system mounted on the chassis of the M48 tank, is an attempt to produce the definitive DIVAD (Divisional Air Defense) system, using the latest in radar and electronic systems (some adapted for the F-16 fighter) allied to dual 40-mm Bofors L/70 guns, each capable of firing 300 HE or PF (proximity fused) rounds per minute.

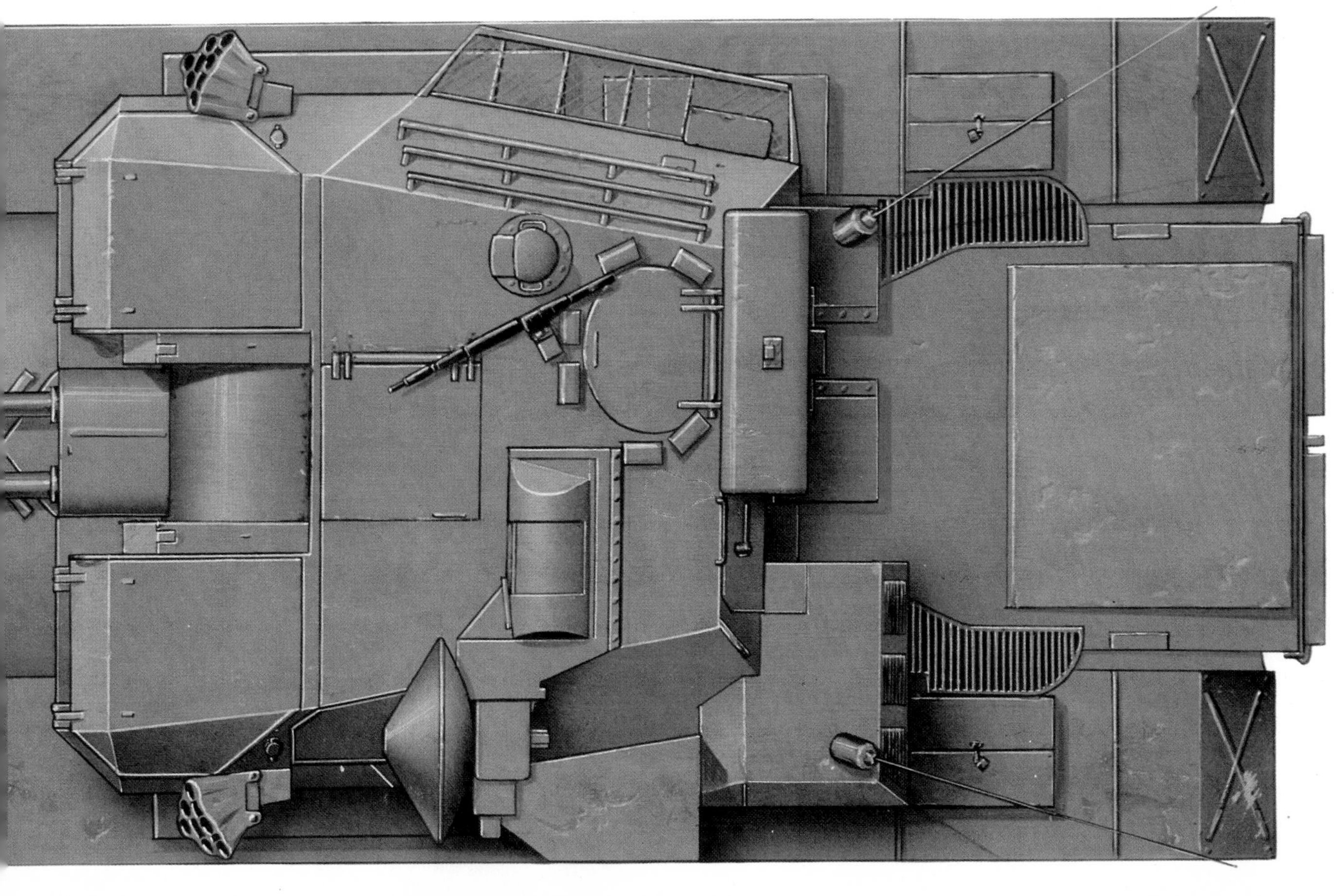

United States Army

systems, pilot aids and armour. As armament, the AH-64 has an inbuilt 30-mm Chain Gun, 70-mm (2.75-in) rocket in pods for ground-fire suppression, and Hellfire anti-tank missiles. Sensors and electronic devices for target-seeking sprout from all parts of the airframe. The first AH-64s have entered service but with a price tag close to $15 million (£10 million) each. While the US Army has an initial requirement for 112 AH-64s, it is unlikely to get even that many if current noises from Congressional budget-watchers are anything to go by, especially since the AH-64 is intended to knock out helicopters and tanks costing far less.

An even louder brouhaha has arisen over the divisional air defence system (DIVADS), inspired by the Soviet ZSU-23-4 air-defence cannon. DIVADS is a radar-guided, twin 40-mm gun system mounted on an M48A5 tank chassis, and is intended to guard field forces against armed helicopters and fighter-bombers. Critics say it has both faults which compromise some weapons systems: it is too complicated to operate and, at $1.5 million (£1 million), it costs too much.

Other examples of the over-elaborate or of 'gold-plating' can be cited, but in the main the US Army is well served by American defence industries, who are now the arsenal of the non-Communist world. What the US Army adopts, other nations adopt, aware that supply, back-up and spares will be forthcoming.

Suppliers of equipment for the US Army include a few which are virtually state-owned. For example, artillery comes almost exclusively from Federal arsenals at Rock Island and Watervilet. Most items, however, come from the nation's well-known private contractors such as Chrysler, Ford, McDonnell Douglas, and so on.

When the US Army assumes a new weapons system, as a rule the replaced equipment goes to the National Guard. But in recent years the National Guard has begun to receive some new equipment ahead of the regular army, a case in point being the M901 Improved TOW anti-tank missile vehicle provided to National Guard units before it was issued to troops in Germany. Most of the equipment of the National Guard and Reserves remains a generation behind that of the regular army.

The US Army: Infantry Weapons

The basic service rifle of the US Army is the 5.56-mm M16A1. Most have been produced by Colt, though some have been manufactured as far away as South Korea, and the type is now virtually a standard rifle

One of the two prototypes of the Sgt York Twin 40-mm Divisional Air Defense System (DIVADS), first production models of which came off the production line in late 1983. The US Army has a requirement for over 600 of these systems, which are based on an M48A5 chassis.

The Hughes Helicopters Apache Advanced Attack Helicopter is to enter service in 1984. This is armed with a 30-mm Chain Gun in the nose and can also carry a wide range of ordnance including packs of rockets and Hellfire missiles that can knock out all known tanks.

American troops duck as a 107-mm (4.2-in) mortar goes off. This mortar is the heaviest in service with the US Army and is normally mounted in the rear of a M106 mortar carrier, a member of the M113 family. In addition to carrying the mortar and its crew the M106 also carries 93 mortar bombs. The 107-mm (4.2-in) mortar has a maximum rate of fire of 18 bombs a minute and fires a variety of mortar bombs including high explosive, smoke, illuminating, gas and tactical CS.

worldwide. As a result of recent NATO ammunition trials the current 5.56-mm cartridge is due to be replaced by the Belgian SS109 cartridge which requires a different rifling pitch, so existing M16A1s will have to be replaced or modified. Already an M16A2 version is on the stocks. At first, the M16 had teething troubles and acquired a reputation for jamming, but these are now history. The 5.56-mm round is said by some not to be a particularly powerful 'man-stopper', but it is easy to handle and produces low recoil.

The 5.56-mm (0.223-in) cartridge is also used for the Squad Automatic Weapon (SAW), chosen as the fire-support weapon for the infantry squad. Soon to enter service, the SAW is a development of the Belgian FN Minimi light machine-gun, a compact weapon with ammunition feed from a side-mounted box magazine.

M14 rifles in 7.62-mm×51 NATO calibre are still found in some National Guard units. The M14 is a modernized version of the M1 Garand of World War II. Its modified sniper version, the M21, is still in front-line service with specialized personnel.

An American infantryman fires his 7.62-mm (0.3-in) M60 machine-gun on a desert range. This is the standard general-purpose machine-gun (GPMG) of the US Army and is also used in helicopters and aircraft. The M60 has a cyclic rate of fire of 550 rounds per minute, and was the first machine-gun in American service to have a quick-change barrel, a vital feature when the weapon is used in the sustained-fire role.

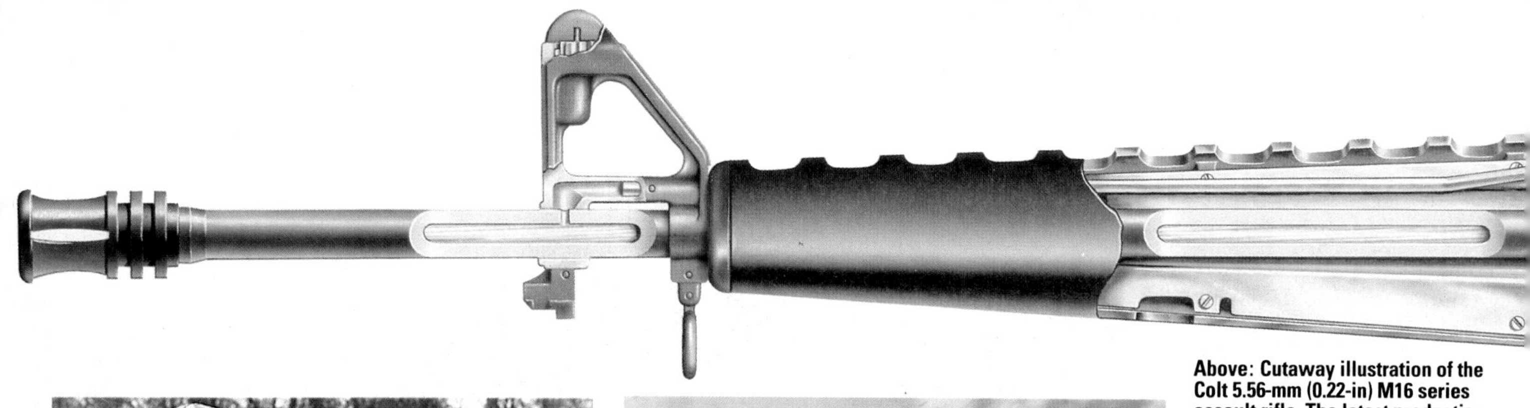

Above: Cutaway illustration of the Colt 5.56-mm (0.22-in) M16 series assault rifle. The latest production model is the M16A2, which is going first to the US Marine Corps. This has a new barrel, will fire the new 5.56-mm (0.22-in) heavier round adopted by NATO as well as having the full automatic feature removed in favour a three-round burst capability, so giving greater accuracy.

Far left: The General Dynamics Viper light anti-tank weapon has recently been rejected by the US Army after extensive trials. Instead the USA may buy the Swedish FFV AT4 anti-tank weapon.

Above left: American airborne trooper takes aim with his M47 Dragon medium anti-tank missile (MAM) which complements the Hughes Aircraft TOW heavy anti-tank missile (HAM). This is the only man-portable anti-tank missile in service with the US Army and was first fielded in the early 1970s. The original manufacturer was McDonnell Douglas, but Raytheon also undertook production at a later time. The Dragon has a command-to-line of sight guidance system, and all the gunner has to do to ensure a direct hit is to keep the cross hairs of the sight on the target. Missile commands are transmitted from the launcher to the missile by wire, the corrections being carried out by 30 pairs of small side-thrusting rocket motors that are mounted in rows around the body of the missile. Dragon is fitted with a HEAT (high explosive anti-tank) warhead that is said to be able to penetrate 20 in (500 mm) of armour at 0°.

The standard US Army machine-gun is still the 7.62-mm (0.3-in) M60, used in the light and heavy machine-gun roles on a bipod or tripod respectively. There are numerous sub-variants of the M60, some mounted on helicopters and vehicles. The basic weapon is a belt-fed machine-gun with an air-cooled barrel. There are features of the M60 which have not stood up too well in service, but the type will remain standard for years to come.

Perhaps the most famous of American machine-guns is the 12.7-mm (0.5-in) Browning HB (Heavy Barrel) M2 machine-gun. This superlative weapon has been in inventory for decades and is still in production. The main reason for its longevity is quite simply reliability and a round that remains among the best of available anti-personnel weapons. The power of the ammunition is such that it can be used against almost any vehicle except a tank, and special armour-piercing ammunition is produced. The M2 can be mounted on a tripod, and also on vehicles and light river craft.

The US Army's array of grenades ranges from the basic M68 hand grenade to the complex family of 40-mm projected grenades. These latter grenades can be fired from the shotgun-like M79 grenade-launcher or the M203 device mounted beneath the barrel of the M16A1 rifle. The weapon is accurate as far as 440 yards (400 m), making these launchers very useful squad weapons indeed. There is now a move to procure automatic launchers for the 40-mm grenade under the designation M19.

To lob projectiles to greater ranges, the US Army uses mortars. The smallest is the 60-mm M224 Lightweight Company Mortar, a new weapon that can throw a 3.3-lb (1.5-kg) HE bomb about 5,000 yards (4575 m). The M224 will replace the heavier 81-mm M29 mortar but a new generation 81-mm mortar is also being sought. The new weapon may well be the British L16, but the latter's delayed trials programme and political difficulties may mean that the M29 and its later M29A1 variant will have to soldier on for some time to come. A point of interest is that American soldiers refer to their mortars as 'cannons'.

Though not primarily an infantry weapon, the largest mortar used by the US Army is the 107-mm (4.2-in) M30, a modernized version of the World War II weapon with the same bore diameter. This differs from others of its kind by firing a spin-stabilized projectile from a rifled barrel, other mortars firing a fin-stabilized bomb from a smooth-bore barrel. The M30 can fire a 22-lb (10-kg) HE bomb to a range of 7,435 yards (6800 m), and is so

An AM General M151 (4x4) Jeep patrols in the desert, armed with a pintle mounted 7.62-mm (0.3-in) machine-gun. The M151 is used for a wide range of roles such as reconnaissance, command and control, and anti-tank (fitted with TOW missiles) as well as for general utility duties all over the battlefield.

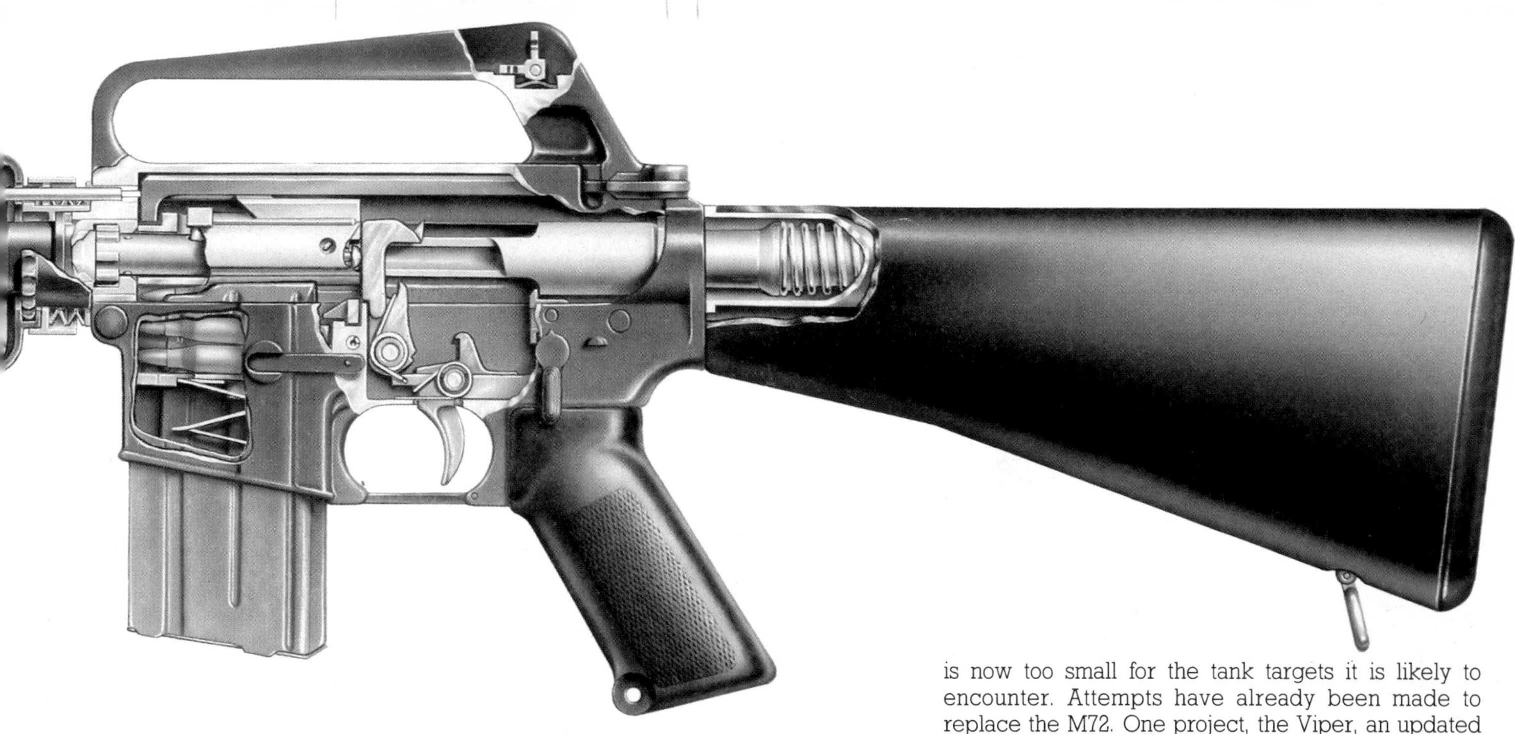

heavy that it is usually carried in a special version of the M113 armoured personnel carrier.

The infantry is well supplied with anti-tank weapons, but trials are under way to select a more powerful, portable anti-tank weapon to cope with the coming generation of main battle tanks, which will have thicker armour. Current weapons include the M47 Dragon medium anti-tank weapon, a heavy missile-launcher requiring a muzzle-mounted bipod to allow the operator to aim and fire accurately. The Dragon missile is wire-guided and aimed by a tracker unit mounted on the launcher tube. Range is about 1,095 yards (1000 m), now seen as insufficient, although the Dragon will remain in service for some time. Inflight corrections are transmitted to the missile along the guidance wires, and corrections are made by firing tiny rocket jets arranged in rows along the missile body, the jets 'kicking' the missile toward its intended path.

The smaller 66-mm M72 family of rocket-launchers carries its rocket in a telescopic tube, the tube being unopened until required for use. Sighting the M72 is simple, and once the weapon has been fired the tube is discarded. The M72's main problem is that its warhead is now too small for the tank targets it is likely to encounter. Attempts have already been made to replace the M72. One project, the Viper, an updated variant of the M72, has been proposed but found wanting. The British LAW 80 is one candidate in the current US Army trials.

Still held in reserve and used by the National Guard, but unlikely to be employed again in anger, are the 106-mm (4.17-in) recoilless rifle, often carried on a Jeep, and the 3.5-in (89-mm) bazooka.

Armour-piercing

Most powerful and best known of infantry-based anti-tank weapons is the TOW heavy anti-tank weapon system. Although not normally carried by soldiers, TOW (Tube-launched, Optically-tracked, Wire-guided) is the most important US Army anti-tank weapon and is currently undergoing a programme to improve the missile's armour-piercing capabilities. The new variant is the I-TOW (Improved TOW) which is said to be capable of piercing the frontal armour of the latest types of Soviet tank. In its basic form TOW is fired from a tube-launcher mounted on a tripod. A tracker unit on the launcher is used to keep the sight cross-hairs on the tank target, and once fired the TOW missile is automatically guided by signals sent along

A well camouflaged Hughes Aircraft TOW anti-tank missile awaits the arrival of enemy tanks. The TOW system is the most widely used missile in the world, and so far some 300,000 have been made for more than 30 countries, including the United States. The original version entered service in 1972 and had a range of 3,280 yards (3000 m), but the current production TOW has a range of 3750 m (4,100 yards) and an improved warhead that will penetrate the frontal armour of even the latest Soviet tanks. In US Army service the TOW is carried on the M151 (4x4) Jeep, but this will soon be replaced by the High-mobility Multi-purpose Wheeled Vehicle.

The M60A3 MBT is fitted with a thermal sleeve for the 105-mm (4.13-in) M68 gun, infra-red/white-light searchlight over the main armament and British-designed smoke dischargers on the turret side. This model also has the new fire-control system that incorporates a laser rangefinder to give a high probability of a first-round hit. Production of the M60A3 has been completed for the US Army, although the weapon remains in production for export.

the guidance wires. The high-speed TOW missile has a range of 4,100 yards (3750 m). It can be mounted on vehicles and is extensively used from helicopters.

Anti-aircraft defence for the infantry is provided partially by the Browning M2 heavy machine-gun on a special mounting or from vehicle pintles, but also by special anti-aircraft missiles. One in-service infantry system is the FIM-43 Redeye, a basic shoulder-launched system firing an infra-red seeking weapon. Although effective, Redeye has severe operational limitations, some of which have been carried over to its intended replacement, the FIM-92 Stinger. The main problem with both is that they tend to 'chase' after an aircraft target, the main source of infra-red emissions being the aircraft's exhaust. This can mean that a fighter-bomber is engaged only after it has passed and dropped its ordnance. The other drawback to both is cost. Each missile costs thousands of dollars. The US Army is currently conducting tests to find a 'fire-and-forget' anti-aircraft missile system suitable for infantry use.

Armour

Once controversial, still costly, but a source of immense pride, the US Army's latest and most advanced main battle tank is the celebrated M1 Abrams. The M1 is an entirely new design owing nothing to earlier tanks like the M60 series, which can trace its ancestry back to the M26 of World War II. With the M1, the US Army has made a quantum jump in tank design with new and novel features like a gas turbine engine in place of the customary diesel powerpack. The gas turbine is more compact for a given power output and provides more rapid power responses, but it also has higher fuel consumption. Thus volume saved in the engine is sacrificed to greater fuel capacity. Also, the gas turbine's reliability is suspect in the long term. Apart from its powerpack, the M1 has a very resilient suspension and combined with its high power-to-weight ratio this produces sprightly performance that is limited not by the capabilities of the suspension but by whatever buffeting the four-man crew can tolerate. In many ways, the M1 Abrams can be said to be a 'sports car'. Initial batches will be fitted with the 105-mm (4.13-in) M68 gun, the American version of the succesful British L7A1, but it is planned to fit later batches with a more powerful 120-mm (4.72-in) smooth-bore gun produced in the United States under licence from Rheinmetall of West Germany. Allied with these guns is a very advanced computer-based fire-control system that uses information from an array of sensors to ensure the all-important first-round hit. Communications and other sub-systems within the M1 are no less advanced.

Current plans are for thousands of M1 Abrams tanks to roll off production lines at the Lima, Ohio Army Tank Plant, and other sources are being investigated. At first regarded as almost scandalous in its cost and complexity, the M1 now enjoys a generally good reputa-

The M1 MBT is seen from rear with commander manning a 12.7-mm (0.5-in) M2 HB machine-gun that can also be aimed and fired from within the cupola. Although heavily criticized by the media, the M1 has been well received by tank crews. Its most controversial feature is the gas turbine engine which has been the cause of most of its problems, although the powerplant is now much more reliable that it was when the tank was first issued. Under development is a Heavy Assault Bridge that will be based on the chassis of the M1 Abrams.

The M551 Sheridan is the Armored Reconnaissance/Airborne Assault Vehicle (AR/AAV) of which some 1,700 were produced for the US Army between 1966 and 1970. In 1984 the M551 remained operational only with one battalion allocated to the 82nd Airborne Division. The M551 is fitted with the 152-mm (6-in) gun/launcher that can fire a Shillelagh missile or a conventional round with a combustible cartridge case.

The M113 Armored Cavalry Assault Vehicle (ACAV) was originally developed for use in Vietnam. It has a 12.7-mm (0.5-in) M2 HB machine-gun provided with all-round protection, and two side-mounted 7.62-mm (0.3-in) machine-guns that are provided only with a shield to protect the gunner.

tion, but cost remains a significant factor. In recent years, the price of the machine has been under scrutiny and criticism, but the vehicle gets no cheaper. Reliability and cost-effectiveness have improved, but it appears unlikely that the army will be able to afford as many M1s as it wants. For all that, the M1 is now in service in Germany and more are arriving every month.

With the M1 Abrams, as with many systems intended for a nuclear war that has not happened, the truth is that nobody knows quite what the thing will do. 'We can't use it under actual conditions,' complains Captain Michael P. Curphey in Wiesbaden. No American soldier since 1950 has seen a real enemy tank coming at him. Ordnance is so costly that many crews have never fired a live round. The M1 Abrams is designed for rough countryside but in densely-populated Germany and Korea, farmers are less than enthusiastic about seeing their crops trampled. In actual combat, a tank would lie in wait for the enemy by driving into a house and hiding beneath its wreckage, a tactic that cannot be rehearsed. Says Curphey, 'most of what we know is hypothetical . . .'

The backbone of American armour forces remains the M60 series, serving as a main battle tank in its M60A1 and M60A3 versions. Both have diesel engines and are armed with the 105-mm (4.13-in) M68 gun, but the M60A3 also has an improved fire-control system. Compared with its Soviet counterpart, the M60 is high, heavy, and inclined to be cumbersome in performance, but improvements and modifications ensure that the M60 will keep its place among more important tank types. The US Army has 9,000 M60s (its total tank strength being 12,130 of all types). To back up this machine, 2,000 M48 tanks remain in service, some with the National Guard. Some of these are armed with a

A Hughes Aircraft TOW anti-tank missile is launched from a M113 APC, the photograph clearly showing the gunner's total lack of protection from small arms fire and shell splinters. The US Army now has over 2,000 examples of the Improved TOW Vehicle (ITV), which has an elevating arm with two missiles in the ready-to-launch position, additional missiles being carried inside the vehicle for rapid reloading.

The M113 is the most widely used APC in the world, over 70,000 having been produced by the FMC Corporation since 1960. The US Army alone has almost 20,000 of these in countless configurations including command vehicles, mortar carriers, load carriers and anti-aircraft vehicles, and as part of various missile systems such as the HAWK and Chaparral. In the case of these last two the vehicles are based on the M548 tracked cargo carrier.

Left: An obsolete M47 tank is about to be hit by a Martin Marietta Copperhead Cannon-Launched Guided Projectile (CLGP) fired well to the rear by a 155-mm (6.1-in) M109 self-propelled howitzer. The introduction of Copperhead will give the artillery the capability of engaging tanks and other armoured vehicles at long range. The introduction of the missile has been delayed, however, by quality-control problems on the production line.

90-mm (3.54-in) gun, but the M48A5 has the 105-mm (4.13-in) gun and can be said to be almost up to M60 standard. No M48s remain in Europe, their main locations being the Far East and reserve/storage.

The US Army currently has no light tank force, a serious flaw when rapid deployment by air is contemplated, but some M551 Sheridans remain in inventory. The M551 was one of the American defence industry's more spectacular failures, intended to be armed with a 155-mm (6.1-in) combined missile-launcher/gun which was never perfected. Some have been stored or converted to resemble Soviet vehicles for exercise purposes, and numbers have been sold abroad. Able to deploy large numbers of main battle tanks today only by sea, the US Army retains its faith in the light tank concept and is seeking machines armed with a 75-mm (2.95-in) gun suitable for the RDJTF, while the US Air Force continues to want the McDonnell Douglas C-17 transport to carry them.

The M48 and M60 chassis are the foundation for a variety of vehicles used to support armoured forces. The M60 provides the basis for the M728 Combat

An FMC Bradley M2 Infantry Fighting Vehicle (IFV) churns up dust as it speeds forward. The M2 is now being produced at the rate of over 600 vehicles per year, and gives the infantry the capability to work with the M1 Abrams MBT as part of the combined arms team concept. The Bradley is fitted with a two-man power-operated turret armed with a 25-mm Hughes Helicopters Chain Gun and a 7.62-mm (0.3-in) co-axial machine-gun. Mounted on the left side of the turret is a twin launcher for the Hughes Aircraft TOW long-range anti-tank missile.

The M3 Cavalry Fighting Vehicle (CFV) is very similar to the M2 IFV but has a five-man crew, greatly increased ammunition-carrying capacity and no firing ports in the rear troop compartment. The M2 and M3 are fitted with a full range of night-vision equipment, have an NBC system and are fully amphibious. They are, however, very complex and expensive vehicles compared with the M113 they are replacing, and it remains to be seen if the US Army can afford all of the vehicles it so urgently requires.

Engineer Vehicle, armed with a 165-mm (6.5-in) demolition gun and equipped with such items as a front-mounted dozer blade and an A-frame jib. The M48 and M60 are used to carry varying sizes of combat bridges. For front-line repair of tank battalion vehicles, large numbers of M88A1 armoured repair vehicles (ARVs) are still being produced. This highly specialized vehicle is equipped with a large A-frame and all manner of special tooling for keeping tanks running. The M88A1 can carry spare powerpacks, wheels and tracks.

Armoured strength is not measured in tanks alone, for the US Army has invested heavily in armoured personnel carriers (APCs) mainly for its mechanized infantry. The principal type is the M113, which has armoured protection for its crew of two and 11 fully-armed soldiers. A simple vehicle, the M113 can be configured for a number of special purposes, some of which have their own designations. One of the most important is the M577 mobile command post. Others are the M106 (107-mm) and the M125A1 (81-mm) mortar-carriers and the M163 armed with a 20-mm Gatling cannon for anti-aircraft use. The most specialized of all M113s is the M901 which has an armoured TOW launcher at the end of elevating arms to enable the missiles to be fired while the vehicle remains behind cover. Numbers of M901s are being issued to units in Germany, and a move is afoot to replace the existing missile with the I-TOW.

On the move

While the M113 is a successful APC with Vietnam battle scars, it lacks provision for embarked soldiers to fight from the vehicle except with machine-guns fired from roof hatches. Modern combat demands that crews fire and fight while on the move. This concept has led to the mechanized infantry fighting vehicle (MIFV). After a prolonged period of vehicle development, the US Army has now been issued with this new type in the forms of the M2 Bradley Infantry Fighting

The Bradley has a three-man crew (commander, gunner and driver) and can carry seven fully equipped infantrymen. In each side of the hull are two firing ports (each with a vision block above) that allow some of the infantry to fire their M231 (cut-down M16) rifles from inside the troop compartment. Seen emerging from the back of their M2, this squad of M16-armed infantrymen are wearing the new pattern Kevlar helmet that first saw action with the 82nd Airborne Division in Grenada.

Left: A Martin Marietta Pershing 1A battlefield tactical support missile leaves its trailer/erector/launcher. Some 108 launchers are now deployed in West Germany by the US Army, and the system is also operated by the West German air force. The Pershing 1A was originally fielded in the early 1960s and fitted with a 400-kiloton tactical nuclear warhead, but it is thought that some of these have now been replaced by a warhead in the 60-kiloton yield range.

Vehicle (IFV) and the almost identical M3 Cavalry Fighting Vehicle. Both are complex APCs able to fight on the move. The M2 IFV has a crew of three and carries six men. Its armament, in a roof turret, is a 25-mm M242 Chain Gun capable of firing a variety of ammunition types at a rate of up to 200 rounds per minute. The M242 is backed up by a co-axial 12.7-mm (0.5) machine-gun, and there is provision on the turret to mount two TOW rounds. The embarked infantry are provided with six special 5.56-mm (0.223-in) automatic rifles fixed to and firing from firing ports in the sides and rear of the hull, and the infantrymen can leave the vehicle through a hatch at the rear; the M3 lacks this capacity.

Without question, the M2 Bradley IFV is a powerful battlefield asset but it is seen, too, as another example of the 'gold-plated' approach, for each M2 costs well over $500,000 (£340,000) in its most basic form, or almost as much as the needed light tank. Thus, the M2 will not replace the M113 but will supplement it in mechanized infantry battalions and cavalry squadrons. The chassis of the basic M2 is to be used for the MLRS artillery rocket system and is already being adapted for other roles.

Missiles and Artillery

Most frightening of the US Army's weapons is the MGM-31A Pershing battlefield missile. This hefty ballistic missile uses inertial guidance to steer its nuclear warhead to a target up to 460 miles (740 km) distant. The Pershing can be towed and used direct from field sites with only a limited amount of preparations. Pershings already serve in Europe, and the US Army has four Pershing battalions, one a training formation capable of taking the field if required. Starting in 1984, it is scheduled that existing Pershings will be replaced by the Pershing 2 with terminal guidance for a superior but smaller warhead, and with improved range. The new model is the fear of peace demonstrators and a volatile new factor in the European equation, reducing to as little as 15 minutes the decision time available to Soviet policymakers when they think it is coming at them. The same ground support equipment as that for the existing Pershing will be used.

Only slightly less powerful than the Pershing is the MGM-52C Lance battlefield support missile. Like the Pershing, the Lance can be fitted with a nuclear warhead, but the US Army also fields large HE warheads for this missile. The range of the Lance is 75 miles (120 km), and the missile is carried on the battlefield by a special launch vehicle, yet another variation on the M113 APC. The Lance is currently being used as the base vehicle for a new generation of battlefield support missiles intended primarily for use against massed enemy armour. This programme is known as Tank Breaker and already a special warhead containing a large number of anti-tank bomblets has been developed and issued. Lance is deployed in Europe with US and NATO units.

A rocket system yet to be deployed by the US Army is the Multiple Launch Rocket System (MLRS). MLRS is primarily an artillery rocket intended to saturate enemy targets with salvoes of unguided 227-mm (8.93-in) rounds. These are transported and issued in six-rocket pallets that also act as the launching frames, carried on the rear of armoured tracked vehicles. The launcher vehicles are equipped with some very advanced battlefield navigation and position-fixing electronics that enables the three-man crew to launch the rockets at targets 32,800 yards (30000 m) distant. Once the rockets have been launched, the vehicles reload from support vehicles close by. MLRS warheads for the initial batch will be fitted with West German AT-2 anti-tank mines. The first MLRS equipments have already been issued and the first battery has been activated.

In artillery, the US Army is now almost entirely equipped with self-propelled items for front-line formations. Largest in calibre is the 203-mm (8-in) M110 howitzer, which has a range of 23,300 yards (21300 m), and in its latest M110A2 form of 31,825 yards (29100 m) with enhanced-range projectiles. The M110 series can

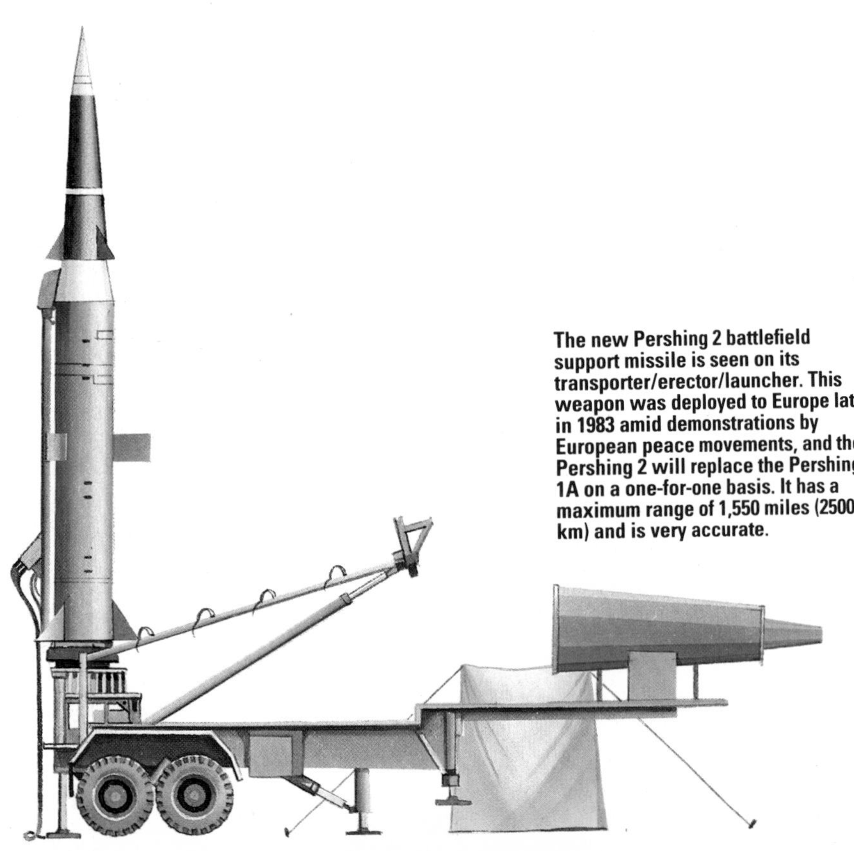

The new Pershing 2 battlefield support missile is seen on its transporter/erector/launcher. This weapon was deployed to Europe late in 1983 amid demonstrations by European peace movements, and the Pershing 2 will replace the Pershing 1A on a one-for-one basis. It has a maximum range of 1,550 miles (2500 km) and is very accurate.

The Lance mobile battlefield missile is launched from a fully tracked vehicle based on the M548 tracked cargo chassis. The US Army has a total of eight Lance battalions, of which two are based in the United States at Fort Sill, home of the Field Artillery, and the remaining six in Europe with a total of 36 launchers. The first production missiles were completed in 1971, and final deliveries were made late in 1980. A number of warhead types can be fitted to Lance, including a tactical nuclear (100 kilotons), high explosive, M251 with 860 bomblets and, in the not too distant future, the neutron warhead.

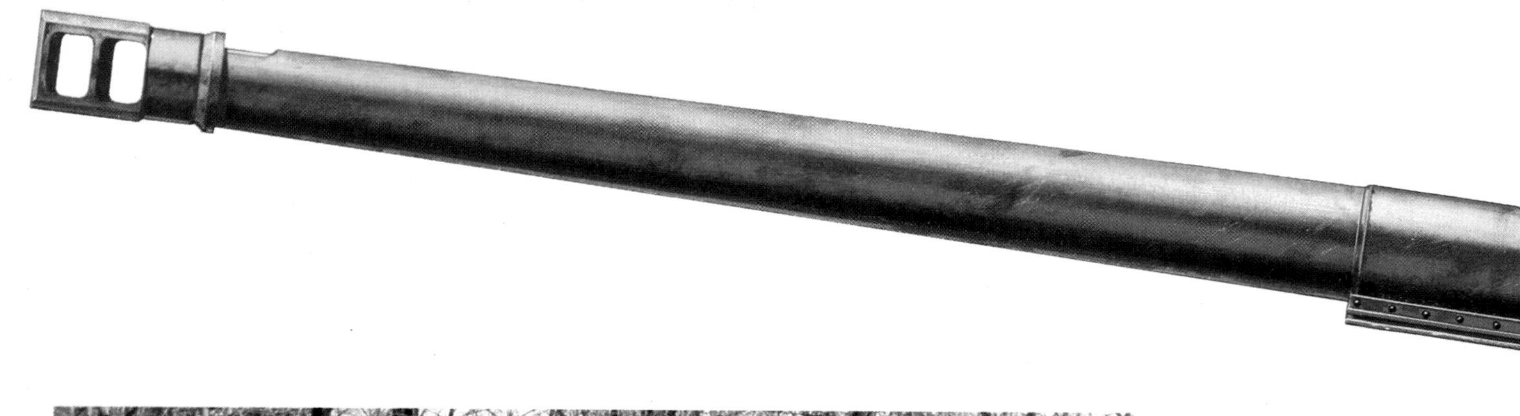

Above: The current version of the M110 is the M110A2, which is essentially the earlier vehicle fitted with a much longer barrel ending in a larger double-baffle muzzle brake, so enabling it to fire new and improved ammunition to much greater ranges.

Side and top view of the 203-mm (8-in) M110A2 self-propelled howitzer in its travelling configuration. The M110A2 is issued on the scale of one battery to each infantry division and one battalion of three batteries to each mechanized infantry and armoured division. In addition to firing high explosive and agent rounds, the M110A2 can also fire a tactical nuclear projectile to a maximum range of 18,375 yards (16800 m).

M110A2 Self-Propelled Howitzer

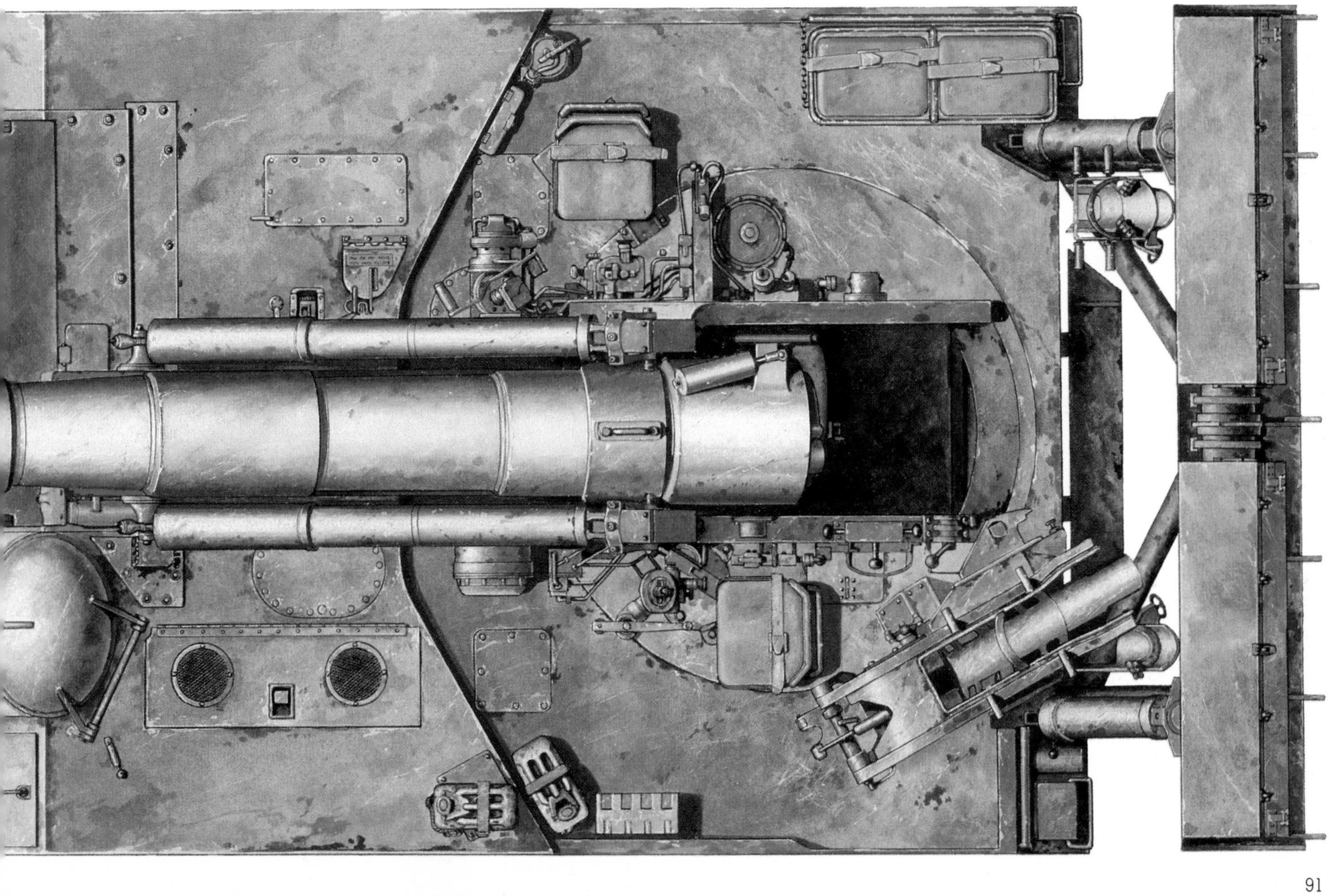

The M102 105-mm (4.13-in) howitzer has been issued to selected US units, including the 82nd Airborne and the 101st Air Assault Divisions. First used in Vietnam in the late 1960s, the M102 has most recently seen action with the 82nd Airborne Division in Grenada.

The original version of the 203-mm (8-in) M110 self-propelled howitzer entered service with the US Army in 1964.

A Vought Multiple-Launch Rocket System launches one of its 12 rockets. This system is already in service with the US 7th Army in Europe, and has also been adopted by the UK, France, West Germany and Italy. The chassis of the MLRS is based on that of the M2 Infantry Fighting Vehicle (IFV) already in service with the US Army.

fire nuclear projectiles. The basic HE shell weighs no less than 20 lb (92.5 kg) and has tremendous destructive potential. The howitzer of the M110 is carried on a special tracked carriage and there is no protection for the gun crew, which consists of five men actually on the gun with more in support vehicles carrying ammunition. The basic M110 has now been replaced by the M110A1 with a longer barrel and by the M110A2 which has the longer barrel with a muzzle brake enabling it to fire more powerful propellant charges.

The most numerous of US Army self-propelled items is the series of vehicles based on the M109 155-mm (6.1-in) howitzers. The M109 has its howitzer in a 360° traversing turret mounted on a chassis that is fitted with armour manufactured from aluminium alloys. The vehicle is thus light for its bulk and is amphibious to a limited degree. The howitzer can fire an HE shell weighing 95 lb (43 kg) to a range of 19,800 yards (18100 m) in the M109A1 version, and the projectiles fired are all standard NATO items that can be acquired throughout the Treaty nations. The original M109 has now been replaced by the M109A1 with a longer barrel to improve range, and the M109A2 is the full production version with the long barrel and other detail internal improvements. The M109A1 is the basic vehicle used by artillery battalions in Europe and a special version known as the M992 Field Artillery Support Vehicle is now being introduced into service. The M992 is an ammunition carrier which is used to supply ammunition to M109s in the field. It carries the ammunition in racks, and from the racks rounds can be moved mechanically and under cover into the recipient M109.

The M109 is in service in large numbers (about 2,500) but already its successor is under consideration: specifications have been drawn up for a new 155-mm (6.1-in) howitzer system known as the Divisional Support Weapon System, or DSWS. The DSWS will have an automatic loader, a computer-based fire-control system, inertial navigation equipment, a very high power-to-weight ratio (a prolonged series of 'shoot and scoot' fire missions is anticipated) and a high rate of fire to ranges up to 32,800 yards (30000 m). While such a weapon would be ideal, costs will be astronomical, so steps are being taken to improve the basic M109's performance and prolong its operational life.

Towed artillery is still widely used in the US Army, with large numbers of M114 155-mm (6.1-in) towed howitzers still in service. The M114 is of World War II

Current US military thinking centres on a requirement to reinforce and resupply troops on the ground as quickly as possible, as well as to deploy and supply units in possible trouble spots at very short notice. To this end, most US Army equipment (including UH-60 helicopters and armoured vehicles) is air transportable, and a large proportion can be dropped by parachute.

The M198 155-mm (6.1-in) Howitzer is a thoroughly modern artillery piece, entering service at Fort Bragg, NC, in 1979. The M198 has since seen action with the Marine Corps in Beirut.

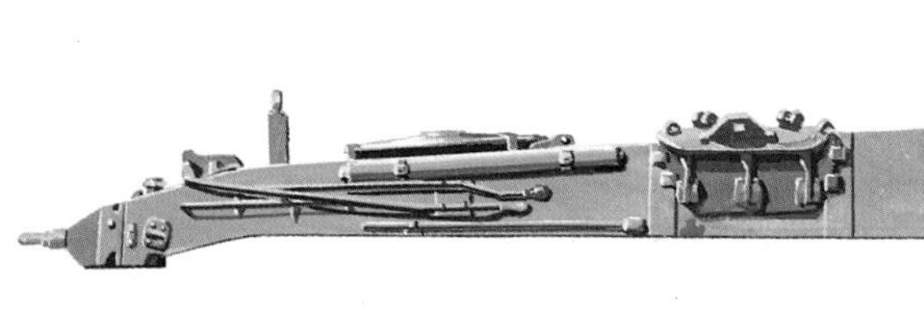

Right: One of the prototypes of the M109 HELP (Howitzer Extended Life Program) is seen with the 155-mm (6.1-in) howitzer in its travel lock. The HELP will extend the operational life of the M109 into the 1990s pending the introduction of the Divisional Support Weapon System, or the Direct Support Armored Cannon System as it is also known. The HELP has a total of 26 improvements over the original vehicle in the areas of reliability, maintainability, survivability and NBC protection. If adopted it is expected that not only will the whole American fleet of 2,500 vehicles be brought up to this standard but also that kits will be supplied to other countries to enable them to upgrade their vehicles to the same standard.

vintage, but with a new and longer barrel on a modified carriage has become the updated M114A2. The basic M114 fires a 95-lb (43-kg) HE shell to a range of 15,975 yards (14600 m).

A more modern 155-mm (6.1-in) howitzer is the M198, intended for use by the RDJTF and airborne artillery regiments. It is a thoroughly modern item with a long barrel and a light carriage. It fires the standard 95-lb (43-kg) shell to a range of 26,250 yards (24000 m). Like other 155-mm howitzers, the M198 can fire the laser-guided Copperhead projectile, intended for use against tanks, but development problems have delayed introduction of this munition, and it may be some time before Copperhead enters service. Meanwhile, a nuclear projectile for 155-mm howitzers is under development, as is a binary chemical-carrying projectile. Cargo rounds carrying explosive submunitions and small mines are already in the 155-mm inventory.

Numbers of towed 105-mm (4.13-in) howitzers are still used by some airborne artillery battalions. The model now used is the 105-mm M102, a weapon specifically tailored for airborne units and firing the time-honoured standard 105-mm (4.13-in) ammunition. The

The 155-mm (6.1-in) M198 towed howitzer is seen in a sandbagged firing emplacement. The M198 is the latest towed howitzer to enter service, and is the replacement for the 155-mm (6.1-in) M114 howitzer developed during World War II. It is used mainly by infantry and airborne divisions, each battalion having three batteries of eight guns. The M198 was first used in combat by the US Marines in the Lebanon in 1983. The M198 is normally towed by a 5-ton (6x6) truck and can be carried slung under a Boeing Vertol CH-47 helicopter.

The Hughes OH-6A Cayuse saw valuable service in Vietnam, armed with Miniguns fired from the rear cabin. Its agility and power make it a useful scout, and it will serve until the end of the decade.

M102 can fire its HE shell to a range of 12,575 yards (11500 m). The M102 has a crew of from four to six, and can be towed or slung from a helicopter.

Army Aviation

Current plans are to extend the number of the US Army's rotary- and fixed-wing aircraft to no less than 9,670 by 1988. In time, these aircraft will be assigned into five main groups.

First will be the scout helicopter. The main type in use will be the Bell OH-58D Aeroscout, a much-modified version of the current OH-58 Kiowa. The OH-58D will have a mast-mounted sensor head which will include a laser sight to designate targets for other attack aircraft or helicopters. The OH-58D will be backed by the slightly less specialized OH-58C and the smaller Hughes OH-6A Cayuse, which is expected to be phased out of service by 1990.

The second category of Army Aviation types will be gunships. The expensive AH-64 Apache is easily the most powerful helicopter in its class. Available in far larger numbers, at greater economy, is the Bell AH-1 Cobra, the gunship development from the well-known UH-1 'Huey'. There are various versions of the Cobra, but most have a Gatling gun and carry up to eight TOW anti-tank missiles.

Troop transports are extensively used by the US Army in the shape of numerous Hueys. The army has thousands of this basic series, and they are set to last for years yet. Soon, they will be supplemented by the larger Sikorsky UH-60 Black Hawk, already in service in some numbers and used in action in Grenada. The UH-60 can carry 11 fully-armed men 375 miles (600 km) without difficulty. External pylons can accommodate extra fuel, Hellfire anti-tank missiles, or such loads as light motorcycles.

Cargo movers are the fourth category, the Boeing Vertol CH-47D Chinook fast becoming the world leader in its class. The CH-47D will be the US Army's only cargo helicopter by the 1990s, and a programme is under way to retrofit earlier models to the CH-47D

Still the most numerous type in US Army Aviation is the Bell UH-1 'Huey' series, which will play an important part in all light transport roles for many years. This example is a twin-engined UH-1N.

An early Sikorsky CH-54A Tarhe demonstrates the load-carrying ability of this flying crane. Although nearing the end of their service lives, the 80 or so Tarhes still in use enjoy a peculiar position, being able to carry out jobs which the more powerful H-47 and H-53 cannot undertake.

Although primarily a transport aircraft, the Sikorsky UH-60A Black Hawk can carry anti-tank missiles on pylons. The army plans to procure over 1,100 of these assault helicopters to supplement and eventually replace the dwindling UH-1 force.

Available in far greater numbers, and at significantly less cost than the Hughes AH-64, the Bell AH-1 Cobra still forms the backbone of the gunship fleet. Armed with TOW missiles, rocket launchers, a Chain Gun and 40-mm grenade launchers, the Cobra can be used in the 'killer' role combined with OH-58 or OH-6 'hunters'. This example is an AH-1S, distinguished by the flat windscreen sections.

standard. The Chinook has a large internal cargo or passenger bay that can take 50 or more men, or loads such as Jeeps and light artillery, but its true cargo-carrying potential is realized only when external suspension points are used. The CH-47D has three external suspension points under the fuselage and from these can be slung portable fuel tanks, trucks, assault bridges and even artillery as large as the M198 howitzer.

Electronic warfare is the final of the five Army Aviation tasks and requires various aircraft, including a version of the Black Hawk known as the EH-60A which can intercept and jam enemy radio frequencies. Fixed-wing aircraft used in this role include a number of Grumman RV-1D Mohawk variants equipped with underslung sensors in long housings, and the Beech RC-12D and RU-21D 'Guardrail' which have aerials protruding from all over their fuselages and wings.

The Bell OH-58 Kiowa has been in use for several years and will continue for some years. Its scheduled replacement is the OH-58D Aeroscout, which is much improved, adding a mast-mounted sight with laser designator. No. 68-16695, pictured here, is an OH-58A with Minigun mounted outside the cockpit. Many OH-58As have been rebuilt as OH-58Cs with flat-pane canopies.

Some electronic warfare aircraft listen in on enemy frequencies; others jam known frequencies. The US Army also has several one-off types of rotary and fixed-wing aircraft used in the electronic warfare role.

Preparedness

At day's end in the darkening expanses of the former dirigible hangar at NAS Lakehurst, New Jersey, a weary Specialist Fourth Class 'locks up' the side-looking airborne radar (SLAR) housing on a Grumman Mohawk and plans to hurry home to catch night TV football. At a barbed-wire enclosure storing chemical weapons at Camp Red Cloud near Uijongbu, Korea, a female MP, bayonet fixed to her M16, scrutinizes the dusk for intruders and mentally rehearses for an MOS proficiency examination which will bring her corporal's stripes. At twilight in Stockholm, at a crowded outdoor reception, a colonel in dress AG-34 greens lifts a glass of ginger ale superficially masquerading as whiskey and speaks politely to the Soviet army attaché hoping that he, the American army attaché, can glean intelligence data from small talk. Near the Korean DMZ and at Germany's Fulda Gap, as they do 24 hours a day and in possession of a grim knowledge the civilian back home lacks, men peer in the direction of overwhelming numbers of hostile armour. These are the people in the modern United States Army doing their jobs.

It is no accident that their tools are named after men who are now ghostly apparitions in the 'long gray line': Creighton Abrams, the gutsy, cigar-smoking, audacious tank commander; Philip Sheridan, a scholar who led sabre charges in the Civil War; Omar Bradley, the folksy field commander of incredibly vast armies in a war so terrible it must not recur.

But recurrence is the stuff of history. If there is a central truth in the final years of the 20th century (as we learn again and again; for instance in the Falklands, as the Americans know) it is that free men must be willing to employ force of arms when tyranny looms. The United States Army is, can, and will.

The Sikorsky UH-60 Black Hawk undertook its first combat action during the invasion of Grenada carrying parties of the 82nd Airborne Division, and Ranger special forces ashore from carriers anchored off the coast.

Battlefield reconnaissance is the main role for the Grumman OV-1 Mohawk, using side-looking airborne radar (SLAR) and electronic sensors. However, tactical loads can be carried on the wing pylons.

The Boeing Vertol CH-47 Chinook has provided the US Army's tactical heavylift capability since the war in South East Asia, and in the shape of the CH-47D will continue to do so until the end of the century.

L 19

United States Marine Corps

With a tradition dating from the days of the Continental Congress of 1775, the United States Marine Corps has a fighting record second to none. Originally maritime soldiers, since the Pacific campaigns of World War II the Corps has become an amphibious warfare specialist. Together with the amphibious squadrons of the Navy, the Marine Corps gives the United States government an extremely potent means of power projection and (if necessary) intervention on a world wide scale.

Left: US Marines storm ashore in a classic amphibious assault. Inheritor of a tradition dating from the first days of the United States, the modern Marine Corps stands prepared to protect American lives and interests worldwide.

Below: Service with the multi-national force in Lebanon saw the Marine Corps occupied in an unfamiliar and thankless task. Tragedy was never far away, and the Marines suffered in a situation not of their making and in which their training counted for little.

Corporal Rick Crudale's parents in West Warwick, Rhode Island, were happy and proud when their flak-jacketed son appeared on *Time* magazine's cover for 3 October 1983 with a story called 'Lebanon: Holding the Line'. Days later, 21-year-old Crudale was dead, one of 226 United States Marines killed in the October 1983 terrorist bombing of their headquarters at Beirut International Airport.

Colonel James P. Faulkner stared grimly at the field radio in his hand, listened to the background chatter of small-arms fire, and made his decision. 'Go!' Faulkner barked into the radio. Moments later, men of Company G, 22nd Marine Amphibious Unit, moved in under fire and stormed the residence of the governor, Sir Paul Scoon, rescuing 33 civilians trapped in the middle in the Grenada fighting.

Crudale and Faulkner, corporal and colonel, are names from two trouble spots where US Marines have faced danger lately. Lebanon and Grenada, however, are only fragments in the story of the US Marine Corps, the elite fighting force popularized by Hollywood, proven on the battlefield, and picked for the tough jobs whenever the spirit and elan of men under arms can make the difference.

The *raison d'être* for the US Marine Corps, formalized in the National Security Act of 1947 and used again and again to justify budget requests to a cost-wary Congress, is amphibious warfare. But, critics ask, is the US Marine Corps really different from the US Army? Is a separate service justified? Supporters of the US

An amphibious LVTP7 (Landing Vehicle Tracked Personnel) comes ashore from an amphibious squadron (PHIBRON) which includes the large USS *Saipan* (LHA-2) and a 'Newport' class tank landing ship. Such squadrons are on station at strategic points throughout the world, providing Marine Corps forces at constant readiness.

Marine Corps will argue that while the Iwo Jima-style beach-head landing may be a thing of the past, a need does exist for a specialized force of fighting men who can accompany the fleet, deploy anywhere at short notice, and move into battle in a Landing Vehicle Tracked (LTV), a twin-rotor Boeing Vertol CH-46 helicopter, or (as men will do as long as there is war) on foot.

Today the US Marine Corps retains its mandate for amphibious warfare and has an added mission: rapid deployment. At the beginning of 1984, its manpower was 192,000. US Marines do not distinguish between 'arms' and 'services' as does the US Army: officially, all US Marines are combat infantrymen. But there is a contrast between the US Marine Corps' ground/sea units and its air arm. And in practice, specializations are inevitable, with some personnel having primarily combat tasks and others holding support functions.

History

The US Marine Corps celebrates 10 November 1775 as its birthday, this being the date when the Continental Congress recognized the amphibious trooper supporting the Navy in the 1775-83 Revolutionary War. The Corps as it exists today was formed by the Act of 11 July 1798, enabling Marines to fight the French in 1798-1801 and the Barbary Corsairs in 1801-5. Marines took an active role in the USA's second war against the British (1812-4), serving aboard practically all American warships of the period.

Marines fought pirates in Cuba in 1824 and participated in the Indian and Mexican wars of the 1800s as well as the 1860-5 Civil War which tore the USA asunder. A noteworthy incident at the beginning of the Civil War period was the participation of Marines in the capture of John Brown and the suppression of the uprising and riot at Harper's Ferry. During the 1900 Boxer Rebellion in China, US Marines from ships on the Asiatic station took part in the defence of the Legation Quarter at Peking, and a regiment of US Marines formed part of the allied relief expedition to Peking as well as taking part in the Battle of Tientsin.

The 20th century, with its seemingly endless conflict, saw a maturing of the US Marine Corps in two world wars and in campaigns in between them. On the morning of 19 February 1945, as men of the 4th and 5th Marine Divisions slogged ashore on an obscure island called Iwo Jima, more than 5,000 men lost their lives in a few hours of struggle for a few hundred yards of ugly, coral-studded beach. A statue of US Marines raising the American flag on Iwo Jima's Mount Surabachi, based upon a photograph by the Associated Press' Joe Rosenthal, looks over the American capital from a green knoll on the Potomac in Arlington, Virginia, not far from the graves of war dead in Arlington National Cemetery and the US Marine Corps' headquarters at Henderson Hall.

When US Marines gather, they talk of Iwo, just as they talk of Belleau Wood, of the dark beginning at Guadalcanal, of blood-smeared Red Beach One at Saipan. They talk of Tarawa and of Inchon. But above all, there was the classic land battle of all American history, fought at the Chosin Reservoir in November 1950 when half a million Chinese troops swarmed down on the 10,000 men of General Oliver P. Smith's 1st Marine Division in the middle of the coldest Korean winter in 144 years. Outnumbered 50 to 1, vehicles and weapons crippled by the sub-zero cold, surrounded by crack Chinese troops in command of the high ground, Smith's Marines fought an offensive war in reverse and came out of the reservoir with all their equipment, all their dead and all their wounded. To have been at the reservoir is to hold a shining place of honour, not merely in US Marine history but in all the annals of American arms.

US Marines intervened in Lebanon on 15 July 1958 in an action which seems innocuous when compared to today's political quagmire in the same country. US Marines fought in Vietnam from beginning to end (1959-73), handling themselves well against a disciplined and dedicated enemy at Hamburger Hill, Hill 881, and Khe Sanh. In all of their battles in this century, US Marine ground troopers (never called soldiers) have been supported by their own air arm. Because the US Marine Corps has always been a volunteer force (in all of its history, accepting conscripts only for a brief period during World War II), the low morale, racial strife and drug abuse of the Vietnam era affected the US Marine Corps less than the other US services. Today, backed by a nation with its Vietnam wounds rapidly healing, the US Marine Corps achieved a tactical success in Grenada but seems, to many Americans, bogged down in Lebanon. Critics argue that the US Marine Corps is poorly prepared for battle in an armour-intensive environment. Still, the US Marine Corps' resolve and dedication have never been stronger.

Organization

Since World War II, the US Marine Corps has traditionally been organized into three ground combat divisions: one on the east coast of the United States, one on

The Sikorsky CH-53 provides the Marine Corps' heavy helicopter lift capability. More than 300 are in use, and funds have been requested for the acquision of the three-engined CH-53E Super Stallion in the next two years.

the west, and one headquartered on Okinawa. Each division has its own aircraft wing.

Rapid deployment

The 1st Marine Division is located at Camp Pendleton, California (supported by the 3rd Marine Aircraft Wing at MCAS El Toro, California), and operates primarily as a component of the Rapid Deployment Joint Task Force (RDJTF), providing a combat force ready to be sent into action in any climate and in any location, at only a moment's notice.

The 2nd Marine Division is based at Camp Lejeune, North Carolina (supported by the 2nd Marine Aircraft Wing at MCAS Cherry Point, North Carolina), and acts as the nucleus of the Fleet Marine Force Atlantic (FMFLant), providing the manpower to support naval operations with the 2nd Fleet in the Atlantic and the 6th Fleet in the Mediterranean.

The 3rd Marine Division is on Okinawa (supported by the 1st Marine Aircraft Wing at MCAS Futema, Okinawa), and forms the nucleus of the Fleet Marine Force Pacific (FMFPac), providing troops in support of the US Navy's 7th Fleet in the east Asian and western Pacific region.

Each division is broken into battalions (nine infantry, one reconnaissance, one armour, one of combat engineers and one for specialized amphibious operations) and has an artillery regiment with towed guns. The aircraft wings supporting these divisions each have up to eight squadrons of tactical jet aircraft, seven helicopter squadrons, and three transport/observation squadrons. Additionally, the US Marine Corps has two independent brigades, one in Hawaii intended for Pacific operations and one at Camp Pendleton as a further component of the RDJTF.

Mention must also be made of the 4th Marine Division, together with its own 4th Marine Aircraft Wing, the former at Camp Pendleton, the latter at NAS Glenview, Illinois. This division is the US Marine Corps Reserve, kept in being by irregular call-up of reservists who train at locations close to their homes. In wartime or in emergency, the President can call the Reserves to active duty.

Among bases where US Marines make their homes

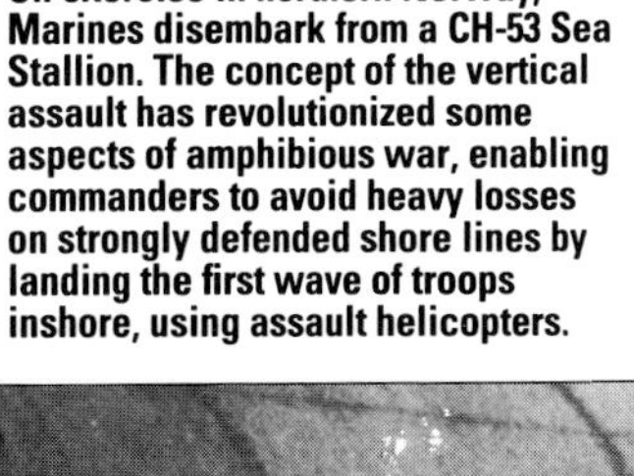

On exercise in northern Norway, Marines disembark from a CH-53 Sea Stallion. The concept of the vertical assault has revolutionized some aspects of amphibious war, enabling commanders to avoid heavy losses on strongly defended shore lines by landing the first wave of troops inshore, using assault helicopters.

Left: Marine peacekeepers march from their utility landing craft (LCU) onto the Lebanese shore in 1982. The LCU 1610 type can land three MBTs, or 170 tons of cargo or up to 250 troops, four of the craft operating from a 'Tarawa' class (LHA) amphibious assault ship.

is the beleaguered US Navy base at Guantanamo Bay in Cuba, where a reinforced US Marine company some 420 strong is used for security purposes. In the Pacific region, some US Marines are station at Subic Bay in the Philippines and at Yokosuka in Japan. In the Mediterranean, another key base is at Naples.

Operationally, the US Marine Corps can be organized into any of three types of formation. The largest is the Marine Amphibious Force (MAF) formed from an entire division plus an aircraft wing. Next in size is the Marine Amphibious Brigade (MAB) one of which, as noted, is kept in being for the RDJTF. The more usual formation is the Marine Amphibious Unit (MAU), based on a composite US Marine battalion and from five to seven US Navy assault ships. Each composite battalion has its own armour, artillery and helicopters. Normally, one MAU is in being at any time in the Mediterranean with another in the Pacific. A variation of the MAU is the Marine Landing Team (MAT), which is a MAU minus the helicopter component. Normally one of these is kept in being in the Pacific region and from time to time another is formed for deployment in the Atlantic. It must be stressed that US Marine forces are formed and deployed as required.

People

General Robert H. Barrow, veteran of three wars and Commandant of the Marine Corps until July 1983, says that the role of the human being is essential. 'The Marine Corps' ability to meet the many challenges and accomplish its mission depends first and foremost on quality people,' says Barrow, 'people who can endure rigorous training, accept firm discipline, respond to sound leadership, and perform with intelligence and adaptability.'

General Paul X. Kelley, Barrow's successor as commandant, agrees. Last year, Americans were touched when Kelley, visiting a Frankfurt hospital to see victims of the terrorist bombing in Beirut, paused over the bunk occupied by a gravely wounded Lance Corporal Jeffrey Lee Nashton. Blinded and unable to move 'with more tubes going in and out of his body than I have ever seen' according to Kelley, Nashton squeezed the general's hand, borrowed a pencil, and wrote *Semper Fi*, short for *Semper Fidelis*, the US Marine Corps motto that means 'Always Faithful'. 'People are our asset,' says Kelley.

The Commandant of the Marine Corps has, since 1978, enjoyed full standing as a member of the Pentagon's Joint Chiefs of Staff (JCS). As one of the nation's five key flag officers, he has the ear of the President and the support of Congress. General Paul X. Kelley is the ideal man for the job: A former commanding officer of the Rapid Deployment Joint Task Force, a US Marine officer since 1950, he served two tours in Vietnam, one as a battalion commander where he earned the Silver Star medal and other awards; 55-year-old Kelley is also a master parachutist. An interesting fact about the commandant is that from September 1960 to May 1961 he was the US Marine Corps Exchange Officer with the British Royal Marines. During this period he attended the commando course in England, served as Assistant Operations Officer with No. 45 Commando in Aden, and as commander of 'C' Troop, No. 42 Commando in Singapore, Malaya and Borneo. As the top-ranking United States Marine, although he technically does not actually command the Corps in his JCS posting, Kelly enjoys enormous respect and rarely has difficulty being heard.

Current troop strength of the US Marine Corps is 198,574, of whom 162,881 serve in the continental USA, including those committed to the RDJTF; 3,467 US Marines are in Europe and 28,858 in East Asia, mostly on Okinawa.

The US Marines have a reputation for tough discipline and hard training. It begins during 'boot camp' at Parris Island, South Carolina, or San Diego, California, where the drill instructor (DI) reigns almost god-like over recruits who have volunteered from civilian life.

Not even the toughest US Marine wants to return to the era of mindlessly stern discipline exemplified by the night march at Parris Island in April 1956 when, because of an error by DI Staff Sergeant Matthew C. McKeon, six men drowned fording a swamp. But the 12-week basic training course, much of it conducted under starkly realistic conditions, is intended to breed an elite fighter. In the US Marine Corps, unlike the other US services, every member is first and foremost a rifleman. No matter what his military occupation specialty (MOS), each US Marine is expected to be ready to be hurled into a pointblank fire fight.

Demanding fitness

Once through boot camp, the typical private first class (salary $109.20 per month, or about £72.00) can be assigned to any one of nearly 500 training schools. These vary from Air Command/Control Electronics (six weeks at Tustin, California) to Journeyman Plumbing and Water Supply Specialist (11 weeks at Camp Lejeune, North Carolina) to Manual More Intercept Electronic Warfare Operator (20 weeks at NAS Pensacola, Florida). But whether plumber or missile technician, every US Marine must meet demanding standards of physical fitness and be prepared to fight on the front line.

US Marine officers come from the 57 colleges and universities which offer Naval Reserve Officer Training Corps (NROTC) programmes, or from officer training programmes within the US Marine Corps itself. The elite regular officer is a graduate of one of the service academies and most come from the United States Naval Academy, the hallowed institution on the Severn River in Annapolis, Maryland, which boasts the world's largest dining room, offers four years of scholarly and military education, turns out good football teams, and produces the future leaders of the US Navy and US

Current Marine armoured strength consists mainly of M60A1 MBTs, considerably older than their army equivalents. A wheeled, light armoured vehicle is being procured but for the time being a light tank, more suitable for an amphibious force, has still to be developed.

Nearly 1,000 LVT7 amphibians used by the Marine Corps are to be upgraded to LVT7A1 standard with new engines and transmissions, and a further 239 new examples are to be procured.

Marine Corps. Annapolis sent hundreds of fresh second lieutenants to command platoons in combat in Vietnam, men like Peter A. Messenies, who won the Medal of Honor for taking out a gun position at An Hoa, and James Webb, much-decorated author of the novels *Fields of Fire* and *A Sense of Honor.*

Like the other services, the US Marine Corps has made increased use of women since the armed forces became all volunteer in 1975. As of 31 December 1982, the US Marine Corps had 591 woman officers (3.1 per cent of its total) and 8,039 enlisted women (4.5 per cent). An 'all-women' crew operates a McDonnell Douglas C-9B Skytrain jet transport assigned to NAS Memphis, Tennessee. Actual combat is legally ruled out for female US Marines, but the ruling might be unenforceable in a sudden crisis, since men and women serve cheek-by-jowl in nearly all units.

Equipment

Equipment at the individual level is much the same for the US Marine Corps as for the US Army. The basic combat weapon used by all ranks is the M16A1 5.56-mm (0.22-in) rifle, and the M60 7.62-mm (0.3-in) machine-gun is the squad weapon. At battalion level the 81-mm mortar is used, and each battalion has its own Dragon anti-tank missiles and Redeye or Stinger anti-aircraft missiles. As a rule, US Marine battalions must operate with less direct support than that provided for other fighting units, so they are less well supplied with artillery than comparable formations. Close support is expected to come from US Marine aircraft wings and from naval gun fire provided by the US Navy. Still, US Marines do have the 155-mm (6.2-in) M198 towed howitzer, and current plans are for some form of auxiliary power unit to be fitted to these howitzers for purely local moves across beaches and the like. The US Marine Corps also has a number of self-propelled artillery items such as the heavy 8-in (203-mm) M110A1 and a sizable force of 155-mm (6.2in) M109A1 howitzers. TOW heavy anti-tank missiles are also in good supply.

For armoured support, the US Marines have 575 M60A1 main battle tanks armed with 105-mm (4.13-in) M68 main guns. These tanks are good combat vehicles but somewhat heavy for amphibious operations (and not easily transportable by air, a problem the US Marine Corps shares with the US Army) so a search is now under way for a replacement, probably to emerge as a light tank with an automatic 75-mm (2.95-in) main gun. For direct fire support, the US Marines recently conducted a series of trials to determine exactly what type of vehicle would be required. This programme was a joint US Army/US Marine project and resulted in the Light Armored Vehicle (LAV), a vehicle planned for production in various forms to suit a number of purposes. In the end the LAV emerged as a variant of the wheeled 8×8 MOWAG Piranha, originally a Swiss design but produced by General Motors of Canada. The LAV will be produced in a variety of forms, from a version with a 90-mm (3.54-in) gun to a version with 25-mm Chain Guns, 81-mm mortars, TOW missile-armed vehicles, and so on. Costs have risen alarmingly, threatening the success of the LAV programme. In any event the M60A1 will be around for some years to come.

The other US Marine Corps armour component is the LVTP-7 amphibious armoured personnel carrier. While the LVTP-7 is a very successful design of its kind, the amphibious requirement makes it a high and bulky vehicle. It does have its own built-in armament in

Seen exercising on a Caribbean beach, personnel versions of the LVT 7 can carry up to 24 crew and troops, or alternatively up to five tons of cargo. Armament consists of a cupola-mounted Browning 0.5-in (12.7-mm) machine-gun.

The amphibious transport dock USS *Dubuque* (LPD 8) is fitted to operate as the flagship of an amphibious squadron, but her main function is to land a Marine battalion of some 830 men with 28 LVT 7s and a wide variety of stores and equipment.

the form of 12.7-mm (0.5-in) machine-guns, and there are specialized recovery and engineer variants.

The replacement 'new-generation' assault vehicle is the LVT7A1 manufactured by the FMC corporation of Chicago in three basic configurations: (1) personnel carrier, capable of transporting 25 combat-equipped troops (in addition to its crew of three) or 10,000 lb (4536 kg) of cargo; (2) mobile command post, equipped as a communications centre; and (3) recovery vehicle outfitted with a hydraulic, telescoping crane with a 6,000-lb (2722-kg) capacity, a 30,000-lb (13608-kg) capacity recovery winch, plus cutting, welding and other portable maintenance equipment. Some 984 earlier LVTP-7 vehicles will be modernized to LVT7A1 standard, and 329 more of the vehicles will be assembled from new production by 1986.

The US Marine Corps is looking even further ahead, however, to a replacement for the LVT7A1, and has eventual plans for a Landing Vehicle Assault (LVA, not to be confused with the LAV), but costs are escalating and it may develop that this requirement will have to be met by a special versions of the US Army's M2 Bradley fighting vehicle.

At present, the US Navy operates only enough specialized assault ships to accommodate one Marine Amphibious Force at any given time, though it is the policy of the Department of Defense under Secretary Caspar Weinberger to prepare for what Weinberger calls a 'Two and a half war (at the same time) capability'. Assault ships are highly specialized vessels with provision for carrying landing boats or LVTP-7s along the sides, and most have internal hangars for further stowage of both. The vessels have helicopter landing decks and extensive communications equipment. Command centres are provided in each ship, but one vessel is usually designated the 'flagship' or overall command vessel and retains the bulk of the command and control facilities. Unfortunately, many of the assault ships are of the LSD-28 class laid down many years ago and now approaching the end of their useful lives.

The US Navy has on charge no less than 65 specialized assault ships of various kinds, but at any one time far fewer are available for use. Top of the command structure are two 'Blue Ridge'-class landing craft command (LCC). Five of the 'Tarawa'-class amphibious general assault ships (LHAs) are in a sense small aircraft-carriers, being able to carry BAe AV-8A or McDonnell Douglas AV-8B Harrier attack planes and CH-46 or other helicopters. Harriers or helicopters can also be carried by the seven 'Iwo Jima'-class helicopter carriers. There are no fewer than 14 vessels of the landing platform, dock (LPD) and 13 of the landing ship, dock (LSD) type. M60A1 main battle tanks are carried in land ship, tank (LST) vessels whose vintage traces to the amphibious campaigns of World War II, there being 18 such vessels of the 'Newport' class in service. To back up all of these vessels are six 'Charleston'-class amphibious cargo ships (LKAs), 44 replenishment ships and 20 depot and repair ships.

The first two vessels of the new 'Whidbey Island' or LSD-41 class of assault ship are now under construction to improve significantly the US Marines' rapid-response and amphibious capabilities. 'Impressive' is the word used by General Barrow for these vessels. The US Navy will build at least 10 of these larger and more modern assault ships, and possibly as many as 16.

The US Navy will also request funds in its Fiscal Year 1985 budget to build a new class ship, the LHD, which

A PHIBRON under way, consisting of (furthest from camera) USS *El Paso* (LKA 117), USS *Shreveport* (LPD 12, USS *Hermitage* (LSD 34), USS *Fairfax County* (LST 1193) and USS *Inchon* (LPH 12). Normal marine complement of such a force would be approaching 4,000, together with most of their equipment.

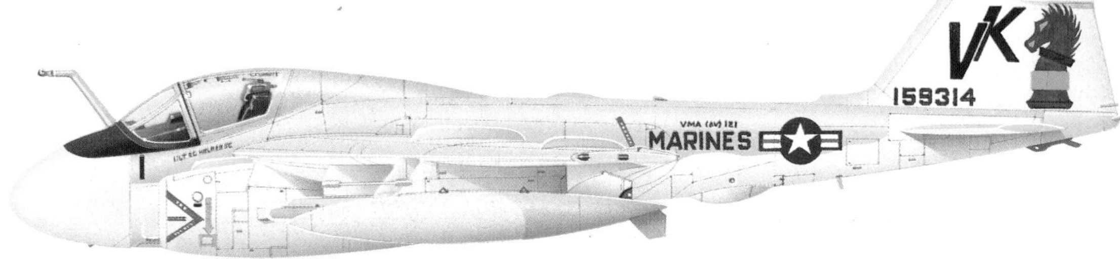

Serving with all-weather attack squadron VMA(AW)-121, based at MCAS Cherry Point, this Grumman A-6E Intruder represents the definitive version of this useful attack aircraft. The Marine Corps maintains five squadrons of Intruders.

will be capable of launch and recovery of other fixed-wing aircraft in addition to Harriers, as well as helicopters. Both the LSD-41 and the LHD will have the capability to carry a new hovercraft, the landing air cushion craft, being procured to support movement of the amphibious force ashore.

Further enhancements in strategic mobility will be achieved through a programme wherein matériel capable of supporting three US Marines brigades will be embarked aboard specially configured merchant ships of the Military Sealift Command. These ships, maritime prepositioning ships, capable of offloading in port or over-the-shore in a permissive environment, will be positioned at strategic locations from which they can be moved rapidly into a crisis area. US Marines would be flown into the area to be joined with their equipment. Deployment in this manner takes advantage of the heavy lift and loiter capability of ships and the speed of airlift to get the US Marine brigade to the crisis area rapidly.

Marine Aviation

The three active force Marine Aircraft Wings have a combined manpower strength of 35,600 men plus a front-line aircraft strength of about 440 aircraft and 102 armed helicopters. Pride of place goes to the fighter squadrons, of which there are 12. In the mid-1970s, the US Marines sought the Grumman F-14A Tomcat for their front-line squadrons, but were forced by Congress to wait longer for a new generation fighter. The F-14A never became part of the US Marine Corps inventory, but because of that disappointment the US Marine Corps was able to win an early place in receiving the McDonnell Douglas F/A-18 Hornet. Three F/A-18 squadrons are now operational. The remaining nine fighter squadrons fly the McDonnell Douglas F-4N and F-4S Phantom. The ageing F-4N model will be retired by February 1985.

The US Marine Corps has 13 attack squadrons, three of which are equipped with the AV-8 Harrier. Though plagued by a series of crashes early in its American incarnation, the Harrier has always enjoyed the full support of US Marine flyers themselves, who now have total confidence in its capabilities. The AV-8C Harrier, a slightly improved version of the operational AV-8A, is now under test. Far more advanced is the AV-8B, the big-wing version of the Harrier scheduled to enter operational service in 1985. The US Marine Corps' 10 remaining attack squadrons include five each with the McDonnell Douglas A-4M Skyhawk and the all-weather Grumman A-6E Intruder. The US Marines have a single photo-reconnaissance squadron flying the RF-4B Phantom and an electronic warfare squadron operating the EA-6B Prowler. All of these air units are expected to maintain the capability to operate from US Navy carrier decks, and periodically deploy to carriers as part of an embarked Navy Carrier Wing.

Standing behind the combat squadrons are the no less important support squadrons. Two of these are Rockwell OV-10D Bronco observation squadrons, and there are also several headquarters and maintenance squadrons with TA-4J and OA-4M Skyhawks. Lockheed KC-130F, KC-130R and KC-130T Hercules aircraft serve with three assault transport and tanker squadrons. Limited numbers of C-9B, North American CT-39G and Douglas C-117D aircraft meet more mundane utility transport and 'hack' requirements.

The US Marine Corps has no fewer than 25 operational helicopter squadrons. Eight of these use the heavy Sikorsky CH-53D and CH-53E, and the US Marine Corps has 168 of these large helicopters with more on order. There are 180 CH-46E and CH-46F Sea

Pictured on the assault ship USS *Saipan*, these McDonnell Douglas/ British Aerospace AV-8A Harriers provide Marine forces with close support over the landing areas and battlefields. The Boeing Vertol CH-46 Sea Knight, at left, continues to provide the Marines and helicopter assault capability along with the Sikorsky CH-53. At top is a visiting Royal Navy Wessex.

One task of the USMC is to provide helicopter transport for the President and other government officials. Along with VH-53s and VH-46s, eight UH-1s have been built or modified to luxurious VIP standard as VH-1Ns.

Knights distributed among 11 squadrons and a couple of training units. The universal 'Huey' is used in the transport role, there being three Bell UH-1N squadrons, and a further three squadrons are equipped with the AH-1T SeaCobra for the armed offensive role, carrying TOW anti-tank missiles. Finally, the US Marine Corps contributes a special VIP squadron to the USAF's 89th Military Airlift Wing at Andrews AFB, Maryland, operators of the President's 'Air Force One' which becomes 'Marine One' when the chief executive is flying aboard a US Marine Corps aircraft; this squadron is equipped with the VH-53D, VH-46F and VH-1N, all of which have been seen landing on and taking off from the White House lawn.

The US Marine Corps also has two air-defence battalions equipped with the Improved HAWK heavy anti-aircraft missile.

The US Marine Air Reserve is kept at a high state of readiness and its 4th Marine Aircraft Wing is formed from four aviation groups, one service group, and one air control group. The 11 aircraft-operating squadrons of the Reserve are equipped with F-4N and F-4S Phantoms, A-4E, A-4F and A-4M Skyhawks, the EA-6A intruder, and the OV-10 Bronco. A combined tanker/assault squadron uses 12 KC-130Fs and is receiving the new KC-130T model ahead of active-duty units. There are 10 US Marine Reserve helicopter squadrons. One of these uses the armed AH-1J, and there are two squadrons operating the UH-1E/UH-1N 'Huey' in the light transport helicopter role. For heavy lift tasks, there are three squadrons with the CH-53A and a further four squadrons operate the CH-46. The Reserve also has an air-defence battalion equipped with the HAWK heavy anti-aircraft missile, and there are a further 32 or so support units of one type or another.

The Support Units

The US Marine Corps has to operate a large number of support units in addition to the combat and air arms. These units accomplish such functions as transport (equipped with much the same types of wheeled transport as the US Army), fuel supply and distribution, special signalling, equipment holding, special maintenance and rearming. Normally, these variegated units are attached to MAUs and other units as and when required, but one special grouping is maintained at Camp Pendleton, California, for the specific support of the 7th Marine Amphibious Brigade and the 1st Marine Division as part of the RDJTF. This is the 1st Force Service Support Group. It contains among its various components a number of units equipped with material-handling equipment that ranges from massive 140-ton cranes to container-handling tractors.

Detachments of US Marines provide security on board US Navy ships, at naval bases, and at 118 embassies and consulates in 103 countries. Service with a Marine Security Guard (MSG) detachment at a US embassy is a sought-after perquisite. But in recent years, MSG members have been held prisoner in Tehran and killed or injured in rioting in Pakistan and Libya.

The Future

The US Marine Corps enjoys the support of the administration and the American public, even when committed to a controversial cause, as in Lebanon. The US Marine Corps has the training, preparedness, mobility and firepower to fight and win on almost any farflung battlefield. With improved artillery and armour support, and enhancement of its combat service support elements (the latter having purposely been given top priority) the US Marine Corps has an assured future. A large proportion of the strength of the US Marine Corps is now involved with the RDJTF and is thus always kept at a high state of readiness. New equipment for this and other roles is on the way. The turmoil and violence of these troubled times will almost certainly guarantee the US Marines a place in the public eye for the foreseeable future. While their long history of achievement on the battlefield is an established matter of record, members of the US Marine Corps believe (and seem to be right) that they will have ample opportunity to add future achievements to their long list of laurels.

Beginning life as TA-4F dual-control trainers, the McDonnell Douglas OA-4M Skyhawks are used by the Marine Corps as forward air control (FAC) platforms for the A-4, A-6 and F/A-18 attack squadrons.

The McDonnell Douglas F/A-18 Hornet has been procured for the Marine Corps. The ability to operate in both air defence and attack configurations (and the ability to change configurations rapidly) give the Marine Corps greater flexibility of operations. Although it is primarily a land-based air force, all Marine Corps pilots have to maintain a carrier qualification.

United States Coast Guard

Though not funded by Department of Defense, the US Coast Guard operates alongside the regular US armed forces, mostly performing civilian-related tasks such as maritime law enforcement, marine safety and environmental protection. But in an emergency it will come under Navy control, with prime responsibility for coastal defence and certain anti-submarine, escort and air/sea rescue duties.

Left: Given the wide range of duties required of the Coast Guard, equipment varies from aircraft to riverine buoy tenders. Co-operation is vital, especially in rescue operations where an HC-130 Hercules might need to direct a medium-endurance cutter, such as USCGC *Confidence* (WMEC 619), to shipwreck survivors.

In cold glaring sunlight above the ice-dotted Bering Sea off Alaska, the Lockheed HC-130H Hercules patrol plane dipped its wing, circled menacingly, and descended upon a Korean trawler harvesting salmon illegally in American waters: The threatening manoeuvres of the aircraft, emblazoned with the blue-bordered red slanting sash of the United States Coast Guard, frightened off the intruder and prevented an incident.

On a fog-shrouded, storm-swept night off the Louisiana coast, a small US Coast Guard cutter swerved abruptly in ranging seas to block the path of an expensive-looking cabin cruiser: shotgun-armed Coast Guardsmen boarded in a quick blunt assault and seized four smugglers and 175 lb (80 kg) of cocaine.

In a rented cinema in Seattle, a Coast Guard petty officer cleared his throat, stood before an audience of local yacht-club members, and began lecturing on safety.

HC-130H aircraft, cutters, shotguns and lectures are among the tools available in the mid-1980s to the US Coast Guard, the smallest and most specialized of the American armed forces.

Master Chief Petty Officer Vincent Constantine, dark-haired, 42-year-old senior enlisted Coast Guardsman, describes his service in three words. 'We're something special,' says Constantine. With major commands in Washington, New York and San Francisco and with 12 regional districts in the USA equipped with cutters, aircraft and boats supported by geographically dispersed shore facilities, the US Coast Guard is not merely special, but unique.

History

When the first Congress under the Constitution passed an act in 1789 calling for the collection of

Below: The first icebreaker built for US service since the early 1950s, USCGC *Polar Star* (WAGB 10) is also, at 12,087 tons (12280 tonnes) the largest ship operated by the Coast Guard. Pacific-based, *Polar Star* and her sister ship *Polar Sea* each carry a pair of Sikorsky HH-52A Sea Guard helicopters.

customs on imports, the foundation of the US Coast Guard was laid. To enforce the act, in the following year Congress created a system of cutters, later named the Revenue Marine and afterward the Revenue Cutter Service. Typical of this service's tasks were the enforcement of quarantine laws (1799), intervention against slavery (1800), and the enforcement of neutrality laws (1818). Historically, the most acclaimed activity of the service occurred between 1919 and 1933, the Prohibition era. The federal law prohibiting alcohol gave the US Coast Guard an almost impossible enforcement task, no less difficult than its efforts against drug-smuggling today.

In 1915, the Revenue Cutter Service and the Life-Saving Service was combined into one organization, the United States Coast Guard. World War I saw US Coast Guard cutters playing a major role in escorting convoys. In World War II, the service expanded from 17,000 personnel at the outbreak to a peak of over 175,000. These men and women performed a wide range of naval missions, including anti-submarine warfare and amphibious operations. Landing craft which went ashore at Normandy had Coast Guardsmen at their helms. During the 1950-3 Korean conflict, US Coast Guard destroyer escorts were stationed in the Pacific to be aircraft rescue sites.

Although primarily an operator of surface vessels, the US Coast Guard has its own aviation arm and has flown aircraft as large as the Consolidated PBY Catalina, the Consolidated P4Y-2G Privateer (a navalized variant of the B-24 bomber) and today's Hercules. A little-known fact is that the US Coast Guard was ahead of the other services in helicopter development. In 1944, tests with Sikorsky HNS-1 and HOS-1 helicopters aboard the ancient cutter *Cobb* were the very first American shipboard landings of helicopters. In the mid-1940s, the US Coast Guard ordered its version of the Sikorsky S-51, the HO3S-1G, while other services debated whether rotary-winged flying machines had any practical role. The US Coast Guard has more recently pioneered the use of hydrofoil naval craft and surface effect ships, though none are in operational use at this time.

People

From his headquarters building at Buzzards Point on the Potomac River in Washington, Admiral James S. Gracey commands a US Coast Guard which has reached its highest strength since the Vietnam War, when Coast Guardsmen fought in riverine operations against the Viet Cong. The US Coast Guard's 38,500 uniformed personnel and 5,400 civilians, with assistance from the 40,000 civilian volunteer members of the Coast Guard Auxiliary, possess a formidable diversity of skills. Gracey, as Commandant, is not a member of the Joint Chiefs of Staff but his organization is beyond question 'a military branch of the armed forces': it says so in Title 14 of the United States Code. Grey-haired, bespectacled Admiral Gracey, who made an extended visit to London in late 1983, holds degrees in mechanical engineering and business administration. He has people working for him who know everything from enforcement of boat safety laws to maintenance of Hercules aircraft.

US Coast Guard people volunteer from civilian life. 'Regular' officers come from the Coast Guard Academy at New London, Connecticut, a history-steeped city also known as a home of submarine builders, and receive a four-year education coupled with an ensign's commission.

The US Coast Guard's Mission

Admiral Gracey's service is under the Department of Transportation in peacetime, and under the US Navy in time of war. The US Coast Guard is fortunate in that its duties are sharply, unequivocally defined, the service being responsible for precisely 13 missions. The missions are search and rescue, boating safety, enforcement of laws and treaties, short-range aids to navigation, radio navigation, bridge administration, port safety, commercial vessel safety, waterways management, polar operations, domestic ice operations, marine science activities, and military operations. 'Military operations' means just that: combat. US Coast Guardsmen have fought in all major American wars and have won their share of awards for valour.

USCGC *Gallatin* (WHEC 721) is a high endurance cutter of the 'Hamilton' class. Powered by combined diesel/gas turbine engines, *Gallatin* has a cruising range (diesel engines only) of some 14,000 miles (22530 km) at 11 kts.

The US Coast Guard's success in search and rescue is but one example of the service's achievements. In 1981, the most recent year for which statistics have been tabulated, the Coast Guard responded to 71,781 calls for assistance, saved 6,339 lives, assisted another 168,278 people and prevented loss of property valued at $2.3 billion (£1.53 thousand million).

To fulfil its law and treaty enforcement mandate, the US Coast Guard now has a major role combating the flow of illegal drugs into the USA. Radar and other electronic sensing devices are coupled with a fleet of small cutters designed for speed and manoeuvrability in operations against fast smuggling boats. The US Coast Guard has added new 110-ft (33.5-m) Surface Effect Ships and Dassault-Breguet HU-25A Guardian patrol aircraft to its arsenal. The new 'Famous' class (incorrectly but better known as 'Bear' class) of 270-ft (82.3-m) medium endurance cutters, although criticized for failings in other areas, will be potent weapons for law enforcement.

Under the short-range aids to navigation programme, the US Coast Guard manages the federal system of over 46,000 lighthouses, buoys, daybeacons, fog signals and radar reflectors. The service also has jurisdiction over 42,000 private aids.

With its radio navigation programme the US Coast Guard establishes, operates and maintains electronic aids to navigation throughout the United States and in other areas of the world. This includes simple radio beacons (some 200) and highly sophisticated radio pulse systems such as LORAN-C and Omega that have world application for vessels and aircraft.

The US Coast Guard was transferred from the Treasury Department to the Department of Transportation when the latter was established in 1967. With the transfer, the US Coast Guard was given the responsibility for bridge administration, no small task in a modern nation whose civil infrastructure is in dismally sad condition, the state of American highways and bridges being a national scandal. Under this programme the US Coast Guard approves bridge altera-

Dating from World War II, the 6,515-ton (6619-tonne) icebreaker USCGC *Westwind* (WAGB 281) operates on the Great Lakes. *Westwind* has led an interesting career, having served with the US Navy and from 1945 to 1951 with the Soviet navy.

A combination of catamaran and hovercraft, the Surface Effect Ship is of interest to the coast guard in replacing the 85-ft (26-m) 'Point' class large patrol boats. USCGC *Sea Hawk* (WSES 2) and *Shearwater* (WSES 3) are capable of 40 knots while fanborne.

tion, grants bridge permits, and regulate drawbridges.

American interests in the Arctic and Antarctic have never been greater. To resupply Department of Defense installations in the Arctic and facilities maintained by the National Science Foundation in the Antarctic, the US Coast Guard operates five polar icebreakers designed to carve a pathway for supply vessels through frozen expanses. Duty on an icebreaker is among the most gruelling and most exciting of US Coast Guard tasks. The service also carries out icebreaking duties on the Great Lakes, in north eastern US ports, and in Alaskan waters, The US Coast Guard has acquired its new 'Bay' class of 140-ft (42.7m) icebreaking tugs to keep maritime trade moving through the winter months.

US Coast Guard Vessels

The US Coast Guard operates surface vessels which range from tiny boats to its 378-ft (115.2-m) 'Hamilton'-class high endurance cutters. The latter are the biggest ships in service, but are an 'older generation' in the minds of today's Coast Guardsmen. USCGC *Hamilton* (WHEC 715) and 11 sister ships are intended additionally to supplement the US Navy's frigate force escorting ocean-borne carrier battle groups, being fitted with sonar, Mk 32 torpedo tubes, a single 5-in (127-mm) gun, and a spacious helipad to accommodate a Sikorsky HH-52A or Sikorsky HH-3F helicopter. Some will be retrofitted with twin 40-mm and twin 20-mm guns. In service since 1967, the low-sitting, rakish 'Hamilton'-class ships were the largest US warships with gas turbine propulsion before the launching of the US Navy's 'Spruance'-class destroyers. The Combined Diesel And Gas turbine (CODAG) powerplant comprises two Fairbanks-Morse 12-cylinder diesels of 7,000 bhp (5220 kW) and two twin-shaft Pratt & Whitney FT-4A turbines of 36,000 shp (26845 kW). One of these sleek vessels, the USCGC *Gallatin* (WHEC 721) in 1977 became the first US warship to have women assigned as permanent members of its crew.

Newer, having been commissioned only on 4 February 1983, and sitting remarkably high in the water for a modern vessel, is the USCGC *Bear* (WMEC 901), the first of at least 13 medium endurance cutters 270 ft (82.3 in) in length. Controversy surrounds the 'Bear' class (properly 'Famous' class) developed in the late 1970s as the US Coast Guard's primary cutter well into the 21st century. Described by Captain William K. Earle as 'stubby, overloaded and short-legged', the *Bear* (of which as many as 23 may eventually be ordered) is armed with a single Mk 75 gun of 3 in (76 mm). It has anti-aircraft and anti-submarine detection systems. It will eventually be retrofitted to carry

The choice of the French Aérospatiale SA-336G Dauphin by the USCG aroused a storm of controversy, notably from Bell Helicopters, but the deal has progressed. For Coast Guard service it has been redesignated HH-65A Dolphin.

the Phalanx CIWS and the Harpoon missile. At a time when Coast Guardsmen feel a need to get deeper into the missile and electronics age, Earle, Captain Robert G. Moore and others say that a far earlier and now defunct generation of cutters like the USCGC *Roger B. Taney* (WHEC 7), which before its 1982 retirement was the only ship still in commission to have engaged Japanese aircraft at Pearl Harbor, sat lower in the water, were designed with greater flexibility, and were more potent. Too high and too slow (19.5 kts), the *Bear* is considered highly effective for fisheries law enforcement but is disappointing as a vehicle for chasing drug smugglers or Soviet submarines.

Criticism of new equipment is being heard less for the simple reason that most Coast Guardsmen are glad to be getting any new equipment at all. Far louder and far more frequent, is the complaint that the US Coast Guard is always last to get anything new. 'We just don't have a high priority when the money is passed out,' says one officer. 'Chances are, we'll get some new item only ten years after the Army, Navy and Air Force get it.' Two decades after the M16 was adopted as the standard American rifle, some US Coast Guard vessels still carry the M1 Garand.

The 'Hamilton' and 'Bear' cutters, already mentioned, are 'top of the line' items with top priority. They are more frequently seen, discussed, debated, than less impressive US Coast Guard vessels, including the 16 medium endurance cutters of the class represented by the 210-ft (64.2-m) UCGC *Reliance* (WTR 615).

The US Coast Guard operates about 50 buoy tenders, including 33 vessels of the 'Balsam' (WLB 62) class which are also designated as oceanographic cutters. These 180-ft (54.9-m) vessels, each with a crew of 58, have recently been strengthened for icebreaking and have been modernized with updated communications and electronics gear.

The US Coast Guard also has eight full-fledged icebreakers, 23 'Cape'-class 95-ft (29-m) patrol craft, and 53 'Point'-class 83-ft (25.3-m) patrol boats. Its assorted seagoing tenders and an assortment of tugs are joined by one of the most unusual and beautiful of active American vessels, the sail ship *Eagle* (WIX 327). A spectacular sight under full sail, this aesthetic, ship-rigged 295.2-ft (90-m) vessel is used for crew-training by the US Coast Guard Academy at New London, is actually a World War II reparation, having been acquired at VE-Day and having been launched in 1936 in Bremen as the *Horst Wessel*!

The US Coast Guard has a strong and active interest in Surface Effect Ships (SES) and has tested some on an experimental basis. None are in inventory at the present time, but the service retains a strong preference to make greater use of more advanced technology, and will almost certainly acquire SES vehicles when funding permits.

Intense competition to find a medium-range surveillance aircraft resulted in an order for 41 Dassault-Breguet HU-25A Guardians, a specially-developed version of the Dassault Falcon 20. The order made history, as it was the first purchase of foreign equipment in the history of the service.

US Coast Guard Aircraft

The latest helicopter in the US Coast Guard's inventory is a rare foreign purchase, the Aérospatiale SA 336G Dauphin, which has been given the American military designation HH-65A. No less than 90 of these machines have been ordered, powered by 710-hp (529-kW) Turboméca Arriel turboshaft engines driving four-bladed rotors 39 ft 1¾ in (11.93 m) in diameter. Though primarily a search and rescue machine and not equipped with the anti-shipping ordnance carried by other nations' versions of the Dauphin, the HH-65A carries advanced maritime search, surveillance and rescue gear. At a time when a 'buy American' policy

Procured for short-range recovery duties from shore bases, icebreakers and Coast Guard cutters, the USCG HH-65A Dolphins are distinguishable by the larger fin and 'fenestron'. Deliveries will continue through 1986.

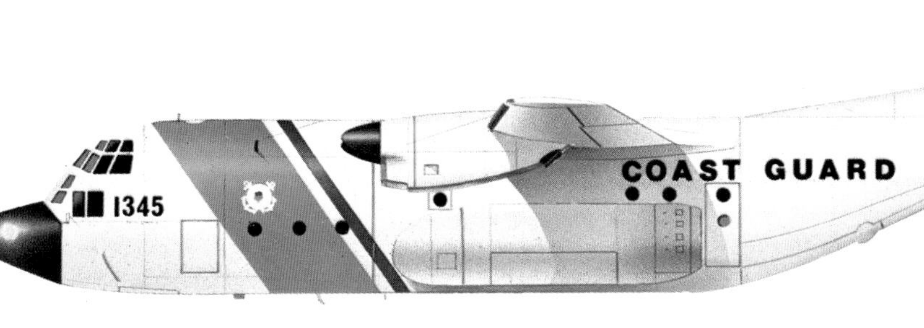

The largest aircraft currently operated by the USCG is the Lockheed C-130 Hercules, which has been procured in two versions. Illustrated is an HC-130B, an SAR version of the C-130B, 12 of which were purchased between 1959-62, with further orders following.

reflects growing protectionist sentiment, the US Coast Guard also has on order another French-designed aircraft, the Dassault-Breguet Falcon, designed as a maritime surveillance and rescue craft and designated HU-25A Guardian.

US Coast Guard aviators also fly 38 Sikorsky HH-3F Pelican and 80 Sikorsky HH-52A Sea Guard helicopters, primarily for search and rescue. To provide executive transportation for Admiral Gracey, the Secretary of Transportation, and other government 'bigwigs', the service has a single VC-4A Gulfstream I turboprop and one VC-11A Gulfstream II jet transport. Plans exist to order at least one Gulfstream III aircraft, which has been given the US Air Force designation C-20A. With the arrival of the French HU-25A Guardian, the veteran Grumman HU-16 Albatross has been retired, the final machine of this type being the first US Coast Guard craft designated for the National Air and Space Museum in Washington. This leaves the service without a fixed-wing aircraft capable of landing on water for the first time in decades. Also on the verge of retirement are the 17 Convair HC-131 transports converted to the search and rescue role.

The eminently successful Lockheed C-130 Hercules is used for cargo hauling and for the search and rescue function. The US Coast Guard operates 25 HC-130B and HC-130H aircraft, and has six more on order.

US Coast Guard aviators are, of course, career officers and receive their initial flight training through the US Navy's facilities. Those who fly the HH-3F helicopter were trained by the US Air Force, which used a similar machine for rescue operations in North Vietnam and still operates the type.

The US Coast Guard's work, largely undramatic, is seen rarely in headlines. All too often, the toil and sacrifice of Coast Guardsmen goes unnoticed. At the small shore installation in Monterey, California, in late 1983, Petty Officer James H. McDowell borrowed several private vessels, recruited and organized a band of volunteers, and led a rescue operation in a blinding rainstorm which saved the lives of four persons on a capsized fishing vessel. When a civilian cargo aircraft ditched off the New Jersey coast at about the same time, US Coast Guard vessels and helicopters saved not only the three crew members but much of the cargo. Though US Coast Guard personnel are not a common sight at the world's far-flung battle fronts, the service continues to perform its other responsibilities while maintaining a high state of military readiness.

The US Coast Guard may be the least known of the American military services, but its achievements are many. *Semper Partus* ('always ready') is the official motto of the United States Coast Guard, and its personnel carry out the spirit of that motto every day.

Illustrating to good effect the colourful and deliberately prominent USCG colour scheme is Lockheed HC-130H Hercules '1600'. The USCG 'H' model differed from its USAF counterparts in that the Fulton Recovery System nose apparatus was removed.

USAF
U.S. AIR FORCE
U.S. AIR FORCE

United States Air Force

The US Air Force is the spearhead of the established defence positions. With fire power available in vast concentrations, the Air Force operates from fixed bases around the world, able to respond massively to any challenge. In addition the service is responsible for the air defence of continental USA and the air space of many of its allies. Now it is developing into space, extending its command of the skies well beyond its previous dimensions.

Left: SAC's finest, and still the fastest aircraft in the world, Lockheed's remarkable SR-71A equips just one squadron of the 9th Strategic Reconnaissance Wing at Beale AFB, California although 'Blackbirds' also operate with detachments at Mildenhall in the United Kingdom and at Kadena in Okinawa.

Below: SAC's heavyweight is the Boeing B-52H Stratofortress, seen here in the form of an aircraft preparing to taxi at the start of a practice alert mission. Introduced to the SAC inventory during the mid-1950s, the B-52 still equips a total of 16 bomber wings in the USA and on Guam.

The Western world's largest and most powerful air arm, the United States Air Force (USAF) operates in excess of 7,000 aircraft, this impressive total being boosted by close to 2,100 additional machines that are assigned to the Air National Guard (ANG) and Air Force Reserve (AFRes), the majority of which could be called to active duty in the event of conflict at the discretion of the President, acting in his capacity as commander-in-chief. No less impressive are the numbers of personnel, figures released for the 1982 fiscal year indicating that regular forces totalled 581,000 whilst reservists comprised 100,000 with the ANG and 64,000 with the AFRes. A further 236,000 civilian personnel are employed by the USAF, many in an administrative capacity, although roughly one-third are responsible for major aircraft maintenance, modification and overhaul work performed by the Air Force Logistics Command (AFLC).

Having had to employ combat aircraft based on the technology of the 1950s for much of the Vietnam War, US Air Force tactical assets have in the past 10 years or so been considerably updated, a process which began with the McDonnell Douglas F-15 Eagle in the early 1970s and continues today; large numbers of F-15s, General Dynamics F-16s and Fairchild Republic A-10s have been delivered in recent years. Procurement of these three types continues, whilst, looking to the future, Rockwell's B-1B will at long last provide Strategic Air Command (SAC) with an infusion of new equipment, terminating a period of what might best be

described as 'make do and mend' in which the veteran Boeing B-52 Stratofortress has been progressively updated to ensure its continuing effectiveness. SAC will also be responsible for another new weapon system, this being the MEM-118 Peacekeeper ICBM (Intercontinental Ballistic Missile), perhaps better known as MX. The subject of considerable controversy in recent years, Peacekeeper will, if present planning is followed, enter service in 1986, although the basing mode to be employed has still to be decided after a long-running saga which comes close to emulating TV soap operas.

Moving to less warlike aspects, airlift capacity has been significantly boosted by the recently-completed programme of 'stretching' Military Airlift Command's (MAC) fleet of Lockheed C-141A Starlifters, the resulting C-141B being a far more capable machine in that it can be refuelled in flight, thus bestowing genuine global capability on MAC's workhorse. MAC is also to receive an infusion of new equipment in the shape of the Lockheed C-5B Galaxy, delivery of the first of a projected total of 50 being due to start in 1986. And Air Training Command (ATC) will also begin to be updated in the latter half of the present decade when the Fairchild T-46 NGT (New Generation Trainer) begins to enter service. Due to fly for the first time in April 1985, the T-46 will initially supplant, and eventually replace, the Cessna T-37 with ATC, an eventual total of no less than 650 being required to fulfil basic training tasks for the remainder of this century. Even further ahead, in the 1990s, the USAF expects to deploy the much-vaunted 'Stealth' technology in the shape of yet another new bomber which is now under development by a consortium made up of Boeing, Northrop and Vought, whilst Lockheed is also understood to be working on another 'Stealth' project, this apparently being a tactical reconnaissance aircraft similar in size to the McDonnell Douglas F/A-18 Hornet. Fighter-sized stealth prototypes are rumoured to have been flying in Nevada since 1978.

Responsibility for control of two of the three elements which form the United States strategic nuclear triad is vested in Strategic Air Command (SAC) with headquarters at Offutt AFB on the outskirts of Omaha, Nebraska. Both of these elements (manned bombers and land-based ICBMs) are to be the subject of modernization during the remainder of the present decade, with older aircraft and missiles being retired from the inventory as new and potentially far more capable weapons are introduced. This process has already begun with a fairly major reorganization of existing bomber assets resulting in the withdrawal of the older Boeing B-52D Stratofortresses. Optimized for conventional bombing duties, the B-52D provided the backbone of SAC activity in South East Asia, and its passing has resulted in some B-52Hs being configured to perform similar tasks as well as sea surveillance duties as part of the SAC contribution to the Rapid Deployment Force. These are, however, unable to carry quite so large a weapons load. Withdrawal of the B-52D has resulted in a contraction of the bomber fleet, the number of active squadrons being scheduled to fall from 25 to 21, operating approximately 270 B-52Gs and B-52Hs plus a further 60 or so General Dynamics

The second bomber type currently to be found in the Strategic Air Command line-up is the General Dynamics FB-111A, which serves with just two wings. The example shown here is about to launch a Boeing AGM-69 SRAM (Short-Range Attack Missile) from its internal weapons bay, which can accommodate two missiles of this type.

Jointly funded by NASA and the Department of Defense, the Space Shuttle will become a very significant tool for the US armed forces. A launch pad has been built at Vandenberg AFB, California, and this will be the main installation, handling military space technology in the future.

The SR-71 'Blackbird' can conduct multi-sensor surveillance at the rate of 80,000 square miles (207200 km^2) per hour, at a speed of around 2,000 miles per hour (3219 km/h) and at heights about 80,000 ft (24385 m).

Various specialized variants of the Boeing C-135 are amongst the most sophisticated aircraft now operated by SAC, but relatively little is known of the work undertaken by the RC-135 series beyond the fact that these somewhat elusive machines are engaged on strategic reconnaissance. Blade aerials, antennae and the prominent SLAR fairings spoil the otherwise clean lines of this RC-135V.

FB-111As. Similarly, six Strategic Missile Squadrons (SMSs) with the older liquid-fuelled LGM-25C Titan II ICBM are to be disbanded with the missiles being gradually removed from their silos, a process which began in 1982 and is scheduled for completion in 1987.

SAC structure and units

Operational elements of SAC are organized within two numbered Air Forces: the 9th Air Force with headquarters at Barksdale AFB, Louisiana, and the 15th Air Force with headquarters at March AFB, California. Both possess aircraft- and missile-equipped units, command and control devolving via a number of subordinate Air Divisions to the respective bomber and missile Wing organizations at the various air bases.

Essentially, the 8th Air Force is responsible for those units located to the east of the Mississippi and is predominantly an aircraft-operating command with eight B-52 Bomb Wings, two FB-111 Bomb Wings, two Titan Missile Wings and one Minuteman Missile Wing. Two Air Refuelling Wings, each with two squadrons of Boeing KC-135 Stratotankers, and two single-squadron Air Refuelling Groups make up the remaining operational elements of this command.

Units to the west of the Mississippi constitute the somewhat larger 15th Air Force, an organization with a preponderance of ICBMs, there being five Minuteman Missile Wings and a single Titan Missile Wing as well as seven B-52 bomb wings, a couple of tanker units and two Strategic Reconnaissance Wings, one with the Lockheed SR-71As, Lockheed U-2Rs and Lockheed TR-1s at Beale AFB, California, whilst the other has various marks of Boeing RC-135 at Offutt, operating alongside EC-135s and Boeing E-4s engaged in the airborne command post role. In addition, the 15th Air Force is also responsible for the 6th Strategic Wing at Eielson AFB, Alaska, which has a single RC-135 reconnaissance squadron and also controls the activities of rotational KC-135 Stratotankers assigned to the aerial refuelling mission.

A couple of other SAC units are located overseas, these also falling within the numbered Air Forces detailed earlier. These units are responsible for air refuelling support and strategic reconnaissance: Anderson AFB, Guam, is home to the 3rd Air Division (15th Air Force) which has a single Strategic Wing on the same base with B-52s as well as the 376th SW at Kadena, the latter having some RC-135s with the 82nd SRS and a mixed fleet of KC-135As and KC-135Qs with the 909th Air Refuelling squadron. In Europe, the 7th Air Division (8th Air Force) at Ramstein oversees the activities of a number of units including the 306th SW at RAF Mildenhall, Suffolk, with rotational tankers; the 11th Strategic Group at RAF Fairford, Glos, also with rotational tankers; and the 17th Reconnaissance Wing at RAF Alconbury, Cambs, which in the autumn of 1983 had three of a planned total of 18 TR-1s for battlefield surveillance and other reconnaissance functions. RC-135s from the 55th SRW also routinely operate from Mildenhall and Hellenikon, Athens, on a temporary duty basis, whilst SAC's other reconnaissnce unit, the

Principally intended to fulfil NEACP (National Emergency Airborne Command Post) duties, the Boeing E-4 is essentially similar to the commercial Model 747. Four aircraft of this type are operated by the 55th SRW from Offutt, and all four will eventually be updated to the E-4B configuration as portrayed by this example which is shown in flight near Mount Rainier.

Still perhaps best known as 'the black lady of espionage' by virtue of its long association with the Central Intelligence Agency, Lockheed's U-2 remains a most valuable reconnaissance tool. Recently reinstated in production as the TR-1, it is now in process of being deployed to Alconbury, England for battlefield surveillance tasks.

9th SRW, maintains detachments of U-2Rs and/or SR-71As at Kadena, Mildenhall, Osan (on TDY from Kadena), Akrotiri and Patrick.

With regard to the bomber force, the Short-Range Attack Missile (SRAM) has, in conjunction with gravity-fall nuclear bombs, been the predominant weapon system of recent years but increasing doubts about the ability of the B-52 to survive in the face of Soviet defences has resulted in a shift in philosophy coincident with deployment of the Boeing AGM-86B ALCM (Air-Launched Cruise Missile). Recently introduced to operational service with the 416th BW at Griffiss AFB, New York, and earmarked for some 200 B-52s as well as the forthcoming Rockwell B-1B, ALCM will permit the Stratofortress fleet to operate in either 'stand-off' or 'shoot and penetrate' modes, the former envisaging ALCM-armed B-52s launching missiles from a position of relative safety outside Soviet territory whilst the latter involves firing of missiles before penetration for delivery of gravity weapons. Avionics improvements will enhance the survivability of the B-52 fleet in the near- to mid-term, but long-term planning currently anticipates those B-52s which are still in service in the 1990s being mainly employed in the stand-off role, responsibility for penetration falling upon the B-1B and the 'AT' (Advanced Technology) or 'Stealth', bomber.

Long awaited

Incorporating some elements of 'Stealth' technology, the B-1B will be the first new purpose-built aircraft to join the SAC inventory for over 25 years when it begins to enter service with the 96th BW at Dyess AFB, Texas, during 1985. Current planning calls for the acquisition of exactly 100 aircraft by mid-1988 and it will bring about a significant and long-overdue improvement on both the nuclear and conventional bombing fronts with effect from June 1986, when the first 15 aircraft are expected to attain initial operational capability.

Existing missile forces have also been subject to some improvements in recent years, this effort being devoted mainly to enhanced target selection capability and silo upgrading to provide improved protection against blast and electro-magnetic pulse effects. But once again, the two basic weapons (Minuteman

Right: First deployed some 20 years ago, the LGM-25C Titan is still SAC's heaviest and most powerful missile in terms of throw-weight, although it is by no means as accurate as the Minuteman, and does not possess MIRV capability.

After an interval of more than 10 years, SAC expects to begin to receive the first examples of a new bomber aircraft during the course of 1985, the year in which Rockwell's B-1B is due to enter service with the 96th Bomb Wing at Dyess AFB, Texas. A total of 100 aircraft of this type are on order for delivery between 1985 and 1988.

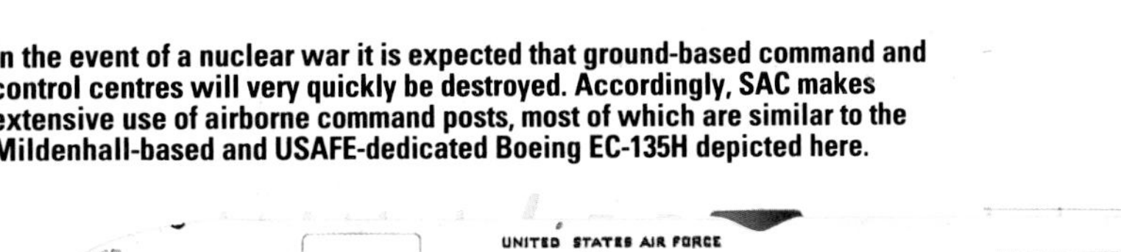

In the event of a nuclear war it is expected that ground-based command and control centres will very quickly be destroyed. Accordingly, SAC makes extensive use of airborne command posts, most of which are similar to the Mildenhall-based and USAFE-dedicated Boeing EC-135H depicted here.

and Titan) are essentially old systems. Deployment of the new MEM-118 Peacekeeper ICBM, each of which will carry 10 independently-targeted warheads, will go some way towards closing the so-called 'window of vulnerability' from 1986, when the first 40 missiles are expected to go on alert. In the meantime, the Minuteman will continue in service, no less than 1,000 missiles of this type being operational with six Missile Wings. Of this total, 450 are single-warhead LGM-30F Minuteman IIs, the balance being LGM-30G Minuteman IIIs with MIRV (Multiple Independently-Targeted Re-entry Vehicle) capability, each having three Mk 12 warheads; plans are now in hand to update 50 LGM-30Fs to MIRV standard, an action which should more than compensate for the loss of 52 LGM-25C Titans. Earmarked for withdrawal by 1987, the Titan is SAC's oldest ICBM, dating to the late 1950s in its original form, and it has been the cause of some embarrassment in recent years as a result of two separate silo explosions. This, combined with the fact that it has become increasingly expensive to maintain, has conspired to bring about the type's gradual retirement from the nuclear arsenal.

SAC is also responsible for providing inflight-refuelling support to all elements of the USAF and currently maintains a fleet of approximately 500 KC-135 Stratotankers in some 32 squadrons, these being ably supported by a further 128 aircraft of this type operated by ANG and AFRes units. The KC-135 is another veteran, and efforts are being made to improve performance and extend service life by means of re-engining and wing-strengthening programmes. Re-engining has thus far been largely confined to installing refurbished surplus civilian Pratt & Whitney JT-3D turbofans on a number of ANG machines, the resulting aircraft being known as KC-135Es, but the most significant proposal envisages fitting brand-new General Electric/SNECMA CFM-56-2B1 turbofan engines to about 300 Stratotankers and a prototype of this model, known as the KC-135R, has now completed flight trials at Edwards AFB. Modified aircraft will be able to remain in front-line service until well into the 21st century, but other efforts to overcome the present shortage of tanker aircraft centre around acquisition of the McDonnell Douglas KC-10A Extender, close to 20 aircraft of this type now being active of the 60 that will eventually be obtained. Tanker capability combines with an impressive payload to make the Extender a valuable addition to the inventory, the KC-10 being particularly useful when operating in support of tactical

Right: With a total of 1,000 emplaced in silos throughout the mid-west, the Minuteman is SAC's most numerous missile and is expected to remain in the inventory for the foreseeable future despite the forthcoming deployment of Peacekeeper.

Far right: The newest ICBM to be developed in the USA, the MEM-118 Peacekeeper will carry no less than 10 warheads when it begins to enter operational service in 1986.

After many years of reliance solely on the Boeing KC-135 Stratotanker, USAF inflight-refuelling capability is in process of receiving a tremendous boost through the acquisition of no less than 60 examples of the McDonnell Douglas KC-10A Extender. In addition to the basic refuelling mission, the KC-10A regularly augments strategic airlift aircraft assigned to Military Airlift Command.

Originally conceived as a lightweight fighter optimized for the air-combat role, the General Dynamics F-16 Fighting Falcon has evolved into a most capable strike fighter and presently equips eight wings in the USA, Europe and Asia. The F-16B shown here is painted in an experimental 'charcoal lizard' camouflage scheme which was not adopted.

aircraft engaged in the overseas deployments which are now a routine feature of USAF operations.

Long viewed by some as the poor relation of SAC, Tactical Air Command (TAC) had the defence of North America added to its duties with the demise of the Aerospace Defense Command and has for the past few years been engaged in a major modernization programme which has witnessed the procurement of substantial numbers of a new generation of combat aircraft to replace older types such as the trusty McDonnell Douglas F-4 Phantom and the Vought A-7 Corsair II. Today, the Fairchild Republic A-10 Thunderbolt II, the McDonnell Douglas F-15 Eagle and the General Dynamics F-16 Fighting Falcon are predominant in TAC's combat echelons, but force modernization has not been solely confined to such elements, another noteworthy recent acquisition being the Boeing E-3A Sentry derivative of the Boeing 707 for airborne warning and control duty.

In terms of numbers of personnel assigned, SAC still maintain a position of superiority, but TAC is by far the largest USAF command with regard to the number of aircraft on hand. These are engaged in a multitude of missions encompassing virtually all areas of tactical air power, ranging from forward air control through air superiority to close air support and reconnaissance. Accordingly, TAC's fleet consists of several widely disparate types, of which most are optimized for a specific task, a situation far removed from that of the 1960s and early 1970s when the albeit highly versatile F-4 Phantom reigned almost supreme as a 'maid of all work'.

Atlantic and Readiness Command

Making a substantial contribution to the Rapid Deployment Joint Task Force (RDJTF), TAC elements in fact constitute the USAF component of two of the specified commands responsible to the Joint Chiefs of

After some 10 years of front-line service with Tactical Air Command, most of the surviving examples of the Vought A-7D Corsair have been passed on to the Air National Guard. This picture shows a pair of 175th TFS, South Dakota ANG Corsairs setting off on a practice bombing mission during a 14-day European deployment.

A clutch of ALCMs (Air-Launched Cruise Missiles) are gathered around an extended pylon of a B-52. They are evidence of a curious game; the pylon has been obviously extended beyond the leading edge of the wing so that they can be seen by Soviet surveillance satellites – all part of the highly charged arrangements with the Soviets to prevent war starting and to convince them that it is not winnable.

Below: Launch of a GLCM (Ground-Launched Cruise Missile). In time of crisis the TELs (Transporter/Erector/Launcher) carry four missiles and, with their associated LCC (Launch Control Centre), will make their way from their well-known storage bases to conceal remote and secret launch sites, screened from satellite surveillance. It would make any Soviet pre-emptive nuclear strike much less effective.

General Dynamics F-111A

One of the most controversial warplanes ever developed, the General Dynamics F-111 eventually 'came good' and is now one of the most potent elements in the TAC and USAFE inventories. Optimized for sustained operation at low level, the F-111 excels in the deep-strike interdiction role, being able to use either conventional or nuclear weaponry. The example shown here in the colours of the 474th Tactical Fighter Wing at Nellis AFB, Nevada during the mid-1970s is an F-111A and clearly illustrates the type's impressive payload capability, being loaded with no less than 24 Mk 82 500-lb (227-kg) retarded bombs.

NA
AF 67 064

The shark's-mouth motif and 'EL' fin code letters identify this Fairchild Republic A-10A Thunderbolt II as belonging to the 23rd Tactical Fighter Wing at England AFB, Louisiana, one of three US-based wings which operate this type. Other examples of the A-10 are in service in the United Kingdom, Alaska and South Korea.

Tactical reconnaissance requirements of the USAF are currently fulfilled by the specialist RF-4C variant of the McDonnell Douglas Phantom, and there are no plans to replace these aircraft in the mid-term future. Examples of the RF-4C serve with most major USAF commands as well as the Air National Guard.

Staff, namely Atlantic Command and Readiness Command, and it is therefore possible for TAC aircraft to be ordered into action without referring to the more usual chain of command. TAC headquarters are located at Langley AFB, Virginia, routine administration being effected via two subordinate numbered air forces, these being the 9th Air Force at Shaw AFB, South Carolina, and the 12th Air Force at Bergstrom AFB, Texas. There are, in addition, several units which report directly to TAC headquarters, these mainly being concerned with the development and evaluation of weapons and tactics and with the administration of the various 'Flag' programmes of which 'Red Flag' is probably best known. This is the series of flying training exercises conducted regularly in the vicinity of Nellis AFB, Nevada, with the objective of providing realistic combat training so as to enhance aircrew experience levels and likelihood of survival in any future conflict. Other similar exercises include 'Black Flag' for maintenance personnel, 'Green Flag' predicted on European and Korean theatre operations and 'Blue Flag' which is concerned with battlefield management and the decision-making process.

New equipment

The operational elements of the 9th Air Force are distributed betwen a total of 10 air bases, two of which (Langley and at Eglin) host F-15 air superiority units, Langley's 1st Tactical Fighter Wing having recently completed transition to the newest variant of the Eagle, namely the F-15C with the so-called 'FAST Pack' (Fuel And Sensor Tactical Package); this unit is now one of those assigned to the RDJTF. TAC's second fairly new type, the A-10A Thunderbolt II with its fearsome General Electric GAU-8/A Avenger 30-mm Gatling-type cannon, equips two units: the 23rd TFW at England AFB, Louisiana, and the 354th TFW at Myrtle Beach AFB, South Carolina, whilst the F-16 Fghting Falcon also serves with two units, these being the 56th TFW at MacDill AFB, Florida, and the 363rd TFW at Shaw AFB, South Carolina. The latter wing's three F-16 squadrons are complemented by one squadron with the RF-4C Phantom, this being a legacy of the 363rd TFW's long career as a purely reconnaissance wing. Shaw is also home for the Cessna O-2As and Sikorsky CH-3E helicopters of the 507th TACW, additional elements of this unit being located at Patrick AFB, Florida, from where they operate O-2As and Rockwell OV-10A Broncos in the forward air control role. The three remaining wings which report to the 9th Air Force all operate Phantoms, two being fully operational units with the F-4E at Seymour-Johnson AFB, North Carolina (4th TFW), and at Moody AFB, Georgia (347th TFW), whilst the third serves in the training role with F-4Ds at Homestead AFB, Florida. This 31st TFW is earmarked for transition to the F-16 in the not-too-distant future as the requirement for Phantom crews diminishes with the type's continuing withdrawal from the front-line inventory.

TAC's second major component, the 12th Air Force, differs quite considerably in composition and equipment, three bases hosting two wings each as well as

Right: A total of 24 Mk 82 500-lb (227-kg) bombs fall from an F-111A of the 366th Tactical Fighter Wing during a mission to the massive Nellis complex of ranges in Nevada. Later models of the F-111 serve with two wings in the United Kingdom and are viewed as a very real threat by the Soviet Union.

In the spring of 1984 the Air Force tested its ASAT (Anti-Satellite) missile. Obviously a vital element in the arsenal, it nonetheless raises substantial political problems. Able to destroy vital Soviet communications equipment, its deployment could be perceived as a prelude to a first strike; the most dangerous Soviet retaliatory missiles rely on such satellites for their navigation.

MO
061

With the retirement of the Douglas EB-66C/E Destroyer in the early 1970s the USAF lacked a dedicated jamming platform, a deficiency which has been made good only in the past couple of years through the introduction of the Grumman (General Dynamics) EF-111A Raven. Entering service initially with the 366th TFW at Mountain Home, the EF-111A is now in process of joining USAFE's 20th TFW.

several with just a single wing. Long-range all-weather strike elements are concentrated within the 12th Air Force, these comprising the General Dynamics F-111As of the 366th TFW at Mountain-Home AFB, Idaho, and the F-111Ds of the 27th TFW at Cannon AFB, New Mexico. After a disaster-ridden early career, the F-111 eventually 'came good' in USAF service and such is the faith now placed in this type that it has formed the basis for the latest defence-suppression aircraft to enter the inventory. This, the Grumman/General Dynamics EF-111A 'Electric Fox', is essentially a much-modified F-111A, some 42 Grumman conversions presently being scheduled for service in the USA and Europe. Initial deliveries have been made to the 388th Electronic Countermeasures Squadron at Mountain-Home AFB, these operating alongside the standard F-111A as part of the 366th TFW. Another defence-suppression aircraft, the F-4G 'Wild Weasel' variant of the Phantom, equips the 37th TFW at George AFB, California, this base also being home for the 35th TFW which operates the F-4E on training, including the training of West German pilots in Phantoms owned by that country. Further Phantoms are to be found at Bergstrom AFB, Texas, although in this instance they are the reconnaissance-configured RF-4Cs of the 67th TRW, whilst the 12th Air Force also parents three F-16 units, namely the 58th TTW (formerly TFTW) at Luke AFB, Arizona; the 388th TFW at Hill AFB, Utah, and the 474th TFW at Nellis AFB, Nevada. The two remaining bases supporting 12th Air Force elements are Holloman AFB, New Mexico, which has the 49th TFW with F-15 Eagles plus the 479th TTW with a mixture of Northrop AT-38A and T-38B Talons, and Davis-Monthan AFB, Arizona, with the 355th TTW's A-10A Thunderbolt IIs plus the 602nd TACW with Cessna OA-37Bs for FAC functions. Of these four wings, the 479th TTW is perhaps the most unusual, this undertaking lead-in and operational conversion training of newly-qualified pilots before assignment to other TAC units, and to provide added realism the T-38Bs are fitted with underwing stores stations in order to carry air-to-ground rockets and/or gun pods.

Weapons training

Direct-reporting units within TAC include the Tactical Fighter Weapons Center (TFWC) at Nellis AFB, Nevada, this being a large organization parenting subordinate group and wing structures. Of these, the 440th Tactical Fighter Training group is probably the most significant for, although it has no aircraft of its own, it is responsible for organizing and managing 'Red Flag' exercises. TFWC's second element, the 57th Fighter Weapons Wing, is, conversely, very much in the aircraft-operating business, controlling a Fighter Weapons School with separate elements using the A-10A, F-4E and F-15 to provide advanced tuition in combat tactics. Other 57th FWW components include two Tactical Evaluation Squadrons, namely the 422nd TES at Nellis with examples of most combat types currently to be found in TAC service, and the 431st TES

AIM-9L Sidewinder air-to-air missiles are carried on the wing-tip rails of this trio of 388th TFW General Dynamics F-16A Fighting Falcons seen in flight near their home base at Hill, Utah. Despite the F-16's remarkable aerial agility, it is principally employed on strike/interdiction duties by the USAF.

Combat experience in Vietnam revealed serious deficiencies in USAF air-to-air combat capability and was directly responsible for the introduction of the 'aggressor' concept in which the Northrop F-5E Tiger II is used as a dissimilar opponent in simulated air combat.

at McClellan AFB, California, with the F-111. There are also two 'aggressor' squadrons with the Northrop F-5E Tiger II for dissimilar air combat manoeuvring training, and these also play a major role in 'Red Flag'. Also reporting to the 57th FWW is the Air Demonstration Squadron, the 'Thunderbirds', which is back in business with the F-16A following a disastrous accident early in 1982 when four T-38 Talons were destroyed during pre-season work-up.

Moving a few thousand miles to the east, Eglin AFB in Florida is home base for the Tactical Air Warfare Center (TAWC) tasked with the development and testing of both weapons and concepts for tactical operations. Only a handful of F-4 Phantoms are operated by TAWC's 4485th Test Squadron, although aircraft of the Air Force Systems Command's armament Division, which is also located at Eglin, are available for use by TAWC personnel as and when necessary. 'Blue Flag' training exercises are organized by TAWC's other subordinate unit, this being the 4441st TTG which, like the 4440th TFTG at Nellis, has no aircraft of its own.

The only other direct-reporting unit within TAC is the 552nd Airborne Warning and Control Wing. This, too, is a fairly large organization responsible for some eight squadrons distributed between no less than five air bases. Wing headquarters are maintained at Tinker AFB, Oklahoma, and it is here that the principal type, the Boeing E-3A Sentry, is concentrated, most of the 34 aircraft presently required having now been delivered. Three Airborne Warning and Control Squadrons (AW&CSs) are to be found at Tinker, with further single squadrons located at the two principal overseas operating centres at Keflavik, Iceland, and Kadena, Okinawa. These latter manage aircraft deployed from Tinker on a rotational basis. Such are the permanent units, but the Sentry has in recent years been despatched to overseas bases on numerous occasions and what seems like a near-permanent detachment is presently active in Saudi Arabia, at Riyadh, pending the delivery of Saudi Arabia's own fleet of five aircraft. Other 552nd AW&CW elements comprise the 7th Airborne Command and Control Squadron at Keesler AFB, Mississippi, with the Lock-

Bathed in an almost unearthly green light, a McDonnell Douglas F-15A of the 405th Tactical Training Wing at Luke undergoes pre-dawn checkout at the start of another flying day. Training of aircrews for all USAF F-15 units is accomplished at this Arizona base.

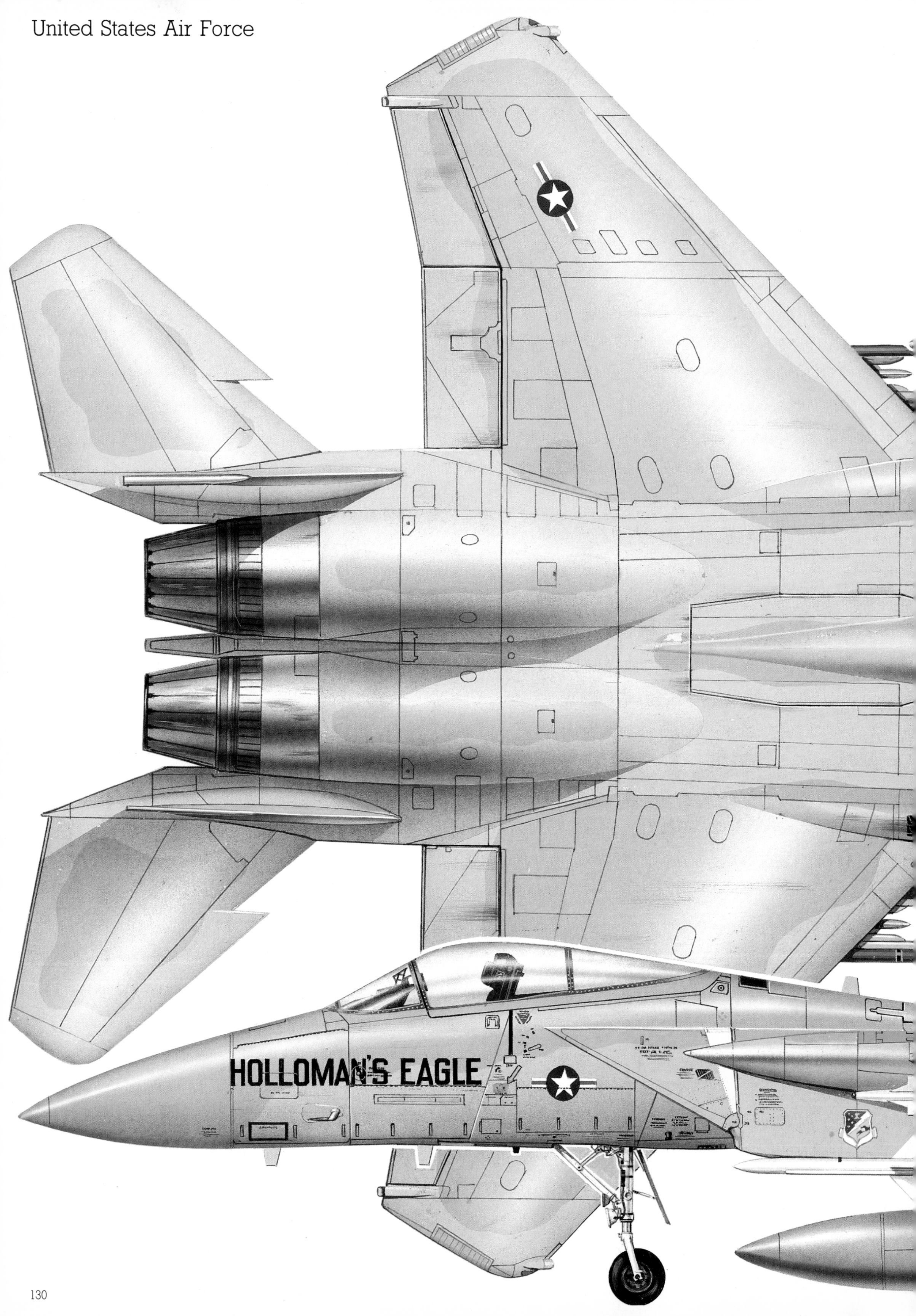
HOLLOMAN'S EAGLE

McDonnell Douglas F-15

Carrying a typical load of four AIM-9J Sidewinders and four AIM-7F Sparrows, this McDonnell Douglas F-15A Eagle was flown by the commanding officer of the 49th Tactical Fighter Wing at Holloman AFB, New Mexico, hence the nickname on the nose section, the multi-coloured fin stripes and the unusual presentation of the serial number on the vertical tail surfaces. In addition to missile armament, the Eagle features an integral Vulcan M61 20-mm cannon buried in the starboard wing root, whilst this example also carries a 600-US gal (2273-litre) auxiliary fuel tank on the centreline stores station.

The backbone of Military Airlift Command's strategic transport fleet, Lockheed's C-141 StarLifter has benefited greatly from the recent 'stretch' programme which resulted in the C-141B. Shown here in the European One camouflage which is now being adopted, the C-141B model currently serves with five airlift wings.

heed EC-130E Hercules for battlefield command activities; the 8th Tactical Deployment Control Squadron at Tinker with the EC-135K; and the 41st Electronic Countermeasures Squadron at Davis-Monthan with the EC-130H.

Following the demise of Air Defense Command during 1979-80, responsibility for the aerial defence of the continental United States passed to Tactical Air Command, and this organization now controls a separate and subordinate element to fulfil this task. Known as ADTAC (Air Defense Tactical Air Command) and managed from Langley AFB, Virginia, by a Deputy Commander, operational assets are confined to six Fighter Interceptor Squadrons (FISs).

Five of these squadrons are located in the USA itself and these are now being modernized, a long-overdue process which is seeing the replacement of the veteran Convair F-106A Delta Dart by the F-15A Eagle. Coincidentally sharing Langley with TAC headquarters, the 48th FIS was first to convert in 1982 whilst the second squadron to re-equip, the 318th FIS at McChord AFB, Washington, received its first F-15A in the summer of 1983. In the early autumn of 1983 the F-106A soldiered on with the other three US-based units, these being the 5th FIS at Minot AFB, North Dakota; the 49th FIS at Griffiss AFB, New York, and the 87th FIS at Sawyer AFB, Michigan. All of these will also eventually receive the F-15.

ADTC's other operational unit is the 57th FIS, stationed at Keflavik, Iceland, and equipped with a dozen F-4E Phantoms. ADTAC is also responsible for management of the Air Defense Weapons Center at Tyndall AFB, Florida, this providing realistic training opportunities in the field of air superiority. One of the major air combat manoeuvring ranges in the USA is located nearby, this extending over several hundred miles of the Gulf of Mexico, where extensive use is made of drones for live missile firing exercises, examples of the Ryan Firebee, North American QF-100D and Convair PQM-102A all being regularly employed as targets.

So as to increase defensive coverage, extensive use is made of detachments, whilst fighter aircraft of the ANG and other TAC units also make a significant contribution to the protection of US air sovereignty.

Long-range lift

The third major US-based element of the USAF is Military Airlift Command (MAC) with headquarters at Scott AFB, Illinois. This, too, has recently undergone its fair share of reorganization, activating a third numbered air force and gaining several units from TAC. As its title implies, MAC is essentially concerned with airlift and, accordingly, it operates a large fleet of cargo-type aircraft, foremost amongst which must surely be the Lockheed C-5 Galaxy, this massive freighter and troop transport being ably supported by substantial numbers of the Lockheed C-141B StarLifter and the Lockheed C-130 Hercules.

Other areas of MAC endeavour include aeromedical airlift, a small fleet of McDonnell Douglas C-9A Nightingales being used in conjunction with regular airlift aircraft to ensure that no US serviceman is more than a few hours from top-quality medical care. This command also performs a valuable humanitarian duty by means of the Aerospace Rescue and Recovery Service (ARRS), which operates helicopters and fixed-wing aircraft on such diverse tasks as local base rescue, combat search and rescue, and weather reconnaissance. MAC also has control of about 130 Rockwell CT-39 Sabreliners which perform routine liaison and communications functions throughout the USA and in Europe. Transport of VIPs is yet another task fulfilled by MAC, from Andrews AFB, Maryland, which lies conveniently close to the seat of government in Washington; it is this unit which operates 'Air Force One' for the President. Numbered amongst the fleet of aircraft and helicopter types operated by the 89th MAW which undertakes this duty are the Bell UH-1N Iroquois, Sikorsky CH-3E, McDonnell Douglas VC-9A, Lockheed VC-140B JetStar, Beech VC-6A, Grumman C-20A Gulfstream III, and the Boeing VC-137B/Cs of the Presidential Flight.

Finally, MAC also now controls several units engaged in highly specialized combat-type operations from bases in the USA, the Far East, the Panama Canal Zone and Europe, these all being fairly recent additions.

As far as airlift operations are concerned, these are the principal responsibility of the 21st Air Force at McGuire AFB, New Jersey, and the 22nd Air Force at

Aeromedical evacuation duties are also assigned to MAC which has a small fleet of McDonnell Douglas C-9A Nightingales suitable equipped to undertake this mission. Most of these are based within the continental USA, although a few are situated overseas where there are large concentrations of US military personnel.

Seen during inflight-refuelling compatibility trials, a Lockheed C-141B StarLifter closes for contact with a Boeing KC-135A. Incorporation of inflight-refuelling equipment took place at the same time as these aircraft were 'stretched' and has resulted in genuine global capability for the 270 or so C-141Bs which are in service.

Military Airlift Command's third major transport type is the highly versatile Lockheed C-130 Hercules, although this is more usually employed on tactical rather than strategic missions. The C-130's ability to operate from rough fields is graphically depicted in this view of a desert camouflaged machine getting airborne from a sandy strip.

Travis AFB, California, serving the eastern and western hemispheres respectively, and both of these organizations feature examples of the three principal cargo aircraft types in their line-up, permitting them to perform all aspects of the airlift mission. Units of the 21st Air Force located on the eastern seaboard of the USA comprise the 436th MAW with the C-5A at Dover AFB, Delaware; the 437th MAW with C-141Bs at Charleston AFB, South Carolina; the 438th MAW with C-141Bs at McGuire AFB, New Jersey; the 317th TAW with C-130Es at Pope AFB, North Carolina. Moving overseas, a subordinate element within the 21st Air Force, known as the 322nd Airlift Division administers MAC activities within Europe from Rhein-Main, controlling rotational C-130s at Mildenhall via the 313th TAG and permanently-based C-130Es at Rhein-Main with the 435th TAW. Other 435th TAW components include a handful of C-9As for aeromedical services within Europe, plus a small number of VIP and communications aircraft at Ramstein, these including examples of the CT-39A, VC-140B, Beech C-12A and C-135B.

A slightly larger command, the 22nd Air Force is similarly equipped, with the 60th MAW operating C-5As and C-141Bs from Travis AFB, California; the 62nd MAW C-141Bs and C-130Es from McChord AFB, Washington; the 63rd MAW C-141Bs from Norton AFB, California; the 314th TAW C-130s (including a training squadron) from Little Rock AFB, Arkansas; the 463rd TAW C-130Hs from Dyess AFB, Texas; and the 616th MAG C-130Es from Elmendorf AFB, Alaska. Also forming part of the 22nd Air Force is MAC's principal jet transport training unit, this being the 443rd MAW at Altus AFB, Oklahoma, with examples of both the C-5A and C-141B, whilst overseas assets in the Far East are grouped together under the control of the 834th Airlift Division at Hickam AFB, Hawaii, and include single squadrons of aeromedical C-9As and airlift C-130Es with the 376th TAW at Clark AB in the Philippines and a further squadron of C-130Es with the 316th TAG at Yokota AB, Japan.

MAC's newest command echelon, the 23rd Air Force at Scott AFB, Illinois, was established recently

Although the type originally entered service almost 15 years ago, it is only recently that the Lockheed C-5A Galaxy has begun to adopt tactical battledress as seen here. Serving with two MAC wings, the C-5A fleet is to be augmented by over 50 essentially similar C-5Bs in the not-too-distant future.

MILITARY AIRLIFT COMMAND
MILITARY AIRLIFT COMMAND
436th MAW
0456
U.S.AIR FORCE

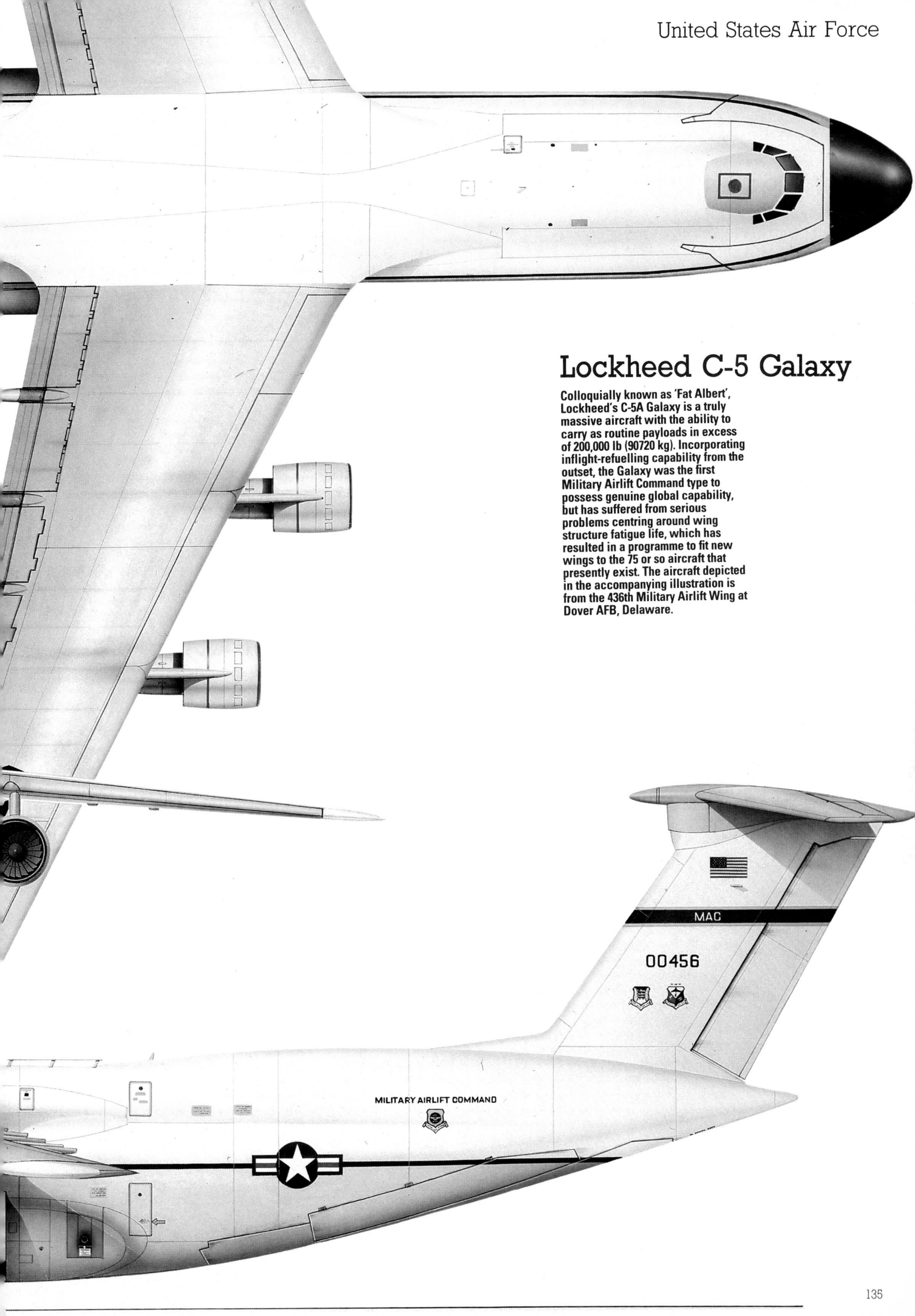

Lockheed C-5 Galaxy

Colloquially known as 'Fat Albert', Lockheed's C-5A Galaxy is a truly massive aircraft with the ability to carry as routine payloads in excess of 200,000 lb (90720 kg). Incorporating inflight-refuelling capability from the outset, the Galaxy was the first Military Airlift Command type to possess genuine global capability, but has suffered from serious problems centring around wing structure fatigue life, which has resulted in a programme to fit new wings to the 75 or so aircraft that presently exist. The aircraft depicted in the accompanying illustration is from the 436th Military Airlift Wing at Dover AFB, Delaware.

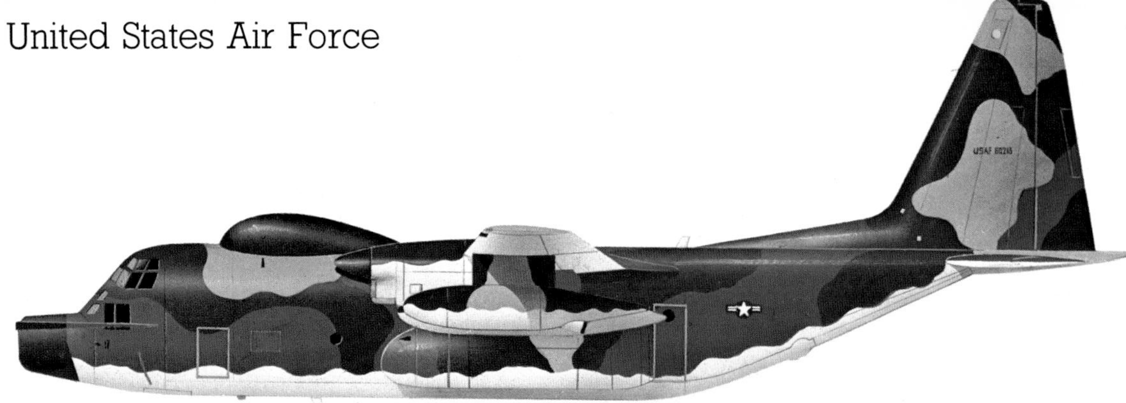

One of three variants of the Lockheed Hercules assigned to MAC's Aerospace Rescue and Recovery Service, the HC-130P possesses dual-mission capability, being able to function as both a rescue aircraft and as an aerial tanker. Special pods located on the outer wing hardpoints contain hose and drogue fuel transfer equipment.

Aircrew recovery capability under combat conditions improved immeasurably in Vietnam, with great strides being made in terms of both tactics and equipment. In this view, a crew member aboard a Sikorsky HH-3E 'Jolly Green Giant' prepares to lower the jungle penetrator device to a downed pilot.

and this now looks after the ARRSs and the small number of special operations units, the former having previously reported direct to MAS headquarters at the same base. ARRSs assets have also contracted in recent years with regard to the chain of command, a couple of squadrons having been eliminated although the number of active elements has remained fairly constant. Extensive use is made of detachments, most operating variants of the highly versatile Bell H-1 Iroquois although a few have the larger Sikorsky HH-3E. The bulk of the rescue forces are grouped together within the 39th Aerospace Rescue and Recovery Wing at Eglin AFB, Florida, this controlling four squadrons, namely the 37th ARRS at F.E. Warren AFB, Wyoming; the 40th ARRs at Hill AFB, Utah; the 55th ARRS also at Eglin; and the 67th ARRS at RAF Woodbridge in Suffolk.

The 37th and 40th ARRSs operates only Bell Huey helicopters, whilst the other two squadrons number the Lockheed HC-130 Hercules, Sikorsky HH-53C/H, Bell H-1 and Sikorsky HH-3E amongst their inventory, some examples of the Sikorsky UH-60A Black Hawk having recently been assigned to the 55th ARRs for training purposes in anticipation of the acquisition of a considerable number of HH-60Ds in the fairly near future.

The 41st Rescue and Weather Reconnaissance Wing at McClellan AFB, California, is the second major ARRS sub-unit, this controlling the 33rd ARRS at Kadena (HH-3E, HH-53C and HC-130) and the 41st ARRS at McClellan (HH-53C and HC-130) plus three weather reconnaissance squadrons engaged in the provision of meteorological data and forecasts as well as the more hazardous task of hurricane tracking. Two squadrons (the 53rd WRS and the 54th WRS at Keesler

Possibly the greatest single improvement to recovery capability came with the development of inflight refuelling for helicopters, for this permitted the radius of operations to be greatly increased. Here an HH-53C receives fuel from an HC-130P Hercules tanker.

Without doubt one of the most fearsome weapons to be developed and deployed during the Vietnam War, the gunship remains in use today although the number of aircraft available has diminished greatly. This picture shows a Lockheed AC-130A of the Air Force Reserve letting fly with one of the 20-mm cannon that it carries.

After years of struggling to make do with the veteran Lockheed EC-121, airborne early warning and control received a major boost in the latter half of the 1970s with the advent of the Boeing E-3 Sentry.

AFB, Mississippi, and at Andersen AFB, Guam, respectively) are equipped with WC-130s whilst the third (the 55th WRS at McClellan) has WC-135Bs.

In addition to these, the 23rd Air Force also exercises control over a fairly widespread collection of special operations units inherited from TAC, USAFE and PACAF, these being grouped together under the auspices of the 2nd Air Division. Briefly, these consist of the 1st Special Operations Wing at Hurlburt Field, Florida, with three squadrons operating MC-130ES, AC-130Hs and CH-3Es respectively; the 1st SOS at Clark in the Philippines with the MC-130E; and the 7th SOS at Rhein-Main AB, West Germany, also with MC-130Es.

The only other front-line combat organizations situated on US territory is Alaskan Air Command (AAC) which has as its main purpose the detection of an impending air attack on the USA and Canada. Consequently, it is responsible for managing many radars, communications centres and other facilities of which perhaps the most widely known is the DEW (Distant Early Warning) Line. Continuing exploration for and development of the plentiful natural resources in Alaska have helped to make this somewhat bleak and desolate state of increasing importance to the entire North American continent, and it is hardly surprising in view of this that the small number of aircraft-operating combat units have recently been dramatically updated with an infusion of McDonnell Douglas F-15 Eagles and Fairchild Republic A-10A Thunderbolts.

Located at Elmendorf AFB, AAC headquarters co-ordinate the activities of a small number of tactical units, foremost of which is probably the 21st TFW which shares the same base, having one squadron of F-15 Eagles for interception and air superiority and one squadron of vintage Lockheed T-33As for communications, ECM chaff duties and target-towing. The F-15 squadron keeps a small number of aircraft on alert at Elmendorf and also maintains separate detachments for air defence duties at Eielson AFB, King Salmon airport and Galena Air Force Station.

AAC's second major tactical echelon is the 343rd Composite Wing at Eielson, this controlling one fighter squadron with the A-10A for close air support plus a Tactical Air Support Squadron with a mixture of Cessna O-2As and Lockheed T-33As for forward air control tasks. In addition to these AAC-dedicated forces, both SAC and MAC have a permanent presence in Alaska, operating from Eielson and Elmendorf respectively and details of these can be found in their respective sections.

As well as combat elements within the continental USA, the US Air Force also has two major overseas

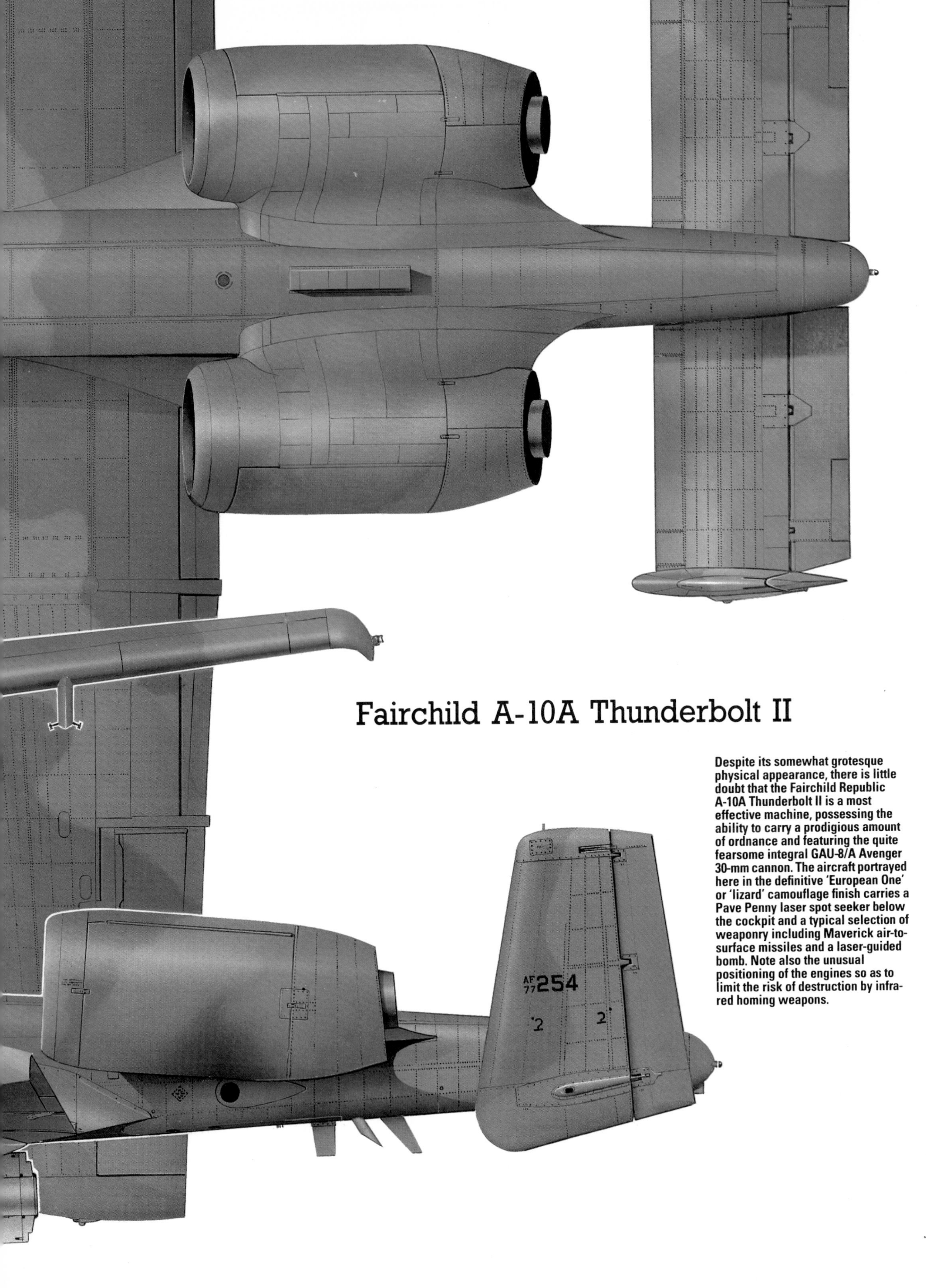

Fairchild A-10A Thunderbolt II

Despite its somewhat grotesque physical appearance, there is little doubt that the Fairchild Republic A-10A Thunderbolt II is a most effective machine, possessing the ability to carry a prodigious amount of ordnance and featuring the quite fearsome integral GAU-8/A Avenger 30-mm cannon. The aircraft portrayed here in the definitive 'European One' or 'lizard' camouflage finish carries a Pave Penny laser spot seeker below the cockpit and a typical selection of weaponry including Maverick air-to-surface missiles and a laser-guided bomb. Note also the unusual positioning of the engines so as to limit the risk of destruction by infra-red homing weapons.

The wolf's head motif visible just aft of the cockpit of this General Dynamics F-16A Fighting Falcon signifies assignment to the celebrated 'Wolf Pack' at Kunsan Air Base in Korea. Much reduced in size since the heyday of the Vietnam War, PACAF is still nevertheless a most powerful fighting force in its own right.

commands, Pacific Air Forces (PACAF) and the United States Air Forces in Europe (USAFE) and these being primarily tactical organizations. And like TAC they have been considerably updated in recent years, the F-4 Phantom giving way to A-10s, F-15s and F-16s in substantial numbers.

Now little more than a pale shadow of the massive organization which existed at the height of the Vietnam War, PACAF is still nevertheless a most powerful force and one that consists of two numbered air forces plus a couple of smaller direct-reporting elements on the island of Oahu, Hawaii. Strategically located in the Pacific Ocean, the chain of islands which constitute the state of Hawaii has a special significance in US military history for it was here, at Pearl Harbor, that the Japanese attack was directly responsible for bringing the massive American war machine into World War II in December 1941. More recently, Hickam AFB, Hawaii, was an important staging post in the supply lines to South East Asia during the Vietnam War and Hickam still serves as PACAF headquarters today.

Korean capability

In terms of size, the 5th Air Force at Yokota, AB, Japan, is the most significant component of PACAF, and this organization exercises control of three fully-fledged fighter wings via two Air Divisions. At Kadena AB, Okinawa, the 313th AD administers the 18th TFW with three squadrons of F-15C Eagles plus a single squadron operating reconnaissance RF-4C Phantom IIs, the latter also maintaining a small detachment at Osan AB in Korea.

Sharing Yokota with the 5th Air Force headquarters is the 475th Air Base Wing, essentially a support organization tasked with ensuring smooth running of the air base itself although it also operates a handful of Bell UH-1F Iroquois helicopters and Rockwell T-39A Sabreliners mainly on communications tasks.

Elements of the 314th Air Division, which has its headquarters at Osan AB, are rather more widely dispersed, being distributed between four air bases in Korea. At Kunsan, the 8th TFW (the celebrated 'Wolf Pack') has two squadrons of F-16 Fighting Falcons, this wing having been reduced in size when it re-equipped with the F-16, losing one squadron to the 51st TFW. Located at Osan, the latter controls four squadrons in all, these being fairly widely scattered and comprising one F-4E Phantom II squadron at Taegu; one A-10A Thunderbolt II squadron at Suwon; one F-4E squadron at Osan itself and one Rockwell OV-10 Bronco squadron for forward air control duty, also at Osan.

By comparison, the 13th Air Force at Clark AB in the Philippines is a fairly puny command, for this has just one major aircraft operating element, namely the 3rd TFW with single squadrons operating the Northrop F-5E Tiger II for aggressor training, the F-4E for close air support and limited air superiority, and the F-4G for defence-suppression. All three squadrons use Clark as their main base, but the F-5Es frequently deploy to other bases (most notably Kadena) to spread the air combat manoeuvring gospel to other PACAF elements and to combat units of allied air forces in this part of the world.

Although much reduced in size in recent years, PACAF has been significantly updated with regard to equipment, and limited expansion is very much in mind for the future, a process which will witness the return of USAF combat aircraft to mainland Japan in about 1985 when a two-squadron wing of F-16s is to be established at Misawa.

European theatre update

After years of seeming neglect in deference to the demands of the war in South East Asia, the US Air Force's second major overseas command, USAFE, is now in far better shape, having received a long-overdue infusion of new and more modern equipment whilst at the same time being expanded somewhat with regard to overall size. Control in peacetime is vested in USAFE headquarters at Ramstein, West Germany, but it should be noted that virtually all of the units which make up this command would come under NATO auspices in the event of conflict and, accordingly, some of the more senior commanders are 'dual hatted', a good example of this being provided by the

Right: A brace of lizard camouflaged Fairchild Republic A-10A Thunderbolt IIs of the 81st Tactical Fighter Wing undergo 'last-chance' checks before departure on a routine training mission. USAFE's largest tactical wing in terms of the number of aircraft operated, the 81st TFW makes extensive use of forward operating locations within West Germany.

Pictured moments after take-off on the return flight from Taegu, Korea to Mountain-Home, Idaho in August 1976, this 366th TFW General Dynamics F-111F was part of the American response to the so-called 'tree-cutting' incident of that year in which two US Army officers were killed by North Korean troops.

The only other tactical unit at present located in Korea is the 51st TFW which has its headquarters at Osan although the four attached squadrons actually operate from three different bases. Combat capability is mainly vested in the McDonnell Douglas F-4E such as that shown above, but one squadron is equipped with the Fairchild Republic A-10A.

Commander-in-Chief of USAFE, whose NATO role is that of Commander, Allied Air Forces Central Europe.

With approximately 60,000 personnel and some 700 aircraft on charge, USAFE organization follows largely geographical lines, each of the three numbered air forces being responsible for operations in a specific area.

In the United Kingdom there is the 3rd Air Force, predominantly equipped with the General Dynamics F-111 for long-range strike duties, the 20th TFW at RAF Upper Heyford being a three-squadron wing with the F-111E model whilst the 48th TFW at RAF Lakenheath has four F-111F squadrons. Expansion in the size of this force is imminent, Upper Heyford having been selected to receive approximately 20 examples of the EF-111A 'Electric Fox' for electronic countermeasures duties in support of strike elements during 1984, and the 1st ECS may well have begun to form by early 1984.

A fairly recent addition to the USAFE inventory, the Fairchild Republic A-10A Thunderbolt II, equips the 81st TFW which is stationed at the so-called 'twin base' complex of Bentwaters and Woodbridge, these two separate and distinct airfields being just a few miles apart. Currently the largest operational wing in the entire US Air Force, the 81st TFW has no less than six squadrons and a total fleet of 108 A-10As, about a quarter of which are usually deployed in West Germany where this wing maintains four Forward Operating Locations (FOLs), each with about eight A-10s attached on a constantly-rotating basis. Detachment One is located at Sembach, other FOLs being at Leipheim (Det. 2), Norvenich (Det. 3) and Ahlhorn (Det. 4).

Aggressor services for USAFE's combat echelons are fulfilled by the 527th TFTAS at RAF Alconbury operating Northrop F-5E Tiger IIs, this forming part of the 10th TRW which also has a single McDonnell Douglas RF-4C Phantom II-equipped reconnaissance squadron, whilst RAF Mildenhall's 513th TAW provides support services for transient MAC aircraft, and for rotational MAC Lockheed C-130 Hercules and SAC Boeing KC-135 Stratotankers. The 513rd TAW also looks after the 10th ACCS which has a fleet of four Boeing EC-135H airborne command posts.

Other facilities under 3rd Air Force control are the support bases at Greenham Common, Sculthorpe and Wethersfield, all having been used in recent years for exercises or to permit runway repairs to be performed

RESCUE

General Dynamics F-16A Fighting Falcon

Carrying a mixed load of Sidewinder air-to-air heat-seeking missiles and bombs, this General Dynamics F-16A Fighting Falcon of the 50th Tactical Fighter Wing at Hahn Air Base, West Germany is typical of this, the newest fighter type to enter the operational USAF inventory. Already in service with no less than eight wings throughout the world, the F-16 remains in quantity production for both US and export markets whilst with improved variants in prospect there is little doubt that the type will assume ever greater importance in years to come.

The task of exercising control of tactical assets over the battlefield is still largely entrusted to the Rockwell OV-10A Bronco such as that depicted here in the European One camouflage scheme.

This F-5E Tiger II is based at RAF Alconbury, England, and is operated by the 527th TFTAS. Painted in 'Soviet'-type colours, its task is to provide training in dissimilar air combat tactics for USAFE units.

at the major bases already detailed. Greenham Common has been chosen to serve as a base for the BGM-109G Ground-Launched Cruise Missile (GLCM), the 501st Tactical Missile Wing having already been established to operate this highly controversial weapon. Extensive construction work at this base reached completion towards the end of 1983, with deployment following shortly after.

Southern flank

Elements within close proximity to the Mediterranean report to the 16th Air Force, located at Torrejon AB, Spain, the smallest USAFE command in terms of combat aircraft at its disposal, possessing just one fighter wing. This, the 401st TFW at Torrejon, has operated F-4 Phantom IIs for many years, but is at the time of writing well advanced in the process of transition to the General Dynamics F-16 Fighting Falcon. Other 16th Air Force assets comprise the 406th Tactical Fighter Training Wing at Zaragoza AB in Spain, the 40th Tactical Group at Aviano AB in Italy and TUSLOG (Turkey/US Logistics) at Ankara and Incirlik in Turkey, all of these overseeing the activities of tactical aircraft deployed from other USAFE commands on a rotational basis for training purposes. The 7206th Air Base Group at Hellenikon (Athens Airport) also provides support and command services for USAFE elements active in Greece and to Boeing RC-135s deployed by SAC for the acquisition of electronic intelligence, whilst Comiso AB in Sicily has been selected to serve as a base for cruise missiles and these will come under the control of the 487th TMW when deployment occurs in due course.

Numerically the largest USAFE echelon, the 17th Air Force has its headquarters at Ramstein AB in West Germany and has also undergone its fair share of modernization recently, a process which is expected to continue with additional F-16s being anticipated in the mid-1980s. With the exception of a single F-15 squadron, the 32nd TFS, at Soesterberg in The Netherlands, all 17th Air Force forces are located in West Germany, being distributed between six major bases. Responsibility for air superiority rests largely with the F-15Cs equipping three squadrons of the 36th TFW at Bitburg, this more sophisticated model of the Eagle having only recently supplanted the F-15As delivered to this wing in the latter half of the 1970s. At Hahn, the 50th TFW is now fully operational on the F-16 Fighting Falcon following conversion from the F-4E Phantom II during 1982-3, and this wing retains strike and close air support as its primary tasks although it also has a secondary air-to-air function, operating in conjunction with the F-15 which has a far more capable radar.

Spangdahlem's 52nd TFW will be the last USAFE unit to operate fighter Phantoms, currently controlling two McDonnell Douglas F-4E squadrons plus a third with the F-4G 'Wild Weasel' defence-suppression variant while, at Ramstein, the 86th TFW also has two F-4E squadrons, although these are expected to be replaced by the F-16 in the near future, at which time a third squadron will be activated. Reconnaissance requirements of the 17th Air Force are met by the 20 or so RF-4Cs of the 26th TRW at Zweibrücken, whilst control of air power is undertaken largely by the 601st Tactical Air Control Wing from Sembach, the latter unit having two Rockwell OV-10A Bronco FAC squadrons as well as one Sikorsky CH-53C squadron to assist in mobility of the various ground-based control centres which form part of this very large wing.

In addition to those elements described here,

Suppression of surface-to-air missile sites is the principal task of the F-4G 'Wild Weasel' variant of the McDonnell Douglas Phantom, epitomized here by an aircraft of the 81st TFS at Spangdahlem, West Germany. Weaponry normally employed in this most hazardous mission consists of beam-riding missiles such as Shrike and Standard ARM.

An impressive array of electronic equipment is used by the F-4G in its task of defence suppression, such apparatus enabling the crew to detect and locate enemy missile radars before attacking them with missiles or conventional ordnance. This particular F-4G is from the 81st TFS, 52nd TFW at Spangdahlem.

One of several USAFE bases situated in West Germany, Bitburg is home to the McDonnell Douglas F-15C Eagles of the 36th Tactical Fighter Wing. In this fine study, a trio of Eagles flies within the Arctic Circle whilst operating on detachment to Bodo during a NATO exercise.

USAFE can also call upon SAC and MAC aircraft (either permanently-based or operating on a temporary duty basis) to assist in fulfilling its duties. Details of these can be found in the relevant sections.

Training

Responsibility for the training of personnel to man aircraft and undertake ground support functions rests with the Air Training Command (ATC) at Randolph AFB, Texas. One of the largest commands, ATC has a total of 14 major bases in the USA as well as close to 100 training detachments and operating locations in the USA and throughout the rest of the world. Possessing about 1,600 aircraft, it is also one of the major aircraft-operating elements of the USAF and its influence can truly be said to extend to every area in which the US Air Force is active, tuition encompassing all aspects of military education following the absorption of the Air University during 1978.

By far the greater part of flying centres around undergraduate pilot training, the USAF's demand for newly-qualified aircrew being nearly insatiable. Basic flying instruction is handled by the civilian-operated Officer Training School at Hondo Municipal Airport, Texas, potential pilots undergoing a 30-hour course on the Cessna T-41 before progressing to the Cessna T-37 for a further 90 hours of what might best be described as intermediate training. Finally, they move on to the Northrop T-38A Talon for 120 hours of proficiency standard flying, this being followed by assignment to an operational command for specialist mission training on the type that they will eventually man.

To limit the disruption which might arise from frequent reassignment for different phases of instruction, the six Flying Training Wings (FTWs) which are concerned with undergraduate pilot training operate both of the two major training types of aircraft, these being the 14th FTW at Columbus, Mississippi; the 47th FTW at Laughlin, Texas; the 64th FTW at Reese, Texas; the 71st FTW at Vance, Oklahoma; the 80th FTW at Sheppard, Texas; and the 82nd FTW at Williams, Arizona. It is also worth noting that training is not limited to pilots for the USAF, several friendly nations sending potential aircrew for instruction in the USA. Most of this tuition is undertaken at Sheppard and Williams, the former being unique in that the T-37s and T-38s based there are owned by the West German government although they are in fact operated in full USAF insignia.

To ensure that sufficient suitably-qualified instructor pilots are available ATC also has one wing engaged solely on the production of instructors; this is the 12th Flying Training Wing at Randolph AFB which, in addition to T-37B and T-38A Flying Training Squadrons, also has an Instrument Flight Center with the Bell TH-1F Iroquois being used to train helicopter instructors.

Training of navigators also falls within ATC's sphere of influence, the 323rd Flying Training Wing at Mather AFB, California, using Cessna T-37Bs and Boeing T-43As for practical lessons on conclusion of initial

Screening of candidates for the USAF's undergraduate pilot training programme is accomplished on a fleet of Cessna T-41 Mescaleros operated by a civilian school of Hondo, Texas. Successful applicants log 30 hours on this type before progressing to the Cessna T-37.

training in ground-based simulators. No study of ATC would be complete without mention of the Air Force Academy at Colorado Springs. Offering four-year courses for career officers, the Academy has a separate basic flying school with the Cessna T-41 at Colorado Springs, more advanced pilot and navigator training being performed on T-37s and T-43s operating on detachment from Mather.

Specialist trade training is performed by technical training centres located at Chanute, Illinois; Lowry, Colorado; Sheppard, Texas; and Keesler, Mississippi. The last also caters for overseas students. Some of these facilities employ redundant airframes in order to provide practical 'hands-on' experience of aircraft handling and maintenance procedures.

At Maxwell AFB, Alabama, the Air University provides a variety of specialist facilities, serving as home for the Air War College, the Senior NCO Academy, the Air Force Institute of Technology and the Air Command and Staff College amongst others, whilst the increasingly important field of survival training is more than well catered for by the 3636th Combat Crew Training Wing (Survival) with separate elements at Fairchild AFB, Washington; Eielson AFB, Alaska; Homestead AFB, Florida, and Nellis AFB, Nevada, these between them being able to provide realistic training in temperate forest, jungle, arctic and desert environments.

Increasing sophistication of the combat echelons has been matched by improvements to the many and varied means of communication available to the USAF, both for routine day-to-day running of affairs and for the exercise of command and control in times of war. Responsibility for installing, maintaining and operating such systems is entrusted to the Air Force Communications Command (AFCC), a large organization with several hundred operating sites whose brief extends throughout the communications spectrum, encompassing such diverse aspects as air traffic control, navigational aids, telecommunications equipment and radars. Headquartered at Scott AFB, Illinois, AFCC's organization centres around a total of six so-called Communications Areas (four in the continental USA plus one each in the Pacific and Europe) although there are also several independent elements, these comprising groups or squadrons tasked with meeting the special needs of certain areas of major USAF activity.

Essentially a ground-based command, AFCC does operate a small fleet of aircraft, these being assigned to three Facilities Checking Squadrons which ensure that certain navaids and ground-controlled approach systems are correctly calibrated and functioning satisfactorily. Co-located at Scott, the 1868th FCS has four examples of the Lockheed C-140A JetStar and is responsible for the entire USA, whilst the other two squadrons (the 1867th FCS at Clark AB in the Philippines and the 1868th FCS at Rhein-Main AB in West Germany) each have a single Rockwell T-39A Sabreliner.

Entering service with the US Air Training Command in 1957, the Cessna T-37 continues to fulfil an important training role, though its days are numbered with the choice of the Fairchild T-46 as replacement. All of the initial T-37A models were upgraded to T-37B standard, this being the model illustrated.

Research

Although not engaged in operational duty in the more usually accepted context of the term, there can be little doubt that the Air Force Systems Command (AFSC) plays an important role in the modern US Air Force, and some idea of its true worth can be gained from the fact that it usually receive close to one-third of the total annual USAF budget appropriations.

Engaged principally in the fields of research, development, test and evaluation, AFSC is responsible for the design, construction and purchase of aircraft, weapons and other items of military hardware, controlling some 200 operating locations from its headquarters at Andrews AFB, Maryland. Many of these locations are extremely small, consisting of just a few scientists or technicians, but AFSC also has several major centres of activity. Probably the best known of these is the Air Force Flight Test Center at Edwards AFB, California, for it is here that new aircraft are

Right: Advanced pilot tuition is presently accomplished on the Northrop T-38A Talon, about 120 hours being logged on this type before the pilot is assigned to an operational command. Extensively used by the Air Training Command, a variant known as the AT-38 serves with TAC on 'lead-in fighter' training tasks which include gunnery, weapons delivery and formation flying.

Responsibility for the training of US Air Force and US Navy navigators is now entrusted solely to Air Training Command, and is accomplished by the 323rd FTW from Mather on the Cessna T-37 and Boeing T-43, an example of the latter being illustrated here.

U.S. AIR FORCE
00576

Originally procured by the US Air Force for military training tasks, the North American T-39 Sabreliner soon acquired the additional roles of communications and VIP transport. Illustrated is a T-39A as operated by Det. 3 of the 1402nd MAS, 375th AAW in 1978.

exhaustively evaluated before production authorization. Such work is generally undertaken by temporary organizations known as Joint Test Forces made up of personnel from the civilian contractor responsible for the product under review, from the designated user command and from other AFSC components such as the Aeronautical Systems Division at Wright-Patterson AFB, Ohio.

Systems and logistics

The activities of AFSC encompass all aspects of US Air Force endeavour, noteworthy additional facilities including the Space and Missile Systems Organization (SAMSO) at Los Angeles Air Force Station with its associated test site at Vandenberg AFB, California; the Armament Division at Eglin AFB, Florida; the Electronic Systems Division at Hanscom AFB, Massachusetts; and the Air Force Contract Management Division at Kirtland AFB, New Mexico. This command also has a fairly sizable fleet of dedicated test aircraft, principal centres of flight activity being located at Edwards AFB, California, Eglin AFB, Florida, and Wright-Patterson AFB, Ohio, which between them operate examples of most combat types to be found in the US Air Force inventory.

Once a weapons system (aircraft or missile) attains operational status the Air Force Logistics Command (AFLC) assumes responsibility for purchase, supply and maintenance requirements on a global basis. Headquartered at Wright-Patterson, AFLC is largely civilian-manned, with most of the personnel assigned to the five Air Logistics Centers (ALCs) located in the continental USA. These are concerned mainly with the performance of overhaul and modification work, and each ALC usually has sole responsibility for several specific types, an example being provided by the Ogden ALC at Hill AFB, Utah, which deals with the F-4 Phantom and the F-16 Fighting Falcon, Minuteman and Titan ICBMs, and guided weapons such as the AGM-65 Maverick. Other ALCs are to be found at Tinker AFB, Oklahoma; McClellan AFB, California; Kelly AFB, Texas; and Robins AFB, Georgia, but perhaps the best-known AFLC activity is the Military Aircraft Storage and Disposition Center (MASDC) at Davis-Monthan AFB, Arizona, where roughly 5,000 aircraft from all elements of the US armed forces are held in open storage at any given time. Often erroneously referred to as 'the boneyard', MASDC is an extremely sound investment and one that provides a significant return by virtue of the fact that it is an important repository for valuable aircraft spares, especially for older types which are no longer in production.

AFLC also manages the Air Force Museum at Wright-Patterson AFB, Ohio, there being about 100 aircraft and missiles on display and many more held in reserve. But despite the fact that the command nominally has responsibility for close to 6,000 aircraft at any time it is essentially not an aircraft-operating organization with just a handful assigned, these including some F-4s, F-106s and T-38s plus one F-15.

In distinct contrast, the two second-line elements of the US Air Force are very much in the aircraft-operating business, possessing close to 2,000 between them.

Although the Air Force Communications Command has a large number of personnel, most of these are engaged in ground-based duty and only about half a dozen aircraft are actually operated. Assigned mainly to calibration tasks, these include a few examples of the Lockheed C-140A JetStar such as the camouflaged specimen shown here.

One of the most important USAF agencies, Air Force Systems Command conducts operations from a number of locations and has a large fleet of aircraft, most of which are normally engaged on test programmes of various kinds. These are represented by a preproduction Fairchild Republic A-10A of the Armament Division at Eglin AFB, Florida.

With about 420 aircraft, the Air Force Reserve (AFRes) at Robins AFB, Georgia, is the smaller of the two commands and is mainly engaged in the transport role although combat types have been added in recent years. Organization follows the usual lines, AFRes controlling three numbered air forces, namely the 4th Air Force at McClellan, the 10th Air Force at Bergstrom and the 14th Air Force at Dobbins, these each being responsible for co-ordinating the activities of several subordinate wings and groups.

Airlift assets are distributed between the 4th and 14th Air Forces, and include the so-called 'Associate' wings by which AFRes personnel man USAF C-141B StarLifters and C-5A Galaxies, so operating alongside regular MAC squadrons. It is worth noting in this context that the AFRes now provides almost 50 per cent of flight crews for these two types. The AFRes also has a number of airlift units with their own aircraft, the Lockheed C-130 Hercules being the predominant type assigned to these although some de Havilland Canada C-7 Caribous are still on charge.

Tactical components are grouped together within the 10th Air Force, and include five squadrons of McDonnell Douglas F-4 Phantoms, three squadrons with the Fairchild Republic A-10A Thunderbolt II and one squadron with the Republic F-105D Thunderchief, although the last will give way to the F-16 early in 1984 as part of the continuing process of modernizing second-line forces. The 10th Air Force also controls three Boeing KC-135A tanker squadrons, two 'Associate' squadrons providing crews for SAC McDonnell Douglas KC-10A Extenders and a single Special Operations Squadron with the Lockheed AC-130A Hercules gunship.

Inventory development

The remaining 1,600 or so aircraft which are assigned to second-line elements are all operated by the Air National Guard (ANG) which maintains its headquarters at Andrews AFB and which has also been the subject of some modernization in the past few years, examples of new production aircraft such as the A-10, A-37 and C-130 having been turned over straight from the factory, whilst one squadron recently converted to the F-16A, receiving aircraft which had seen service with the regular US Air Force but which had been brought to virtually the latest modification standard before delivery to the ANG.

Although the fin-code letters 'WR' would appear to indicate that this McDonnell Douglas F-15A is assigned to the 81st TFW at Bentwaters, it is actually operated by the Warner-Robins Air Logistics Center, one of five such facilities in the Air Force Logistics Command.

Air National Guard inflight-refuelling resources are quite substantial, consisting of 104 Boeing KC-135 Stratotankers distributed between 13 squadrons. This particular KC-135A is from the Ohio ANG's 145th Air Refuelling Squadron at Rickenbacker.

The Vietnam war led to a USAF order for an armed version of the Cessna T-37 trainer. Designated A-37B Dragonfly, the aircraft had several modifications including IFR capability. From 1970 the aircraft were passed to ANG units, a 104th TFS, Maryland, ANG aircraft being illustrated.

Organized on a state basis, with at least one flying unit in each of the 50 state plus others allocated to Puerto Rico and the District of Columbia, the ANG at present has 91 squadrons engaged in a variety of missions and with a commensurate variety of equipment. Like the AFRes, the ANG unit would report to a 'gaining' command in the event of mobilization, tactical and air defence units joining TAC, airlift units going to MAC and tanker squadrons reporting to SAC. Under the recently introduced 'total force' concept, ANG units are expected to achieve and maintain a state of combat readiness in order that they can respond immediately to mobilization orders. That the ANG takes its duty seriously is reflected by performance in recent years, ANG elements achieving consistently good results in competitions such as 'William Tell', in 'Red Flag' exercises and in overseas deployments, the last being a regular aspect of the year's work. Types at present operated by the Air National Guard include the Lockheed C-130, Boeing KC-135, Vought A-7, Fairchild Republic A-10, Cessna OA-37, McDonnell Douglas F-4/RF-4, General Dynamics F-16 and Convair (GD) F-106.

Finally, with the future very much in mind, the US Air Force recently established a new command, the first for many years. Known as Space Command, this is at present engaged in activities of what might best be described as a passive nature, monitoring the ever increasing number of satellites in orbit and keeping an eye on all the other debris known to be circling the Earth, from headquarters in the Cheyenne Mountains North American Air Defense Command complex. At present far removed from the type of pyrotechnics associated with 'Star Wars' and other films of that genre, Space Command may, however, acquire the means to destroy other satellites in the foreseeable future, for it is known that research work into the possibilities of using lasers as weapons is making progress.

If (or perhaps it should be when) such weapons become available, it will be fair to say that the sky is no longer the limit as far as the US Air Force is concerned.

Right: Seen against the impressive backdrop of the Golden Gate Bridge, this unusual near head-on view of a Military Airlift Command Lockheed C-5A Galaxy does little to convey the truly massive size of this type.

No less than 66 per cent of the total air-defence resources within the continental USA are contributed by the Air National Guard, types assigned to such tasks comprising the McDonnell Douglas F-4 Phantom and the Convair F-106 Delta Dart. This fine picture shows an F-106A of the 119th Fighter Interceptor squadron, New Jersey ANG returning to its home base at Atlantic City.

U.S. AIR FORCE

United States Rapid Deployment Force

Faced with the prospects of unstable regimes interrupting vital US commodity supplies and interests around the globe, President Carter launched the concept of a highly mobile, integrated multi-service force that could intervene at short notice. This highly visible force now frequently exercises overseas – notably in the Middle East – serving notice on nations not to lightly interfere with US interests.

Left: Ready and able: a C-141 StarLifter stands by for its next mission. It could be to Central America, the Middle East, the Gulf, Korea, Europe, the Caribbean, Africa, Pakistan, the Philippines or a hundred other places. The only certainty is that it will be somewhere, for the USA's interests girdle the globe and it is dedicated to protection of those interests, whatever the challenge.

Below: StarLifters display not only their ability to airdrop, but also the USA's ability and preparedness to deploy her armed forces around the world to protect her interests.

As from 1 January 1983 the American Rapid Deployment Joint Task Force became a new Command known as US Central Command, or USCENTCOM, under the control of the US Joint Chiefs of Staff. This upgrading to command level of a force that has grown in numbers and importance since its conception during the term of office of President Carter is significant for it marks the 'coming of age' of a force that had more than its fair share of being a political football, and it also marks the arrival on the global scene of a new factor on the chess board of world military power.

The new command is still widely known by its abbreviated designation of the Rapid Deployment Force (RDF), and the new command title will gradually be assumed and become more familiar as time progresses. Its future is now certain, despite many political attempts either to do away with it entirely or to attenuate its numbers and scope; but it is still in the throes of organization and establishment, so some of the planned details given below may yet be altered.

Headquarters and tasks

The headquarters of the RDF is at MacDill Air Force Base in Florida. The commander is a lieutenant general of the US Army and under his command he has 230,000 personnel under a unified command that embraces US Army, US Navy, US Air Force and US Marine Corps units. The task of the RDF is wide and largely undefined, based mainly on the fact that the RDF will be called upon to protect the interests of the United States

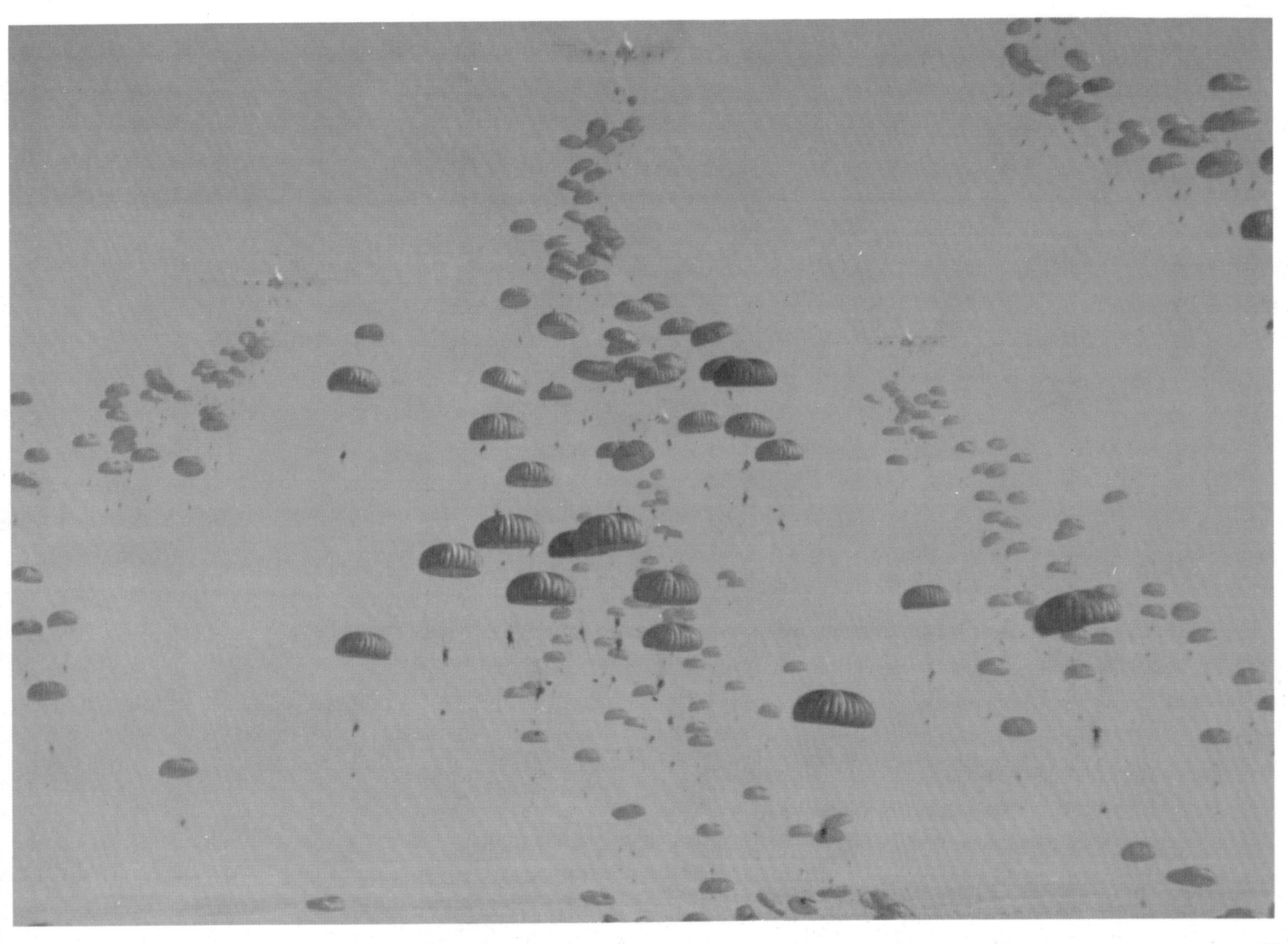

and its allies in an area known as South West Asia (SWA). This operational area takes in 20 countries but specifically excludes Israel. The main centre of interest centres on the area containing the Middle East oilfields and includes such sensitive nations as Iran and Iraq (already at war with each other) and the other smaller Persian Gulf states. Put bluntly in such terms the RDF appears to be but a force to protect American business interests, but the wider intention is to deter Soviet aggression in the area, for one of the more important Soviet foreign policy objectives has for many decades been the establishment of a blue-water port as an outlet to the Indian Ocean.

The headquarters is at present a long way from its intended theatre of operations and already moves have been made to establish a forward headquarters somewhere in the SWA region. To date these efforts have been unsuccessful, mainly as a result of the political considerations that make the region such a source of potential conflict. The plan for a full move to the region has now been replaced for the time being with a scheme to establish a much smaller forward headquarters of only about 200-300 personnel in the SWA theatre but in mid-1983 negotiations for this were still in progress.

Composition

When completely established, the full RDF will be a powerful force in the SWA region. Current plans are for the following units to be part of the RDF by the end of Fiscal Year 1984, but some of these units have been part of the RDF since its inception. Some of the units mentioned have not yet been fully equipped or manned for their new role.

Each of the three main forces (US Army, US Navy and US Air Force) has its own separate headquarters, while the US Marine Amphibious Force operates under the control of the US Navy headquarters.

For several reasons it is not possible to place precise unit allocations to the RDF. To date several units have been involved at one time or another, and the usual policy is to rotate units to and from the role for training and other commitments. It is known that units involved to date have included the 82nd and 101st Airborne Divisions, the 7th and 25th Infantry Divisions and for the US Marine Corps the 31st Marine Amphibious Unit. One known US Air Force unit is the 1st Tactical Fighter Wing at Langley Air Force Base, Virginia, which is equipped with 68 McDonnell Douglas F-15C and F-15D Eagles with their special long-range FAST (Fuel And Sensor Tactical) packs.

One other factor to be borne in mind is that the US Army infantry division is now in a state of transition from its current to a new organizational basis (Infantry Division '86). It is planned to make all current US Army units conform to the new '86 pattern, which includes a structure and equipment revision to make all the units involved more flexible and mobile while at the same time increasing their combat potential and firepower. The High Technology Light Division is a new concept being undertaken by the 9th Infantry Division at Fort Lewis, Washington. It will be an air-transportable division, without tanks and based around 10 infantry battalions, only two of which will have any vehicles. It will be an ideal addition to the RDF.

Deployment and supply

The heart of the RDF concept is that the bulk of the forces involved will be able to move to the SWA (South West Asia) region of action and, when there, continue to be supplied. This is the RDF's weakest point, for to deploy forces on the scale that the RDF mobilization will entail is currently beyond the scope of the US Air Force Military Air Command (MAC), even if the Civil Reserve Air Fleet (CRAF) becomes involved. Also involved in this massive move would be the finding in the region of sufficient reliable bases from which to operate.

The latter point can be considered first as American policy planners are currently involved in the preparation of several ports and airfields in the SWA theatre. These facilities have been obtained by local discussions leading to the active updating of existing sites to make them usable on the scale that any move by the RDF will involve. There are several of these locations scattered around the Indian Ocean and others en route

Soldiers from the 101st Air Assault Division wait in line to board incoming UH-60 Black Hawk helos. The 101st specialize in helicopter assault, whilst their comrades in the 82nd Airborne Division are skilled in air drop. These two are the Army's major contribution to the Rapid Deployment Force.

Right: In a deployment to the Middle East, immediate supplies of Army equipment such as this M113 can be flown in with the front-line troops. Further kit will be shipped forward from pre-positioned stores (principally from Diego Garcia and at sea). But the bulk will have to come in from continental USA by aircraft and ship.

to SWA. At all of them the US Army Corps of Engineers has overseen the construction and modification of all manner of airfield and port facilities at Ras Banas in Egypt, Masirah Island off Oman, Mombasa in Kenya, Berbera in Somalia, the island of Diego Garcia and facilities in the Azores. Kenyan airfields involved are Embakasi and Nanyuki, and in Oman more facilities will be provided at Seeb airfield, Thumrayt, and the ports of Mutrah and Salalah.

Most of these locations will be used as staging bases and staging posts. Many of them already have oil storage facilities or will be provided with them. Payment for these facilities is made in a variety of ways from direct cash to economic and military aid.

To move a force the size of the RDF involves more than air transport, as the bulk of the RDF's equipment is such that sea transport is involved. For this purpose no less than 17 heavy cargo carriers are scheduled to be based in the SWA region, most of them at Diego Garcia, already loaded with the heavy supplies needed by RDF units. More shipping is earmarked in the continental United States for the task, and the experience gained during the recent Falkland Islands campaign is being examined for any possible lessons. The Military Sealift Command has no fewer than 37 dry cargo vessels in service with a further 29 in the Ready Reserve Fleet. To these can be added 167 other reserve vessels, but not all of these will be available all the time.

The airlift potential of the US forces, although considerable, is now insufficient for the RDF requirement and is currently being reinforced by the purchase of a further 50 Lockheed C-5B Galaxy heavy-lift transports and some other aircraft, including a substantial quantity of McDonnell Douglas KC-10A Extenders.

To these and other aircraft in the inventory can be added 215 passenger aircraft and 109 cargo aircraft from the Civil Reserve Air Fleet (CRAF), and this total is to be increased if funds become available.

Equipment

The RDF will be equipped with the same weapons as all other branches of the US armed forces, but already moves are being made to introduce newer equipment that will produce greater mobility without any sacrifice of firepower. Much of this new equipment will take the form not of weapons but rather of support equipment such as bridging, fuel supply systems, and water supply and purification systems. Already much training has been carried out in the SWA area, including such relatively large-scale exercises as 'Bright Star' (three of which have been carried out in Egypt) and 'Jade Tiger' (carried out in conjunction with Somalia, Sudan and Oman). Some of these exercises have been carried out on a relatively small scale but have still involved some large airlifts and taught some invaluable lessons. One was learnt during the first 'Bright Star' when over one quarter of MAC's strength was involved in moving a single battalion plus its support from the United States to Cairo. Such lavish deployments will be 'out' in future.

In general, US Army divisions will be light on armour and those involved will be based around the M60 main battle tank. The US Marines will gradually introduce their new LAV (Light Armoured Vehicle) based on the Cougar wheeled vehicle. Support artillery will be towed instead of self-propelled (although some M109A2s will be involved for the time being), the weapon mainly involved being the M198 towed 155-mm howitzer. Numerous proposals for other support weapons for the RDF have been mooted, including such things as 'miniature' MLRS long-range rocket-launchers, towed DIVADS 40-mm anti-aircraft guns and special Chaparral SAM carriers, but these all depend on funding, and extra funding over and above

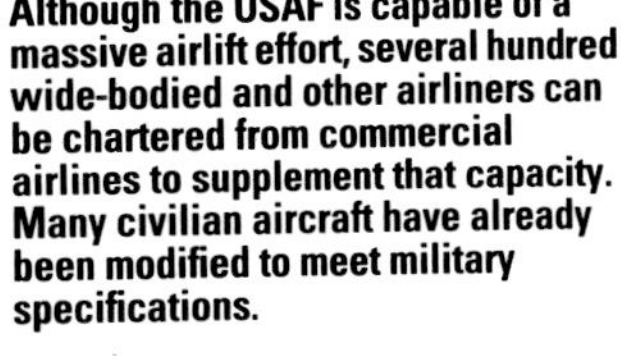

Although the USAF is capable of a massive airlift effort, several hundred wide-bodied and other airliners can be chartered from commercial airlines to supplement that capacity. Many civilian aircraft have already been modified to meet military specifications.

the huge sums already involved is unlikely.

The US Air Force, other than the MAC involvement, is likely to be based on a mix of McDonnell Douglas F-15 Eagles and Fairchild Republic A-10 Thunderbolt IIs for direct support, and on General Dynamics F-111s and Boeing B-52s (probably operating from the continental USA) for bomber support.

The US Navy is already operating in the Indian Ocean, with at least one carrier-based battle group on station at any one time. The US Navy is already deeply involved in a major re-equipment programme and is unlikely to make any major RDF changes, but already under way are a new class of amphibious assault ship (the first of which is the LSD-41 *Whidbey Island*) and a new multi-purpose amphibious assault ship known as the LHD. Involved with these will be new special crane ships and lighters, including hovercraft for the assault and supply role.

The US Marine Corps is currently reorganizing itself around a new Light Armoured Vehicle (LAV) battalion, and the air component of their amphibious force is now the BAe AV-8A Harrier or the Vought A-7 Corsair. In future these will be supplemented (or replaced) by the McDonnell Douglas AV-8B Harrier II.

To control all these various formations the American forces are also deeply involved in a programme to provide a flexible and capable C[3] (command, control, communications) series of systems, but nothing definite has yet been agreed. It is known, however, that considerable use of Boeing E-3A Sentry AWACS aircraft will be involved. Some of these aircraft have already been based in Egypt and Sudan on occasion.

Any substantial action overseas will depend on a massive sea lift from east- and west-coast US ports. During their Falklands campaign the British found that they needed a supply line of around 100 ships to keep around 5,000 troops fighting ashore and a small (by US standards) fleet operating at sea. Any major American intervention would involve a far bigger maritime effort.

Airborne forces proudly pose in celebration of their successful operation on Grenada. But Grenada was a small and relatively unopposed operation; RDF interventions in the Middle East would provide a much tougher and more substantial challenge.

Air Force F-16s overfly the pyramids of Egypt during a 'Bright Star' exercise, symbolizing the new relationship with that country, following many years of Soviet-inspired antagonism. The political instability of the Middle East necessitates very flexible and mobile disposition of US forces in the area.

INDEX

Page numbers indicating a picture are in **bold**

A

B

C

D

E

F

G

H

I

J

K

L

M

N

O

P

Q

R

S

T

U

V

W